A MATERIALISM FOR THE MASSES

D1292490

INSURRECTIONS: CRITICAL STUDIES IN RELIGION, POLITICS, AND CULTURE

Insurrections: Critical Studies in Religion, Politics, and Culture

Slavoj Žižek, Clayton Crockett, Creston Davis, Jeffrey W. Robbins, editors

The intersection of religion, politics, and culture is one of the most discussed areas in theory today. It also has the deepest and most wide-ranging impact on the world. Insurrections: Critical Studies in Religion, Politics, and Culture will bring the tools of philosophy and critical theory to the political implications of the religious turn. The series will address a range of religious traditions and political viewpoints in the United States, Europe, and other parts of the world. Without advocating any specific religious or theological stance, the series aims nonetheless to be faithful to the radical emancipatory potential of religion.

After the Death of God, John D. Caputo and Gianni Vattimo,
edited by Jeffrey W. Robbins

The Politics of Postsecular Religion: Mourning Secular Futures,
Ananda Abeysekara

Nietzsche and Levinas: "After the Death of a Certain God,"
edited by Jill Stauffer and Bettina Bergo

Strange Wonder: The Closure of Metaphysics and the Opening of Awe,
Mary-Jane Rubenstein

*Religion and the Specter of the West: Sikhism, India, Postcoloniality,
and the Politics of Translation,* Arvind Mandair

Plasticity at the Dusk of Writing: Dialectic, Destruction, Deconstruction,
Catherine Malabou

Anatheism: Returning to God After God, Richard Kearney

Rage and Time: A Psychopolitical Investigation, Peter Sloterdijk

Radical Political Theology: Religion and Politics After Liberalism,
Clayton Crockett

Radical Democracy and Political Theology, Jeffrey W. Robbins

(continued on page 241)

A MATERIALISM FOR THE MASSES

Saint Paul and the Philosophy

of Undying Life

Ward Blanton

COLUMBIA UNIVERSITY PRESS

NEW YORK

Columbia University Press
Publishers Since 1893
New York   Chichester, West Sussex
cup.columbia.edu
Copyright © 2014 Columbia University Press
All rights reserved
Library of Congress Cataloging-in-Publication Data
Blanton, Ward.
A materialism for the masses: Saint Paul and the philosophy of undying life /
Ward Blanton.
pages cm.—(Insurrections: critical studies in religion, politics, and culture)
Includes bibliographical references and index.
ISBN 978-0-231-16690-4 (cloth: alk. paper)—ISBN 978-0-231-16691-1
(pbk.: alk. paper)—ISBN 978-0-231-53645-5 (e-book)
1. Bible. Epistles of Paul—Theology. 2. Christianity and politics.
3. Christianity and culture. 4. Paul, the Apostle, Saint. I. Title.

Bs2651.B54 2014
227'.0832—dc23

2013022765

Jacket design: Noah Arlow
References to websites (URLs) were accurate at the time of writing. Neither the
author nor Columbia University Press is responsible for URLs that may have
expired or changed since the manuscript was prepared.

For those most sublime and forceful of the Paulinist paradoxes of my life, Sophia and Zoe. When the time is right, little ones—and when you are not so little—remember that when we think, love, joke, and incite we reveal the vibrancy of the *worlds* in which we believe.

But the struggle against Plato, or to express it more plainly and for "the masses," the struggle against the Christian-ecclesiastical pressure of millennia—for Christianity is Platonism for "the masses"—has created in Europe a magnificent tension of spirit such as has never existed on earth before: with so tense a bow one can now shoot for the most distant targets.

—Friedrich Nietzsche, *Beyond Good and Evil*

The fact that this materialism of the encounter has been repressed by the philosophical tradition does not mean that it has been neglected by it: it was too dangerous for that. Thus it was very early on interpreted, repressed and perverted into an idealism of freedom. If Epicurus' atoms, raining down parallel to each other in the void, encounter one another, it is in order to bring out, in the guise of the swerve caused by the *clinamen*, the existence of human freedom even in the world of necessity. Obviously, producing this misreading, which is not innocent, suffices to preclude any other reading of the repressed tradition that I am calling the materialism of the encounter: whenever one sets out from this misreading, idealist interpretations carry the day, whether what is in question is just the *clinamen* or all of Lucretius, as well as Machiavelli, Spinoza and Hobbes, the Rousseau of the second Discourse, Marx and even Heidegger (to the extent that Heidegger touched on this theme). What triumphs in these interpretations is a certain conception of philosophy and the history that we can, with Heidegger, call Western, because it has presided over our destiny since the Greeks; and also logocentric, because it identifies philosophy with a function of Logos charged with thinking the priority of Meaning over all reality. To free the materialism of the encounter from this repression; to discover, if possible, its implications for both philosophy and materialism; and to ascertain its hidden effects wherever they are silently at work—such is the task that I have set myself here.

—Louis Althusser, "An Underground Current of Materialism"

CONTENTS

PREFACE TO POLITICS
AS MATERIALIST SPIRITUALITIES

For a Postsecular "Return" of Paulinism

> Industrial factories used the body, forcing it to leave the soul outside the assembly line, so that the worker looked like a soulless body. The immaterial factory asks instead to place our very souls at its disposal: intelligence, sensibility, creativity and language.
> —Franco Berardi, *The Soul at Work*

> Resurrected as a spiritual body (*sōma pneumatikon*) . . .
> —Paul, 1 Corinthians 15.44

TO WONDER EVEN AT HISTORY, TO BE PERPLEXED OVER ALWAYS elusive origins and ends, is to think, with all the danger and hilarity this word implies. As historians, too, we begin as we will ourselves also have ended, as variations of a thought and of its curiously related excess of matters which that thought itself will of course never have understood or captured. Rambunctious souls, we ever live, die, and live again always at least minimally as a meandering and mendicant fragment of temporality which is itself never *merely* located in the past, the present, or the future. Tremble or laugh in the face of this simple beatitude of our common life, it is as if we are always enquiring into, bringing forward, or participating in an excess over a stability which our defensive naming and ritual maintenance of discrete positions and identities cannot exhaust. Even as historians, in other words, we traffic in a becoming which was, is, and will be more monstrously wonderful than to remain, simply, '*in*' the proprietorial limits of time.

No wonder my philosophy often turns to Paulinism and my Paulinism to philosophy. I have always been drawn to those whose taste for becoming incites them—again, in danger and hilarity—to call the dead the living, the singular a new collective, or a surprisingly compelling form of being-together the undying itself.

Several intuitive axioms in the form of questions, indications of what is to come:

What if that name, Paul, or that figure Paulinism, were not naturally linked to metaphysical dualisms, to brutally supersessionist anti-Judaisms, or to the economies of salvation with which both of these are tied? What if, in a word, we were to trace a Paul who, as a force of thought, did not play the guarantor in relation to all those tropes and tricks that Nietzsche diagnosed so beautifully with the gloss: "Platonism for the masses"?

As part of the counterfactual or suppressed story I am developing, what if a consistently creative—but ultimately marginal and shortlived—praxis of Paul the partisan Jew had not been co-opted and buried beneath what can only be called a weaponized form of Platonic-historical narration which came to dominate accounts of the foundations and origins of that name, Christianity, within lastingly influential writers like Eusebius of Caesarea? In terms relevant to the opening quotations of both Nietzsche and Althusser, what if the figure of Paul had not been swallowed up by early Christian stories of a supersessionist conversion from one idealist economy of salvation to another? What if the very *problēmata* of idealist—which is to say calculable or guaranteed—economies of redemption had not become the most important organizing apparatus by which Paul's life and writings came to be repeated, refused, or offered freely to others?

What if early Jewish and, eventually, Christian groups had cared about (and for) the various modes in which Paul's peculiarly risky social experimentations evidently failed to last more than several decades? What if the

ephemerality of Paulinism as a form of processual collective experimentation had become the most important legacy of this apostle? What if Paul
had become in the stream of cultural memory not the cornerstone of a
new foundation for a new religion (one which soon enough aspired to be
a new empire), but rather the exemplar of unexpectedly and riskily creative openings immanent to tradition, identity, and the panoply of techniques which constitute these? Why has this stream of cultural memory
not remembered—why has it been *essential* not to remember—that such
strikingly subtle transmogrifications of life emerged as a movement which
maintained itself in blissful vibrancy and exposure to risk and weakness
before passing away as other impassioned contingencies reshaped life in
other ways?

Well, what if the only way latter day Paulinists were to imagine that this kind
of originary Paulinism could be repeated, therefore, was at tangents or
in fits and starts, in the oddly singular or vibrant comparison as coding
networks shift and swerve, opening and closing, folding and unfolding
ecological spaces for a time of life immeasurable because without original
version, authorized copy, or prefabricated purpose? What new Paulinists
would arise!

Or, differently put, what would have emerged were Paul to be for us
resurrected thus outside the theologico-political frame of the old "Platonism for the masses"? And if such thoughts were to have been provoked
by and provoking of a life which is itself unowned and undying? And if
we were to find ourselves in such a moment of encounter, would we have
become revisionist historians, challenging inherited forms of thought
about the past? Would we have become sharers in a becoming we might
name apostolic, at any rate Pauline? Or would we have become benefac-
tors, so many patrons and patronesses funding a decidedly different form
of new life than that instantiating and grounding the old bulwark of Western idealist metaphysics? Would we have invested in a different form of
life, eluding the other form's otherworldliness and (necessarily) accompanying persecutorial tendencies against all those "merelies" from which
it saves, or against which it attempts to inoculate itself (e.g., the merely
animal, the merely human, the pre-Christian)?

And what if we could not locate a difference within these options which
would naturally stand in as a guarantor of judgement about which meta-
morphosis is about the past of another and which about a temporality
which is strangely our own? What if we were to find, rather, that we had
slipped into transformative potentialities which are not be so easily locat-

able, not so readily owned, as if existing in relation to place and property neither here nor there, neither then nor now?

And if we were to find ourselves marked by that uncertain and unsafe mixture of capacity and desire to seduce such a transformative newness from out of the world as we know it, would we say yes, would we gesture for it to come closer? Already we see that our judgment of an ancient historical figure in these respects must entail a judgement we ourselves will not escape.

This book is a solicitation, just a beginning, to a *metanoia*, that turning, twisting, spiraling of mind which is itself hard to localize and impossible to own.

Nietzsche's ear to the ground, he seemed always to hear better than the rest a humming from an enormous cultural machine, one which manufactured docile humans, fitted them up with perceptions, certain kinds of sociality, experiences, readymade or originary debts, and—above all—their own proper judgements about their own appropriate limits. This machine, which he imagined as a pop Platonism named Christianity, operated by fitting up its creations with origins and identities capable of sustaining an increasingly virtual or speculative system of credit and obligatory debt. This fiduciary tale, we might say, was always both deeply religious and deeply economic, so it is no wonder that Karl Marx responded similarly to the desiring hum he also sensed resonating throughout economic life, a desire he glossed as the "massive phenomenon" of Western Christendom.

Is one being audacious, or is one simply awake, when one declares that the religion of the future will be keyed to difference, ecological interrelations, and the emancipation of new kinds of worldliness? This future religion (if we should still call it that), not to mention its future Books, will set in motion experimental series of bodies that are both creative and material, materially creative. These bodies, exemplars of a life that is common—unowned and undying—must necessarily skew received maps of materialism—which tend to be reductive and representational—and spirituality—which tend to represent newness as an ideal category or a category of *another* world, a world somehow free, unrelated, or saved from all that which comes always to be imagined retroactively as "merely" "here below". My solicitations, my thoughts, emerge neither from a friendship to a reductive materialism nor to an idealist or otherworldly religiosity.

Even more importantly I think, the economies of redemption, so many promises of salvation peddled by friends of the one or the other metaphysical option are not at all what is at issue for me. If there is an emancipation to be discussed, then let it be the emancipation of ephemeral—and therefore unexpected and uncoerced—happenings, events, processes as instances of an undying *life* which is in itself not subjected to the need for a redemptive translation into another sphere of tabulation. We believe, therefore, in a redemption (if we should still call it that) which does not go anywhere, does not need, as we like to say today, to cash out.

For this *world in which we believe*, this world without end, this eternal life, we must now struggle and invent, calling on old archival allies to weave together promising collectivities which have, to this point, remained loose ends or squashed prospects.

Heidegger was not wrong in his questioning of technology or in his updating of both Nietzsche and Marx: the *life of faith* would appear most clearly in a world without *objects*, in an *oikoumenē* constituted by exposure to risk, a world whereby being itself is neither objectified nor subjectively invented but rather conjured by new creations of new attunements to, or participations in, ecological or deeply relational events which are themselves processual, wholly relational, and constitutively open. Trying to conjure—ever by hook and crook—affective links between strata of objects, lives, bodies and futures, the investments of our new faith have neither targets to shoot for nor territorialities to own, both of which obfuscate our hope in new forms of the common, the shared, and—in that sense—the universal.

In thinking of Paulinist events in a world without objects, I have often felt that I am posing only a few fundamental political questions for our time, questions associated with instances that remain to me as crystalline and simple as they are problematic. For example, while the exemplary instance of this question could be different (there are plenty to choose from, unfortunately) or updated (we have not stopped producing them), one of these questions concerns whether, on being coralled and sequestered and rendered generally ineffectual during our protests in New York City against the invasion of Iraq (can you still remember?), we should have not started to throw rocks. Or, perhaps, once I heard the politicians' dismissive speech about our place in the political liturgy of a society of the spectacle ("isn't it wonderful that our proud spirit of protest is alive . . . nevertheless in the real world . . . "), I should have not organized a group of people to return to the streets with rocks in hand. Or something, somehow to materialize at different levels a *kerygma* about the lives of scores of thousands of Iraquis who would surely be lost if that remarkable force which is the US military were to be loosed. How could such a moment have been eventalized rather than spectacularized, made "historical" in a completely different way than the way it actually became so? In a world in which the apparatuses of the production of profitable death often seem so much more alive, vibrant, and resilient than the "living" who try in vain to resist them, Paul has become for me a beloved touchstone. Above all, I wonder with and against him about how to snatch an undying life from imperial apparatuses which have, somehow and much to our horror, become more living than the living.

Perversely faithful to the counter-intuitive *para-doxa* of the Stoics, Paul liked to curl up inside the apparatuses themselves, hollowing out within their irresistibly effectual machinations the space of something like a downfall, something like an end, a kind of strangely invested or *vibrant suspension* of the machine or power in question. Such aggressivity—the *vibrancy* of this suspension—is not to be lamented, then or now. In fact, it seems to me that today is more than ever the time to take seriously some of his oddly antinomic or paradoxical fascinations, not only his anti-Platonic "spiritual bodies" (cited above), but also the accompanying "spiritual weapons" which are in keeping with an interventionist Pauline *détournement* of governing dualisms. For me, Paul returns as a figure of inevitably forced and troubling participations in systems of power which are nevertheless—this is the perverse gift implied by the Stoic spiritual exercises—susceptible to being creatively folded over into improper zones of unexpected solidarity. Spiritual weapons of the Paulinist are for me those performances of solidarity capable of feeding off a transformative theft of autonomy from power.

As an instance similar to my mention of this recent manufacture of horrors abroad and slavishness at home, while writing this book I have also felt pressed to wonder comparatively about our participation in affective economies and the proliferation of all those forms of work which now readily overflow working days—not only in the sense that they creep into our "off" hours, but also in the sense that they constantly remetricize (or polemicize differently) the spaces and times of our working life itself. While, once again, other examples are ready to hand, my recent wonders about the shifting function of labor have matured in the midst of life in which hard work so often seems to yield only the weakest of buffers against the demand for *more work*, a demand always linked to a generalized threat that some contingency (of economy, of organizational involvement in economy) could retroactively invalidate currently valued forms of work. In the ongoing crises of finance capitalism, debt appears always in the form of unexpected catastrophe or the unexpected necessity of a new sacrifice, in our case a retroactive manufacture of new debtors-for-life. Such phenomena are never far from my reflections on Paul and his paradoxical tweaks of the old philosophical question: how *do* we know the difference between freedom and slavery?

In other words, there is a pressure at the heart of simple, fundamental questions and their exemplary instances, something I often describe with the language of vibrancy. A faithful witness to selected pressures, I am not at all opposed to doing with my education as critical theorist of culture, as scholar of the cultural history of the European study of religion, and as biblical scholar, what Nietzsche did with his education in Classics, namely, to weaponize it against some of the more atrociously enabling lies of the cultural moment. And, since I am mobilising an education in biblical studies rather than in Classics per se, when it comes to Paul I definitely think I can do Nietzsche one better. He promised to pillory Paul as the horrid inventor of a "Platonism for the masses"; I think I can emancipate Paul from a few of the metaphysical and sacrificially controlling apparatuses constitutive of Western governance. Or, differently, the pressure constituting our moment suggests to me that we *must* outdo Nietzsche in this way, outdo his cultural diagnosis of a pop Platonism in order to think about and with Paul concerning—you guessed it—a "materialism for the masses."

The moment for such a thinking, for such a *metanoia*, arrives all vibrant with the halo of a world which must come. One day there will be a "mass" movement, this (often a good Paulinist) I believe. And so, buzzing with this vibrancy we think—comparatively and archivally—even as we live as so many laboratories of new collectivities. This mode of thinking life which we could name "materialist spirituality" is yet ahead of us, to come, but it is not just that. It is rather waiting in the wings, getting closer, here now in the very form of our uncertainty about whether it is the case.

A MATERIALISM FOR THE MASSES

PLATONISM FOR THE MASSES

On the Sacred Cement Shoes of Paul the Apostle

The text, however, as we find it today tells us enough about its own history [*seine eigenen Schicksale*]. Two distinct forces, diametrically opposed to each other, have left their traces [*ihre Spuren*] on it. On the one hand, certain transformations got to work on it, falsifying the text in accord with secret tendencies [*geheimen Absichten*], maintaining and extending it until it was turned into its opposite. On the other hand, an indulgent piety reigned over it [*eine schonungsvolle Pietät über ihm gewaltet*], anxious to keep everything as it stood, indifferent to whether the details fitted together or nullified one another. Thus almost everywhere there can be found striking omissions [auffällige *Lücken*], disturbing repetitions [*störende Wiederholungen*], palpable contradictions [*greifbare Widersprüche*], signs of things the communication of which was never intended [*Anzeichen, die uns Dinge verraten, deren Mitteilung nicht beabsichtigt war*]. The distortion [*der Entstellung*] of a text is not unlike a murder. The difficulty lies not in the execution of the deed but in the doing away with the traces [*ihre Spuren*].

—Sigmund Freud, *Moses and Monotheism* (trans. Katherine Jones)

It is confirmed likewise by Caius, a member of the church, who arose under Zephyrinus, bishop of Rome. He, in a published disputation with Proclus, the leader of the Phrygian heresy, speaks as follows concerning the places where the sacred corpses [τὰ ἱερὰ σκηνώματα] of the aforesaid apostles are laid: But I can show you the trophies of the apostles [τὰ τρόπαια τῶν ἀποστόλων]. For if you will go to the Vatican

or to the Ostian Way, you will find the trophies of those who laid
the foundations of this church [εὑρήσεις τὰ τρόπαια τῶν ταύτην
ἱδρυσαμένων τὴν ἐκκλησίαν].

—Eusebius, *Ecclesiastical Histories* (2.26.6,7)

A SPECTER IS HAUNTING EUROPE—THE VERY UNRULY SPIRIT OF A
Paulinism we believe ourselves to have isolated safely in the past. This
spirit oozes up through the very cracks in the floorboards of our triumphal institutions. All the powers of the West have entered into an alliance to exorcise the evident danger of this specter, this genie who seems
capable of emerging from any of its bottles. International banks demand
of democratically elected officials that they call up outsourced policing
agencies to quell our rebellions against a diffuse machinery of life and
labor, of domination and co-optation by the wealthy. Where are the lively
partisans of undying, resistant life who are not decried as having dangerously failed to understand the fact that old messiahs and their emancipatory movements are manifestly failed, now safely dead and buried? Where
is the vibrant movement of opposition and stubborn attachment to alternatives which is today not declared by all to be outlaw and unjustified?

There is, for reasons that will become clear, an elusively expansive cultural revolution curled up, as if still sleeping, within narrations of Christian origins. This surprising possibility remains so, even now, despite
much repeated claims of having become secular (as if we knew any longer what this means) and despite the institutional gatekeepers of religions
claiming, yes, it *is* time for a return, here and to me! I suggested in the
preface that we need to think of a Paul and an accompanying "Christian
origins" story that skews received maps of materialism—which tend to be
reductively or dogmatically foundational—and spirituality—which tend
to represent newness or freedom as an ideal category or a category of
another world, a category saved and safe and unchanging in relation to
the actual happenings of transformative becoming. As we might expect
(though also as we have not tended to note), these two modes of thought
have dominated the history of the narration of "Christian origins." On
the one hand, as a way of opposing "religion," a great deal of the modern
impulses to "immanence" and our "material" imbricatedness within evo-
lutionary, biological, and economic processes tended to map onto discussions of the "religious" in the form of deflationary critique imagined in the
form *this reduces to that*. On the other hand, and in part to preserve the

kernel of enjoyment of "religion" from such reductions, there emerged a rather intense fascination with the unrepeatability and transcendent or safely grounded value of religion in this tradition, a fascination which produced some of the most lastingly influential monuments of the study of Christian origins. This latter mode of understanding promoted the heroism of origins, but at the cost of its shareability or its capacity to indicate that the very surprise in question might occur again, here, now.

When philosophies of difference moved increasingly toward nonrepresentational categories of singularity, there awoke a new model of thinking about both materiality and exceptionalism that has only recently begun to see how it might understand both its own politics and "Christian origins" stories very differently. This shift indicates a massive potential to rewire the proprietary rights, as it were, of the origins or legacies of Christianity, a potential which I would never hesitate to call revolutionary, certainly not (this is the whole point) reducible to a discretely formed sphere of what we usually call religion. Pier Paolo Pasolini, Alain Badiou, Slavoj Žižek, Roberto Esposito—only a few names in an emerging movement that is not distinguishable from the insight that "materialism" and "religion" are shifting into the other, could do so, might do so, and with massive consequences for what has constituted the political history of the "West." I won't say that there is a great deal which needs to be done. It is rather that, given the shifts in the philosophical and political fabric of things which these thinkers register, there is a great deal *now ready to happen*. Historians of early Jewish and Christian traditions have a remarkably important role to play, though only inasmuch as they realize how empirical historical reconstruction participates in a more comparative, reflexive, or hermeneutical economy. Philosophers, on the other hand, do not seem to me to have yet realized how, in keeping with their programs to leverage political categories of "the West" by way of reworked Christian origins stories, their own movements—potentially *mass movements*—have only just begun. But these are just initial framing gestures awaiting a genealogy, which is to say the conjuration of a new past.

CONFESSIO

For a long time I have secretly suspected that not even the original psychoanalytic sleuth realized how important his diagnoses of the Western cultural memory of Moses were for also effecting a radical reworking of Paul, imagined founder of Christianity. In this respect, Freud for me remains very close to Nietzsche, who, even more than the analyst, failed radically to transform—rather than simply to excoriate or lament—the ongoing cultural and political functions of the Pauline legacy. I confess, too, that increasingly I have felt pressed, constrained even, to incite new forms of philosophy, critical theory, and biblical scholarship which will not let the matter rest there where these two thinkers left it.

And perhaps not just *where Nietzsche and Freud* left it. No doubt my feeling of pressure to write differently is related also to the fact that I think a radicalized repetition of *Moses and Monotheism* in relation to the life of a Western Paulinism has in crucial respects failed to occur in important recent philosophical explorations of Paul as a new figure of solidarity and evental engagement for a biopolitical or definitively postcommunist epoch of political economy. Whether one turns to Paul for the unearthing of testimonies about what Eric Santner describes as a "biopolitical pantheism"—a politics of immanence "that would not be *over* life but *of* life" (e.g., Gilles Deleuze, Roberto Esposito)—or a "creaturely messianism" (e.g., Walter Benjamin, Santner himself), we have only just begun to see what is possible in such genealogical interventions.[1] As in Nietzsche and Freud, more recent work by Giorgio Agamben, Alain Badiou, Itzhak Benyamini, Daniel Boyarin, Stanislas Breton, Simon Critchley, Michel Foucault, Theodore Jennings, Michel Onfray, Jean-Michel Rey, Bernard Sichère, Jacob Taubes, and Slavoj Žižek (just to name the authors of a few other texts I admire deeply) still seems to me to remain starstruck to one degree or another by a narrativized spectacle, an instauration of a particular biblical and early Christian tradition that Freud's Moses already taught us in 1939 to suspect as the ghostly or sublimated afterimage of a brutal act of repression. This repression, I will explain, operates around the narrations of Paul as the first Christian and foundation of an emergent Christianity, a retrospective interpellation of the figure which is much more suspicious than seems to have been worked through in our working through of Paul as an odd comparative figure of the (bio)political.[2]

My feeling of being something like a witness to an ancient crime I don't want to cover up was deepened as I organized with Hent de Vries a collection of extraordinary multidisciplinary pieces about the Pauline legacy in and around philosophy, *Paul and the Philosophers*. In a word, observing the range of philosophical *problēmata* constituting recent philosophical encounters with Paul led me to see more clearly ways our thinking is not yet attending to some background discursive economies which have both organized and been solidified by the name Paul, a name which—we must never forget—has functioned (and continues to function) as a founding and foundational exemplar or organizational *apparatus* of Western culture. What the apparatus illumines in its organizational captures of life, not to mention what it captures in its illuminations, is something this literature is only beginning to understand.[3] *A Materialism for the Masses* is for me a further step in my own work on Paul and philosophy, a step intending to engage more pointedly in a transformative diagnosis of some of those intertwined discursive economies and material strata within which Paul returns, both serially and again very recently as a topic of exceptional importance, an exceptionality which always indicates a material forcefulness or a psychic symptom that is never *just* about the past.

As a diagnosis or negotiation of the force of cultural memory, the figure of Paul affords us similar resources as those Hans Ulrich Gumbrecht, Caroline Walker Bynum, Regina Schwartz, and Jonathan Goldberg have found in the materialities of medieval and early modern religious texts, fragments and histories of material actualities which are all the more "with" us the more we abandon them to operate as unthought, undertheorized comparative potentials.[4] Or, as thinkers like Clayton Crockett, Jeffrey W. Robbins, Roberto Esposito, Eric Santner, and Arthur Bradley have also diagnosed very aptly, Pauline texts afford an intriguing comparative touchstone by which to think about a kind of excess of life (a "surplus of immanence"), an irreducible excess *in* life itself, an openness or freedom within things which is not without important philosophical, therapeutic, and political consequences.[5] Some of the discursive or comparative networks that I want to discuss in that vein are more strictly historical in relation to the Paul of ancient Mediterranean culture, but as I was finishing this book I began to find myself with a growing collection of my own readings of the oddly material spiritual agencies of Paul, a characteristic which has important implications that I want to develop in relation to Paul's "spiritual exercises," his creative partisanships, or his experimentations in concrete universalism. But these ancient studies finally seemed to me to take the current project, which is more focused on the "afterlives" of Paul in relation to more recent genealogies of a new materialism, too far afield. At any rate, the book would have been too long to be wieldy, so these sketches I will collect as a kind of companion to the book you are holding. The companion volume will concern itself primarily with ancient philosophical readings of the ancient Paul in relation to the same themes which also occupy me in this book, namely biopolitics and spiritual exercises. The thought is pleasing to me, as it is certainly time that we had more historical readings of Paul for the era of the posthumanities and the biopolitical, readings I feel we must approach, incidentally, by way of a more detailed encounter with the materiality of *ancient* religiosity.

For the moment, and in addition to those thinkers already mentioned, the book you have in hand is also comparable to the diagnostic, comparative, or genealogical approach to Paul found so compellingly in the recent work of Giorgio Agamben, Roberto Esposito, and Eric Santner, all of which has enacted encounters between Paulinism and high modern or contemporary cultural economies.[6] The name Paul in these encounters functions as a site on which to analyze more rigorously some high modern and contemporary paradoxes of power that are in this respect indistinguishable from an ontology of contemporary social life. Still, to think such things by way of a comparative touchstone always transforms our thinking of the present in unexpected ways and with important effects. The Pauline past will not be extricable, finally, from our biopolitical and posthuman futures.

THE (AUTO-IMMUNE) ORIGINARY

With that larger roadmap in mind, I want initially to attend to Freud, and also to Nietzsche, to suggest how we can extend the genealogical projects of these key thinkers beyond what they themselves imagined to be the scope and limits of their interest in the cultural figure of Paul. So I want to start with an assertion, a hypothesis with implications that have been inadequately explored, whether by Nietzsche or Freud or more recent philosophical and political encounters with Paul. The assertion, a working historical or comparative hypothesis with philosophical implications, is that the apostle—imagined as the foundational hero of a historiographical archive constituting (as early as Eusebius in the fourth century) Christian origins—is just this, *a hero invested with a foundational greatness to the same degree as key threads of his legacy needed to be forgotten.*

The notion of an original Christianity is a narrative device which always carefully mirrors, shelters, and incites a more strategic metaphysical dualism. Note how Eusebius initiates his lastingly influential *History of the Church* with a paradigmatically important discussion of the divine humanity of Jesus. Eusebius's Platonic dualism or doubling of Jesus is repeated and reinforced in the narrative structures or teleologies that constitute Eusebius's history writing itself, a narrativizing that—I will claim—constitutes the real heart of Paulinism as a kind of "Platonism for the masses." Eusebius writes: "My account of what follows will therefore be complete if I begin my exposition of his entire story with the basic and essential points of the doctrine. By this means, both the antiquity and the divine character of Christian origins will be demonstrated to those who imagine them to be recent and outlandish, appearing yesterday for the first time. To explain the origin and worth, the very essence and nature of Christ, no language could be adequate" (1.1.2.2f.).

In other words, Eusebius will cope with a supposed ineffability of the divinity and worth of the beings in question by way of a historical narration which will supplement the otherwise impossible quest for an origin that is indistinguishable from a guarantee of the "worth" of the hegemonic doctrine for which Eusebius struggles. Read this way, the "divinity" of the story in question is what necessitates a kind of repetition compulsion, always and ever returning to the spot to find, locate, designate that unknown X as, yes, the reason for Christianity's *dis*continuity with its histories or pasts. Or, turned around, narrative discontinuity will always have been structurally demanded by a metaphysical dualism whereby the "truth" must itself be represented as safe, saved, and saving, unscathed by the very world it must denigrate.

Of course, the canonized occlusion of worldly links, a beatification which is by necessity a shrewd form of coverup, becomes an exemplary one in discourses of the West, paradigmatic and therefore profoundly powerful in its capacity to organize forms of thought and action. That an issue *of historical narration* might have such a capacious organizational reach might at first blush seem unlikely. But consider the way that Freud's Moses, like all founding figures and all fathers in the psychoanalytic archive, is split between an instituting and instituted violence, the *archē* itself constituted by a gap separating its actuality and what this actuality forecloses or actively represses. Jacques Derrida rightly begins his reflection on that simultaneously beatified hero and murdered patriarch with an axiom of Walter Benjamin about law, heritage, and tradition, which is of course also significant for my story of Paul's incorporation within what has always been a *politics* of memory glossed as "Christian origins." Derrida writes of the relation between the emergence and maintenance of systems of information and power:

> An exergue serves to stock in anticipation and to prearchive a lexicon which, from there on, ought to lay down the law and *give the order*, even if this means contenting itself with naming the problem, that is, the subject. In this way, the exergue has at once an institutive and conservative func-

tion: the violence of a power (*Gewalt*) which at once posits and conserves the law, as the Benjamin of *Zur Kritik der Gewalt* would say. What is at issue here, starting with the exergue, is the violence of the archive itself, *as archive, as archival violence.*

It is thus the first figure of the archive, because *every* archive, we will draw some inferences from this, is at once *institutive* and *conservative.* Revolutionary and traditional. An eco-*nomic* archive in the double sense: it keeps, it puts in reserve, it saves, but in an unnatural fashion, that is to say in making the law (*nomos*) or in making people respect the law. A moment ago we called it nomological. It has the force of law, of a law which is the law of a house (*oikos*), of the house as place, domicile, family, lineage, or institution. Having become a museum, Freud's house takes in all these powers of economy.[7]

For this reason, after the institution of a new organizational mode, Derrida asserts, "From this point on, a series of cleavages will incessantly divide every atom of our lexicon."[8] Indeed, as we will see in the next chapter, the assumption will remain integral to Derrida's notions of writing, which in his early work he associated with a kind of new materialism as a thinking of the aleatory and the contingent. For the moment, however, recall also that Giorgio Agamben in turn will imagine that Benjamin's very reflections on the *division* between instituting and instituted violence constituted an effort by Benjamin to locate his own thinking as close as possible to the *archē* of what had become effectively *a perennial nomological paradox* capable of floating free of its discrete historical contexts in order to situate itself elsewhere, in revolutionary discussions above all. This *archē*, of course, was a Western Paulinism, and, read this way, Benjamin's work on the internal divisions of power in the institution of new norms was an effort to navigate the perennial or nomological question of power by self-consciously inhabiting that paradigmatic Pauline moment of law/nonlaw in that also paradigmatic story of a "new start," namely, the origin of Christianity. In a word, Agamben argues that, with his reflections on constituting and constituted power at the origin of a political constitution, it is as if Benjamin were regaling himself in the attire of the apostle, conjuring his "return" in a mimetic performance that would perhaps repeat differently, opening up new forms of paradigmatic thinking about origins.[9]

Benjamin, precisely in his diagnosis of the ambivalence of law, of the force of law but also of the power of origins per se, in this sense, locates himself alongside, in, and in some sense *as* Paul, his repetition or afterlife.

This Agambenian reception of Benjamin aside, it is certainly the case that Jacob Taubes performs himself this way, effectively becoming a new Paul as a mannerist intervention against Carl Schmitt's not unrelated depictions of constituting power and the origins of political change. Already the point about our necessarily genealogical encounter with Paulinism should be clear: if the figure of Paul can recycle or return in such modes, then in some sense these specters of Paul are always *already* there at, say, the Benjaminian or Freudian "origin" stories. The legacy has lent and continues to lend itself to repetition in diverse cultural spheres, which is to say that the legacy is effectively powerful in its capacities to organize huge swaths of discursive territory. But this openness to repetition is simultaneously an indication of the way the legacy is also open to transformation, to being repeated differently. It is in this sense that I have wanted to say that the contemporary study of Paul must attend to the Pauline "signature," those instances of an effect that is neither merely historical nor merely conceptual but some quasi-transcendental apparatus putting both into operation at one go.[10] We should not just refuse the historico-metaphysical dynamics of someone like Eusebius: we might also steal from his bag of tricks, repeat his story differently. And if his tale of origins seamlessly repeats and reinforces a two-tiered universe of sovereignly stable forms, then we know already that the story can change.

As we will see in the next chapter, Derrida's splitting of the power of every archon, the division of every *archē*, constitutes a Derridean interest in the *materiality* of cultural memory. But it is my assertion that in what could have been extremely important and transformative encounters with the signature of Paul, Derrida failed to register or contest the interlocking genealogical and philosophical issues, those emerging along a quasi-Pauline gap separating being from act, community from revolution, Judaism from Christianity, and idealism from materialism. As we have already begun to see, the name of Paul will (like it or not) slide along the history of such distinctions, as an operator both guaranteeing and guaranteed by the effective force of the distinction in question, lending it a strangely diffuse and yet strikingly common—even perennial—discursive force, a forcefulness of a repetition compulsion I call the Pauline signature.

To say the least, the opacity of a repetition with such apparent compulsion is of course a crucial issue for the cultural analysis of the figure of an "originary" Paulinism. It is, we must know, not *simply* ancient Christians who were—in my Freudian invitation to the study of this apostolic signatory—engaged in a cover-up. Why, I will ask, have some of the great

bearers of a tradition of genealogical contest and subversion not articulated more clearly the interrelationships, borrowing, secret sharings, over-
and underdeterminations, those generally unspoken obligations and debts
that constitute the significance, the forcefulness of talk about an ancient
apostle? Why have we continued to read Paul as *related to* the Freudian
psychohistorical drama of origins, but without claiming that *Paul himself*
must be read as a *type* of Freud's Moses, hyperinvested with ambivalent
or contradictory tensions constituting the elusive "origin" as such? This
shift in focus is of acute importance, and it is in this respect that I think
we must effectively press diagnoses of Paulinism as a cultural touchstone
well beyond those those undertaken by Nietzsche, Freud, and Derrida
alike. Even when these thinkers want to read Paul as a kind of original
antihero (e.g., as Nietzsche's most guilty originator of a "Platonism for the
masses" or Derrida's very similar first-Christian purveyor of anti-Jewish
metaphysical dualisms), it is still the fact that they read Paul as the one
who knows, the one who founds, the one who is himself the guarantee of
an ideal (even if self-deceptively imagined) origin named Christianity. In
Heidegger's famous and brilliantly counterintuitive reading of Nietzsche,
he describes Nietzsche, that great antimetaphysician and anti-Platonist,
as—despite himself—the last metaphysician and even the greatest Platonist. I would add here only that, in reading Paul in the way they do, both
Nietzsche and Derrida may be likewise be described as the "last Christians," true acolytes of Paul as originator-of-Christianity.

This is by now to me an exceedingly astonishing cultural fact, all the
more problematic if the signature of Paul, as it were, repeatedly stands in
as a kind of quasi-transcendental or paradigmatic exemplar of the very
moment of splitting that is the origin, the very cleft of the *force of law* (and
it is hard to argue against Taubes or Agamben in their comparative articulations of Paul on this general, comparative, or genealogical point). Given
the working assumptions about origins, difference, order, and exemplarity
among our genealogists, it is extraordinarily odd that Paul would ever be
allowed to remain unscathed and not really under scrutiny by those detectives of "the original." This phenomenon is so odd, in fact, that one must
begin to recognize the complicity—of Freud, of Nietzsche, of Derrida, and
of more recent interpreters—involved in their allowing Paul to remain *in
the place of* the origin, at the origin of Christianity, as the exemplary onto-
theologian, the real purveyor of a "Platonism for the masses," and so on.
On my reading, it is this *leaving Paul unscathed at the site of origin* that
obscures a materialist philosophical engagement with a crucial swath of

Western religious and philosophical history, thereby obscuring important resources for a new materialist philosophy of life which is a pressing need within our a biopolitical or posthumanist epoch.

The issue is not at all whether one should or should not be so brash as to make ready to hand criticisms of an apostle. Of course such actions are both possible and readily available, even all worked out and well trodden. Today one can even find iPod "apps" which feed would-be anti-Paulinists of a number of different niche or identitarian markets with useful fodder for this enterprise. No, the issue here is very different. To put it provocatively and in terms of the new materialism, it is not Paul's fault that he is not, like the traditional God of ontotheology (or the ideas of the demiurgic creator in Plato), an identity existing out there, autonomously, on his own, living to imprint his self-existing concepts onto the passive flesh of matter. Rather, the problem is our own, whether we ourselves will remain faithful to handing over *our figures of thought* to a world within which— whether ancient Mediterranean creators of crafts or technicians of texts, whether the LORD of Genesis or the modern psychoanalyst as therapist of our souls—*we* are no longer seeking solace in the imaginary space of the Author, Analyst, Creator as external or self-identical guarantor or fulcrum of the processual flux of reality itself.[11] The problem of refusing to repeat engrained Platonisms isn't any more difficult in the case of Paul than it is with Plato, Western traditions of subjects-making-things, or analysts holding the key to the real me—nor is it any easier.[12]

Consider the case of Derrida's missed transformative encounters with Paul, which I will explore further on. Why is it that Derrida deconstructs— or reads in what he calls a "materialist" mode—Platonic assumptions about intentionality in craft production or authorship in text production (realizing that these models so powerfully inform Platonic models of thinking itself), even as Derrida *simply rejects and lampoons* what he perceives to be the retrograde dualistic metaphysics of the apostle? The difference in treatment here is stunning and not without profound implications for the ongoing discursive life of cultural power: Plato's dualistic metaphysic is worked *into* a model of complex material immanence, whereas Paul is simply expelled as a purveyor of a Platonism for the masses, a thinker of "the veil," and therefore left undeconstructed. Derrida shows how Plato is, despite himself (in slips of the pen, in the talk of *pharmakon* and the "supplement" of presence), a kind of secret anti-Platonist, indeed a kind of Derridean. But Paul never gets the same treatment, is never invited to be otherwise than what he seems to want to be (which is always to say than what perhaps Derrida wants him to be). All this implies that Derrida's Paul remains unanalyzed and unthought in relation the aporetic immanence driving Derrida's early deconstruction. These are psychocultural dramas to which we must attend. To allow the figure of Paul to remain in *our* thinking or analysis as the original founder of Christianity, more or less, is to allow our own most intimate modes of the search for understanding to remain marginalized, as if stuck on the outside of a Western ontotheological or metaphysically idealist cultural complex that one might very well *criticize or lampoon* but that one would not have *understood in one's own terms, which is to say, transformed from its ontotheological coordinates.* As I have said already, I think this problem is the essential issue which demands that we move beyond Nietzsche, Freud, Foucault, and Derrida in a genuinely transformative encounter with Paulinism, this touchstone of Western figures of the new start, the beyond of law, and the free community of spirit. Beyond dismissal or excoriation, there must be a more fundamental *working through* than our philosophical and historical traditions have yet enacted.

Or, to put the matter of repetition compulsion and its working through more provocatively still—and to borrow a line from that post-Kantian philosopher and scandalous New Testament scholar Albert Schweitzer— a new materialism cannot simply criticize or exclude Paul; it must rather *become* him. A still undertheorized moment in the modern political history of biblical scholarship, it is worth mentioning Schweitzer's statements about Paul which would later appear both as a reading of Jesus and also as a fierce diagnosis and critique of modernity's propensity to develop a metaphysical Calculation of all calculations. On this occasion in 1903, Albert Schweitzer, a young professor at a Christian seminary, wrote a letter to his girlfriend, Helene Bresslau. At that point Schweitzer was already emerging as an important biblical scholar and was shortly to enact what he imagined to constitute a critical judgment against European culture by turning from the European academy in order move to Lambaréné, Africa as a physician and humanitarian. That career change and move to Africa had everything to do with Schweitzer's ongoing destructive interpretation of a nineteenth-century tradition of biblical scholarship, theology, and philosophy he summarized as both "modern" and "liberal." Without being led astray by a longer conversation, we should note that a central part of Schweitzer's multifaceted critique of these traditions was a reading of Paulinism as an ambiguously passivist/activist "mysticism of the everyday," this naming the very medicine modernity must take (he argued) to cure itself of its obsessive desire to reduce Paulinism (and, indeed, all reality) to some mode of cosmic economic exchange.[13]

For our purposes, note the way Schweitzer's early private confession to a girlfriend foreshadowed the way his own Paulinist mysticism of the everyday would eventually be imagined by Schweitzer to be a variety of Nietzscheanism. Without salve for tragic loss and without hope or need of the sacrificial substitution, the young seminary professor, about to become a famous New Testament interpreter, confided in the letter: "In Nietzsche was something of [Paul's] spirit of Christ; to say this is a sacrilege. It is, however, true; in the end, only the blasphemous is true. But he [Nietzsche] lacked action; for this reason, his "pride" paced inside a cage like a captured lion; instead of coming out of his cave to attack his prey, he tore himself to pieces in the end. But he was noble, this man. Had he lived twenty centuries earlier, he could have become Saint Paul.[31]"

My own framing of concerns will never be more or less than this, to search for those ready to be the least and greatest of Paulinists. In undoing a history and apparatus of thought and life, we perform it differently, a process of emptying and expansion that remains endemic to the genealogical encounter of philosophy with its exemplary figures.[14]

NARRATIVE PLATONISM FOR THE MASSES: ANOTHER "KILLER APP" OF WESTERN DOMINATIONS

Archival specificities or the exigencies of historiography mean, of course, that Paul's generally unrecognized splitting into hero/repressed, his being covered over or buried under the very aura of the story of "Christian origins," occurs differently from the way Freud imagined a similar thing to have happened to Judaism and what he calls the "greatest of its sons."[15] Interestingly, for example, on my reading the simultaneously doubled beatification-and-occultation of Paul within Western cultural memory happened most effectively by way of a retrospective *historical narration* of Paul as founding figure of a new religion, as someone who named a profound break (and therefore a new start) in relation to Judaism. I agree with Nietzsche's diagnoses of cultural history that Paul is perhaps the "greatest son" of Christianity, its favorite guarantor of a pop Platonizing worldview. But Nietzsche (like Freud after him) did not seem to recognize the way both the popularity and the idealism at issue for Nietzsche's own philosophico-cultural critique of Western logocentrism emerge not at all directly from Paul as the simple *archē* or origin, but from a massive machinery of intellectual and political organization which captured and placed Paul in the simplicity of a ruthlessly ingenious form of historico-theological narration. To name Nietzsche's critique with a term from the triumphalist Niall Ferguson, if there is in Paul an empowering "killer app" for Western power, it is an app whose effectiveness relies very heavily on the repetition of a *narrative* of Christian origins, a narratological supplement which itself teaches across cultural spheres how to embody a pop-Platonic metaphysic or how to remain docile and placidly secure in the imagined security of an inherited structure of life.[16] In keeping with the language of an organizing app in Ferguson (or, to very different ends discussed below, in Agamben and Delueze), it needs to be pointed out that, *just as it was for Freud's Moses*, the most important genealogical or interventionist point to make in relation to the politics of cultural memory here is that for Paul also it is not so much this individual, but rather the *place* or the *site* at which a cultural machinery inscribed this name onto a flesh of a cultural landscape. Once more I ask: why has such a fundamental issue not been made blisteringly clear, in Nietzsche, in Freud, in Derrida (chapter 1), in Michel Foucault (chapter 3), or in more recent philosophical/genealogical readings of Paul like Žižek and Badiou? What are the complicities at stake in *our* failure to unravel and analyze the genealogical story whereby Paul, like all of us presumably, becomes *inscribed into* the cultural memory, thereby becoming a vexed and ambivalent site of both instituting and instituted violence? As I have suggested, it is extremely problematic for Derrida to want to "split" every "atom" or constitutive particle of foundational reality even as he, on important occasions, tends to take Paul as the "original" Christian without further analysis.

At an important level, I think this phenomenon is related to the fact that early Christianity so effectively effaced some of the traces of its own emergence. The pressure readers feel (even now, even after so much ink has been spilled opening up alternatives) to find in the New Testament something like a harmonizable perspective on the "origins" of Christianity must be remarked and challenged. In this respect, and very simply, one must here remain committed to the Marxist-Freudian strategy of discerning historical and structural *difference and agonism* at the level of the emergence of a hegemonic picture of the movements in question. As I keep saying, the sublimating election of an element of a system into a lynchpin of that system's operativity, systematicity, or very framework is what is at issue here, and that is an operation which is *never simply about what we so quickly call "the past."* We will not escape the question of our own complicity in the effective machinations of this aged machinery, the serial repetition of this culturally organizing "app." Nevertheless, initially we do well to remind ourselves of some of the essentials of modern biblical scholarship, essentials which have been discussed in that field for a long time now and which are forgotten *to the same degree* as recent philosophical readings of Paul begin to fall under the spell of a "Christian origins" story that no longer holds sway within the best historical scholarship, scholarship that capitalizes, precisely, on multiplicity or diversity and contingency (though often, as I always say, without seeing the formal or philosophical implications of such an interpretive move).

As we consider the tale in question, remember that with the app language I want to suggest how it is an early Christian form of historical *narration* that most effectively suppresses the open-ended actuality of historical figures, *a repression* that most effectively repeats this misinterpreted actuality as an otherworldly idealism (or *sublimation*). Both together constitute a pop metaphysical machinery that underwrites effective history against a persecuted minority in Galilee and Judea. Platonism for the masses, in other words, is an app that turns repression into sublimation with an eye toward enforcing a very specific *politics*, a very specific "Jewish question," and a very specific mode of imagining power's relation to historical actuality.

In saying things this way, we can begin to catch a glimpse of how my focus enables a subtle but profound displacement of Nietzsche's massive genealogical critique of modern European politics. Nietzsche, for example, always imagined Paulinism as a perverse weaponizing—a turning against *itself*, paradoxically—of the forces of immanent historical actuality. In Nietzsche's view, as a good pop Platonist Paul invents another, imaginary world where redemption is kept, with humanity merely "here below" as those beings who must necessarily declare themselves guilty, always guilty for—by definition—not being part of that other world. But this implied for Nietzsche that those guilty of being in the actual world were caught up in an effort *to turn against* the *actual* inequalities of master-slave relations within the sphere of real, rather than imaginary, life. In this respect, however, Nietzsche was still reading Paul too much like a good pietistic Lutheran precisely inasmuch as the philosopher read Paul as the site of the origin-and-value of Christianity. There is in Nietzsche's story a profoundly ironic, but also profoundly problematic, echo of Eusebius's Platonic narration, on which I have previously remarked. Nietzsche no more than Eusebius analyzes the narrative capture, operationalization, or weaponization of Paul within an emerging ecclesiastical and narrative-based metaphysic, though of course Nietzsche otherwise analyzes and lampoons this two-tiered theologico-political economy within Western culture in very important ways. What Nietzsche is missing here is a way to address the fact that a popularizing metaphysical praxis is more appropriately linked not directly to Paul as the "origin" so much as to an emerging Christian narrative. More importantly, and with fateful consequences, Nietzsche further misunderstands the ancient narratological praxis, the popularization of Platonism, by reading it as a turning *against* historical actuality rather than recognizing what it tended to be, namely, *a brutally effective turning against early Judea and Galilee in their struggle against Roman imperial control.* What Nietzsche's story—and his accompanying critique of European politics—does not register is that Paul only became the (retroactive) founder of "Christianity" over against Judaism with Christianity's own nascent aligning of itself with the effective sovereignty of empire against an increasingly excluded, militarily suppressed minority.

This shift in analytical attention delivers a simple but massive blow to Nietzsche's (and Freud's) reading of Paul as a turning *against* historical actuality or the military might of Rome. Paul, imagined founder of a religion that was (eventually) *not Jewish*, was, after all, precisely the opposite of the one appearing in Nietzsche's story of a turning against life as an imperial "will to power," inasmuch as this fairly early appropriation of Paulinism involved a mode of *siding with* effective colonial power *against* the resistant (and often enough vilified and repressed) minority culture. This aspect of my diagnosis of the Pauline legacy, and of Nietzsche's evaluation of it, coheres very well therefore with Heidegger's genealogical critique of Nietzsche as the real *fulfillment* of a Roman and imperial beatification of instrumental control. After all, was not Nietzsche's disavowal of Paul as Platonism for the masses the most important gesture underlying Nietzsche's own thought of a pure immanence to life imagined as "will to power"? And was not the triumphalist apostolic founder imagined by fairly early ecclesiastical narrations of Christian origins precisely a turning *toward* that historical actuality of imperial life promising to enact a smooth circuit between will, enacted power, and guaranteed security? Heidegger's articulation of Nietzsche is of stunning significance, I think, leading us to formulate an additional genealogical twist: Nietzsche mistook Paul's partisanship with the crucified, his siding with that scandalously failed messiah or his refusal to let the suppressed messiah remain dead, as a bid for a metaphysical guarantee. But this bid for security and control through power—and all of this as "life" in its immanence—has more to do with Nietzsche's doctrine of the will-to-power than it does with Paul's risky partisanship against the imperialism which executed another Galilean messianic figure. Or, put differently, Nietzsche's will-to-power as imagined essence of metaphysics will have more to do with, precisely, the eventual ecclesiastical apostle as triumphalist founder-and-guarantor than the philosopher ever acknowledged. Both options, the church's and Nietzsche's, were grounded in a massive repression of Paulinist actuality, and it is to that burying away in the foundations of these accounts that I want to begin to articulate.[17]

A completely different role of "negativity" and power begins to emerge, which I will explore by way of the philosopher Stanislas Breton (chapter 4). On my reading, Paulinism in its developed Christian-metaphysical (or ultimately Eusebian-historical) form was not about the turning of *ressentiment* against *power* (as impotent or as effective as that turning might be), but rather about a collaborationist turning against the evident *weakness* of the partisans of Judea and Galilee in their struggles against Rome. These Christian origins stories invented a "Jewish problem" that would itself control a thinking of colonial power, an invention Nietzsche's analysis of power and the emergence of Christianity almost entirely ignores. Freud was right: when the origin story starts to smell like a crime, the trick of the detective is to look again to see who has been, who continues to be, investing in the cover-up.

To gesture toward the wider swath of contemporary readers of Paul, I should add that readings as diverse as those of Stanislas Breton, Alain Badiou, Slavoj Žižek, and Daniel Boyarin still seem to me to stick too closely to Nietzsche and Freud, still challenging too little about the way Paul has become a name indistinguishable from *this sublimated type of (weaponized) eventalness within historical process*, the way Paul was as it were murdered and buried in the floorboards, so to speak, of a collaborationist theory of power relations. In the preface I asked aloud what would have happened had second- and third-century Christian apologists not imagined that nailing the texts, tropes, and practices of their tradition onto a *Platonic* philosophical tradition was the most promising way forward in their efforts to achieve cultural recognition within an educated Greco-Roman milieu. I wondered what would have happened if these thinkers had articulated the same impulse by way of a nondualistic historiography like that available in some of the Stoics, Skeptics, or Epicureans.

Much could be explored in this counterfactual mode, a mode that seems to be invited by the frequency with which Pauline tropes are more recently being taken up, precisely, in the context of "materialist" traditions closer to Chrysippus or Lucretius than the traditional Plato. The issue would ultimately be about the modes in which one grounds, guarantees, or territorializes both identity and moments of creative newness. For example, in a fascinating and important recent encounter between Renaissance studies, philosophies of difference, and ancient Epicurean traditions, Jonathan Goldberg summarizes in telling language a Lucretian view of history, decidedly *not* a version explored by our early Christian apologists. In this view: "it is wrong to think of the past in a mode that delimits eras and confines the past to useless error or approximation to later truth. Insofar as supersession is not the way to think of history, [Michel Serres] insists, Lucretius is our contemporary; there always remain the unthought and the rethought. We are no closer to the truth now than we have ever been, and to posit a line dividing before and after, ignorance and knowledge, is to erect a quasi-theological divide like B.C. and A.D."[18]

Indeed. From early on, however, such discursive modes were—decidedly—roads generally untraveled by a historiographical tradition that was about guaranteed proprietary limits serving to ground or secure distinct identities, key components in the apologetic manufacture of politicized and ideal "origins." Or, to echo the initial quotation of Louis Althusser with which I opened this book, it is not *simply* that the tradition took a different path from the "underground current" of a new materialism in its forms of self-presentation. More importantly, philosophical alternatives to the resultant Christian *idealizing* of freedom and power were rejected for reasons that were not at all "innocent."

EXAMPLE: ACTS' NARRATIVE APPROPRIATION OF PAULINISM AND THE EVENTUAL APPARATUS OF A PLATONISM FOR THE MASSES

Already in the New Testament book of Acts, for example, the basic narrative of an emerging group of "Christians" presents a coherent and circumscribed communal identity that originates in Jerusalem under the leadership of Jesus's followers, spreading outward from there even while always remaining both internally coherent and clearly distinguishable from those who tend to be glossed as "the Jews."[19] New names on the stage of world history are often important, little clichés (as Marshall McLuhan liked to say) which—repeated and disseminated—begin to operate as organizing archetypes, apparatuses, quasi-transcendental signatures.[20] Names are certainly important for the text of Acts (cf. 11:26; chs. 9, 13), and there is a fateful discursive shift indicated by Acts' naturalization of these basic narrative coordinates. With Acts' "Christians" and "Jews" we are beginning (though only beginning) to shift from the singularly awkward forms of an experimental multiethnic solidarity (with its necessarily displaced identity markers) that were characteristic of Paul's actual Jewish apostleship to the gentiles. In its place we will have, increasingly, a tale of two distinct groups, two circumscribed spheres of identity, and Acts is, among others, a fateful moment in the retroactive invention of Paulinism as a keystone in the edifice of "Christian origins."[21] It is this narrative dualism of sorts which will, increasingly, displace the more immanently borne pressures, fissures, and risky *forcing into newness* or a new vibrancy of inherited identities, tropes, and ideas that were characteristic of the Pauline movement. The effective dualism will increasingly displace the more immanently borne struggles onto a self-protective representational distinction between identities imagined to be given, received *re*-presented. This safety, in turn, will increasingly occlude the fact that the movement's emerging behaviors, desires, and conceptual systems are themselves *in the act* of invention, forcing without ready-made identitarian ground (or experimenting within an economy wherein *only* the risks of relationalities could appear to justify or condemn the experiments in question). Of course, the soporific givenness of this ready-made identitarian dualism would become increasingly powerful and expansive as an apparatus of capture, gathering ever more and more about the spaces of the present, past, and future into its massive organizational pincers. Indeed, the pincers would eventually become so strong that the *very capacity* to throw representational dualisms back onto a more vexing sphere of borne— politicized rather than instrumental—immanence will eventually be completely misrecognized by Martin Heidegger as the capacity naming *the very difference* between Christianity and Judaism.[22] In this respect, the young Heidegger's fascinating lectures on *The Phenomenology of Religious Life* are a perfect example of what we are diagnosing much more radically than he did, namely, the expansionistic triumph of Acts' new nomenclature, the eventual becoming of Acts' weaponized cliché into an unimpeachable stereotype. After all, Heidegger's remarkable lectures equate the authentic Pauline experience of time with a (modern philosophical) *existential phenomenology as lived immanence*, imagining the neo-Pauline experience to escape from representational structures of Christian ontotheology (in religious terms) and also from foundational metaphysics (in philosophical terms). But it remained inconceivable to Heidegger that the twinned religious and philosophical implosion of representational guarantee (with accompanying revelation of the borne political traumas of existence) in his ancient-contemporary Paulinism should be called anything other than Christian. It is unthinkable to Heidegger that he should describe Paulinist singularity, that form of nonrepresentational risk or faith, with any other phrase than "primordial Christian religiosity."[23] Or, to repeat our earlier exercise in wonder about counterfactual histories, what if Heidegger in 1920–21 *had* dared to name that Pauline singularity without representational guarantee a form of *Jewish messianic solidarity* amidst multiplicity before (precisely) the Christian invention of Jewish-Christian dualism? We can say this for sure: such a gesture would have been worlds more radical than his later suggestions that the fulfillment of this tradition of "primordial Christian religiosity" is a modern European atheism.

Instead, Heidegger remained stuck in a kind of emancipation from representationalism, a kind of religio-philosophical exodus from metaphysics, that would necessarily remain indistinguishable from a lingering "Jewish question," which is itself endemic to all these founding dualisms emerging from texts like Acts. Acts has begun to hit upon a kind of narratological shorthand that would constitute an apparatus of capture from which the singularly partisan Paul would almost never again escape, destined as he was rather to become the "first Christian." Just ask Eusebius of Caesarea, who seems to know Paul is still buried away in Rome, the apostle's sacred corpse stuffed beneath some floorboards in the triumphalist foundations of Rome become Christianity, this hidden corpse the very "trophy" of the success of the enterprise. (With such lovely ambivalence as that, you see by now why we were forced to pair Eusebius with Freud.)[24] Indeed, as Christopher Mount argues in his excellent study, *Pauline Christianity: Luke-Acts and the Legacy of Paul*, Acts may be read as a significant shift in strategies of self-presentation within the Jesus movement, and this precisely as these strategies of self-presentation *occur in relation to Rome.*[25] Mount's study should be read in keeping with the McLuhanesque insight about the media or *forms of repetition* which themselves come to constitute the very form of libidinal investment or ritual maintenance of a particular *type* of Paulinism within the emerging machinery of pop Platonism that Nietzsche so despised. Distinguishing the authorial self-presentation of Acts (cf. Luke 1:1–4, Acts 1:1–5) over against earlier traditions within the movement of authorial anonymity, Mount writes:

> Lk-Acts does not emerge out of the anonymity of public worship of a Christian [*sic*] church community, but out of the intellectual enquiry of an individual, the authorial "I," into apostolic traditions. In speaking in his own voice, the author shifts the literary context of his work from the anonymous interpretive voice of early Christian communities rooted in Judaism to the authoritative voice of an author writing a Hellenistic narrative that is specifically Christian. The author is self-consciously a Christian writer working within the context of Hellenistic literary culture. The traditions of Jesus are no longer conceived as part of an anonymous narrative whose authority belongs to the Christian community, but rather as pieces of the Christian past whose ordering into a narrative depends on the authority of an author writing according to the standards of truth for history in Hellenistic literary culture.[26]

In terms of the history of scholarship on Acts, it is possible to read Mount's work as an interpretive shift from a focus on social religious history to media history, a shift which could (I suspect) ultimately dislodge Mount's own distinction here between "Jewish" and "Christian" traditions. For our purposes it is more important to point out the way in which, within this new authorial/mediating constellation within which the name "Paul" would constitute a narrative weapon against Jews and heretics alike, Acts needs to make the apostle into a kind of first or founding "Christian" (and here the quotation marks indicate Acts' description rather than Mount's).[27] Here the significance of names blurring into narrative structures is subtly effective. Notice that at critical moments along Acts' narrative way, the "Jews" are presented as distinct from this group of "Christians," a politicized reduction of the earlier complexity of negotiation of identity markers among Jews, Gentiles, and Galilean followers of Jesus alike. The nature of this politicizing rhetorical maneuvre is sometimes brutally evident in the way, for example, "you Israelites" or "the Jews" appear—without caveat or specification—as those who used extralegal/Gentile authorities to kill Jesus ("You . . . crucified and killed [Jesus] by the hands of those outside the law," 2:23, 36, 3:12; "you killed the author of life," 3:15; 4:10, 27, etc.), as if "the Jews" had become, somehow, a causal will behind the anti-Jewish violence of Rome itself. Similarly, "the Jews" kill Stephen after his delivery of a fairly standard Hellenistic philosophical invective against the need for temples (cf. 7:51–54). "The Jews plotted to kill" Paul (imagined in Acts as having undergone a radical conversion and possible name change of his own), forcing him to escape Damascus in a basket (9:23), and Jewish rioting is what leads to Paul's being nicked by Roman authorities (21:27–22:30, 23:26–30). Again, it is as if the "Jews" were a causal agent in the enactments of Roman colonial control. Elsewhere the "Jews" become similar culprits in relation to the demise of Paul as they were in the author of Acts' depiction also of the death of Jesus (cf. 21:10–21, 9:16).[28] Moreover, it is in fact the jealous recalcitrance and reactionary violence of the "Jews" which is generally presented in Acts as the very obstruction that ends up functioning as a driving force behind the triumphalist expansion of the Way of the Christians (cf. 13:43, 50, 14:1ff., 25:1, 2), but also (and this is remarkable) as the effective cause of violent outbursts against Jews by the Roman authorities (cf. Luke 19:11–20:19, 21:12–24, 23:28–31).[29] Similarly, as Jack Sanders argues in his still very timely study, *The Jews in Luke-Acts*, in keeping with the earlier presentation of Jesus's relationship to Jewish temple authorities, Acts goes out of its way to present *Jewish* "captains" as the policing mechanism operative in the roundup and persecution of Jesus's apostles (cf. Acts 4:1; 5:24, 26).[30] Indeed, the narrative repeatedly imagines that the machinations of *Roman* policing are altogether safer for Paul than those of "the Jews" in Jerusalem (cf. 25:2–26:32). Moreover, as Christina Petterson argues in her excellent collection of cultural reflections, *Acts of Empire: The Acts of the Apostles and Imperial Ideology*, such narrative distinctions between Paul and the Jews reinforce the text's construction of Paul as an elite "*moral subject*" of empire, the fictive apostle and the fictive Roman dignitaries all sharing the role of public functionaries of a larger rational *beneficence* imagined to inhere in public speaking, respect for the citizenship, and legal structures of Rome.[31] Paul becomes a "hero" in this text to the degree that he becomes an ideal, if controversial, citizen of Rome, an aligning of the apostle *with* Rome and *against* "the Jews" that has an almost mechanical consistency.[32]

The emergence of an apparatus of capture always involves the carrying of a kind of performance, and this type of narrative is no different. Here the *performative element* involved in Acts' evocation of coherently separable groups is to me all the more evident in light of the way that sometimes the text carefully qualifies the multiple layers of identity or practice endemic to the ethnic identifications on offer in the first and early second centuries C.E. For example, the author distinguishes *diasporic* synagogue communities in Jerusalem from, as it were, the local Jerusalem community networks (6:9ff.). The author also distinguishes the "apostles and believers [in Jesus] in Judea" from new followers of Jesus among the "Gentiles" outside Judea (11:1), the Jerusalem elite from those not so invested in currying the external support of Rome (4:27), and "brothers" among the Jesus movement who knew Paul from those who did not (cf. the famous "we" passages at chs. 20ff.). *Most importantly on my reading*, the text can in fact even distinguish between those "Jews" who do and those who do not follow Jesus (cf. 14:1–2). But just here is the essential point: it is the very multiplicity of distinctions that *are* recognized by the narrative which highlights all the more the striking sociological and rhetorical force operative in the *repeated lack of qualification* mentioned in those crucial narrative performances when the totality of identitarian options within the narrative seem to be something like "Christian" or "Jew," or when "Jew" seems to gloss the identity outside of the band of Jesus's followers. It is from the narrative shorthand, from the emerging clichés, that the eventual identitarian archetypes will arise.

These specificities of Acts' narrative enactment are neither accidental nor irrelevant later as part of the emerging machinery of Christian self-understanding. In the repetition of Acts' narrative of Paulinism, first- or second-century audiences end up being captured by Acts' many repetitions of the unqualified references to "you," to "them," "those Jews," the "bad Israelites," and so on. Here we need to be clear. Whatever would have been even a minimally conversionistic or protreptic invitation in such formulations (e.g., to align oneself with the "good" as opposed to the "bad" Israelites, as per Peter's first speech in chapter 2 and elsewhere), the effect of this rhetoric would very quickly have become, as it had already in second-century receptions, a description of the emergence of a group of Jesus followers or "Christians" who were clearly distinct from another group, the "Jews." The nascent idealizing here of two "types" of religion or stably oppositional identity as the implicit explanatory mechanism *behind* the narration of first and early second-century developments constitutes for me an important piece of the operational heart of a machinery that eventually becomes indistinguishable from a Platonism for the masses. It is, we might say, an archetypical reification of identity, identity's retroactive sublimation or imagination as a given, unchanging foundation.[33]

Acts is certainly the tale that co-opts Paul for a "Christian" cause which would have been inconceivable to Paul himself. Here we should repeat an assertion of Nietzsche that is completely *apropos* of such early narratives of two communities, or two identities, namely, the Jewish and the

Christian. Once Paul is taken up into Acts by such narrative machinery, we have reached the *end of Paul as a Jewish partisan and the invention of Paul as the founding Christian* (as will be seen). With Acts' narrative, not to mention that of the explicitly Platonic Eusebius, it is the invention of an identitarian category—and therefore of an idealist or Platonizing capacity for historical representation—which makes possible the Paul of Nietzsche's Platonism for the masses. With this *type* of narrative we have an invention that will install a fateful forgetfulness over the memory of Paul the "Jewish partisan," one among a multiplicity of sectarian options antagonistically and creatively arguing against other options in a bid to suture their partisan model onto that open-ended and shifting identity they often called (like us) Jewish. Indeed, what Nietzsche so beautifully described in *The Twilight of the Idols* as the "'higher swindle' or, if you prefer, idealism"—performed by an imagined stable identity of "another world" which steals or negates the immanence, multiplicities, and ago-nistic bids for hegemony constituting worldly life—is in this forgetfulness fully operational, and not simply because Acts' narrative affords visions of a hereafter or a heavenly doubling of the real world, but because it begins retroactively to baptize Paul as an indication of the move *from one* ideal entity, that of the Jews, to another, the Christians.[34] It is, whatever the ancient author's intentions, the invention of a mode of historical repre-sentation that produces spectators who only receive identities existing, as if fully guaranteed, elsewhere.

As we might expect given the quasi-transcendental or "signatory" func-tion in view with these philosophical or historical repetitions of this pri-mal scene of "Western" culture, telling stories like Acts' about early Jewish and Christian developments is absolutely essential for a larger genealogi-cal story in our purview, even when the focus is almost entirely on phi-losophy. Already in Acts there is a profound transformation of the role of partisanship within irreducible multiplicity into a form of stable, foun-dational, and therefore representationally repeatable identities that exist over time. It is the appearance of a specific type of ownership or propri-etary discourse within historical repetition, and once Acts is canonized in the New Testament it becomes a primary model even for later and more proprietorially rapacious versions of such stories as those of Eusebius of Caesarea. As we will see in chapters 1 and 2, it is the type of historical narration embodied already in Acts, worked out much more elaborately over coming centuries, which tends to preclude our thinking along more aleatory, multiple, or fleetingly material lines about the figure of Paul, that exemplar of origins, or, if you prefer, idealism. In particular, I will argue, we continue to preclude philosophical echoes of a historical tale in which a *subtractive* or *singular* "election" emerges as an auratic performative, an election Jacques Lacan could formalize as an (elusive) object cause of desire or as the subject-constituting event of transferential love. Instead of such a mode of thinking, in repeating early Christian narrations of Paul as the "first Christian" we find ourselves stuck with stories of stable, present, representational entities with no constitutive surprise, emergence, or contingency.[35] Put differently, the future of the discussion about subversive Paulinisms, reworked philosophemes, and a differently constituted "West" depend on our creativity in thinking around the early apologetic self-presentations and their co-optation of Paulinism to these ends.

PAULINIST PARTISANSHIP AND TAUBES

Does such a diagnosis suggest that, were we to leap back "before" such early Christian gestures of appropriation, we might be able to discover Paul the deeply invested partisan within an irreducible diversity? Would we have found, as if working alongside Jacob Taubes, even a kind of (anti-) Schmittian Paul, a figure of exceptional contingencies emerging "from below," and this before the instalment of Paulinism within a massive apparatus of a narrative Platonism for the masses? I certainly think so. For the moment, however, I want to clarify my brief genealogical repetition of Acts a bit further by saying that this early Christian gesture to secure its own identity as a stable imaginary only emerges hand in hand with what I would like to call the *weaponization* of the identity of the postpartisan or the weaponization of the idea of a founding or originary figure. It is in highlighting the weaponization of Paul-the-founder in the early reception history of Paulinism that I want to remember the dense sketches of an intervention of Jacob Taubes within the Western cultural memory of Paul.[36] Above all it seems to me that Taubes was correct in his lifelong intuition that the figure of Paul was precisely the loose thread on which to tug in order to subvert important strands within the still-vibrant Western theologico-political legacy.

To pair our sketch of a reading of Acts with Taubes in this respect, should we not first wonder aloud about whether the Schmittian sovereign that Taubes wanted to undo—or to subvert from within or from below—was not already nicely foreshadowed in the theologico-political narrative of Acts, even if Schmitt's work of course also builds on later centuries of Christian reflection on government and the enemies of the state? Note how shrewdly the identitarian economies of the book of Acts work in this regard. In Acts, as I have already suggested, the Roman authorities are generally presented as if genuinely predisposed to get along with the "Christians," with interventionist violence only appearing as a kind of providentially beneficent *reaction* against a looming threat for an order already imagined in the text as a peculiar unspoken contract or implicit complicity between the "Christians" and the empire of Rome. In this respect I think the most shrill denunciations of recent philosophical readings of Paul and their praise of a "Paulinist universalism" are correct about important dynamics of the received Western-foundationalist Paul, not so much in their denunciatory criticisms of philosophers like Badiou, Žižek, or Ranciere (whose "universalism" is much more nuanced and nonrepresentational than most historians understood), but rather in their diagnoses of a dominant form of historical narration constitutive of early Christian tales of "Christian origins" like those we can already sketch in Acts.[37] After all, does Acts not already lend itself to the perverse projection of a situation in which, precisely, the unruly "Jews" become the figure indicating chaotic threat against the harmonious order of empire, such that willful Jewish self-subtraction from the imperial juridical economy comes to be fantasized as what might evoke the exceptional response of imperial sovereignty in the form of retributive and suppressive violence in order to maintain order?

For example, Shmuel Trigano sees the return of standard modern and also Christian anti-Jewish discursive logics congealing once more around the "return" of a philosophical Paul. But, like Nietzsche and Freud, Trigano consistently reifies rather than contests larger historical apparatuses of capture that operate in the name of the (already) suppressed apostle. Fair enough. Trigano and many others are of course not incorrect in their diagnoses of potential new repetitions of a serially anti-Jewish discourse which is itself well documented and which has often rooted itself in an image of Paul-the-first-Christian. Platonism for the masses has always had at its heart a "Jewish question," and this is what concerns Trigano the most. But Trigano and others do seem to me quite docile in the face of genealogical actuality and, therefore, stuck on the outside of a more radical intervention than any we could constitute by way of a simple denunciation of Paulinism as a narrative Platonism for the masses in search of new sacrifices for its ostensibly foundation-laying mechanisms or its closely allied representational universalisms. Put differently, like Nietzsche and Freud, Trigano also seems to think it was Paul who was himself the first founder, the "origin" of an identity capable of being glossed as the Christian, rather than being yet another partisan in an irreducible plurality of agonistic identitarian potentials. For me, it is with dire genealogical consequences that Trigano and others tend to elide the ways in which it was Paul who was himself suppressed in his partisanship within the multiple in order to be sublimated into the mythical role of origins and foundations. Trigano, in this respect, fails to discern the fact that his Paul has been fitted with the concrete shoes of a weaponized and idealizing mode of tale-telling about "Christian origins," a weaponized sublimation that must become as widespread an object of analysis as Freud's Moses ever was.[38]

Of course, the maintenance of Acts' basic plot and character structures not so long after a period in which many of the "pillars" (as Paul would call them) of the Jesus movement were killed by Roman authorities is not a little awkward, maybe even perfectly comical.[39] One thinks for example of the strangely benign or actively admiring stance of all the Roman officials in the narration of Acts, at least when they are encountering a Christian. "This man was seized by the Jews and was about to be killed by them . . . but I came with the guard and rescued him," Acts imagines the typical interdepartmental Roman memo to read (23:26). Later in the text, caveats aside, Paul is presented as thinking he is safer with the Romans than with "the Jews," preferring to be transferred to Rome rather than to Jerusalem (25:1–12)! Beneficent, just, at one level it is as if the Romans and the "Christians" were destined to become the best of friends, again a wishful projection not without a halo of a brutally effective gamble which we must soon enough name and never forget (cf. 19:37–41, 23:29, 25:18–25, 26:31, 28:30–31).[40]

This type of presentation fits perfectly well with the striking absence, at the end of Acts, of what other early Christian traditions would certainly claim to recall, namely, that when actually taken to Rome Paul lost his life to a Roman executioner there. Such indelicate memories, that sublimely heroic agent of an expansionistic "Way" killed by Rome, would be a far cry from Acts' fantasy of Paul, shuttled along to Rome—at Paul's own request!—as a revered captive settling into a rented Roman apartment where he entertains his many friends under a light house arrest (28:23). Acts further imagines that, teaching from this place, Paul plays the bold parrhesiast, speaking candidly under the nose of Rome herself in order to expand his movement "without hindrance" (28:30f.). As the curtains draw on the drama of Acts, the audience is left with a nice, warm feeling of the Evangel's triumphal spread. The more brutal finality that marked the memory of others in the early Jesus movement in relation to Paul's trip to Rome would, of course, have been a real downer for the author of Acts, hardly a note to end on, and not just for the author's narrative interest in the expansionistic witness to a spreading kingdom of God. Or, to say it in relation to the genealogy of Jacob Taubes's (Paulinist) encounter with Carl Schmitt, the bad news of conflict with imperial power would also have been a real downer for Christianity's emerging and eventual imperial political theology, something we should now discuss.[41]

PROLEGOMENA TO *KATECHON*

Now that we have tabled some brief genealogical glosses about some roles played by the book of Acts in the developing narrative of a Platonism for the masses, it is an obvious moment to repeat the question Freud poses in the epigraph to this introduction to the texts about Moses, asking: what economy of forces could so have effected the cobbling together of such unlikely representations, such strange antinomies, such striking omissions! Here, too, at the level of an introductory sketch of the genealogical suturing of an implicitly aggressive (or necessarily sacrificial) metaphysical idealism onto the tale of Paul the partisan, I want to point out that this particular part of the Freudian/genealogical dreamwork is not so difficult to determine. In fact, I think this is one more occasion when it is safe to say that the story is not at all hidden from recent discussions in historical or biblical studies, even as it is almost nowhere to be found in recent philosophical discussions of Paul. As Paul himself might have said it, the story is neither hidden away in heaven nor buried underneath the earth. And yet, I'm suggesting, it has been hiding away in plain sight—once again, how is that?[42]

To put it bluntly, was not the maintenance of Acts' implausible explanation of power relations not caused rather directly by the expansion and intensification of Roman retributive or counterrevolutionary interventions in Judea and Galilee after that latest (in a series of) Jewish revolts during the sixties C.E.? This basic context of a sometimes virulent prejudice against ostensibly seditious and dissident nature of the Jews begins to yield here a kind of *katechon* myth—Schmitt's beloved touchstone about the sovereign or extralegal maintenance of order—which inflects the *pax romana* with a decidedly different tone that it might have other-wise had.[43] One should say it clearly and brutally: Christian origins stories of the sort we begin to see in Acts always had a great deal more to do with negotiating the ideological aftermath of *this* colonial rebellion and its rapaciously brutal repressions than it ever did with the natural outwork-ing of distinct and distinctly ideal identities, projects, or theologies. Such representational, idealizing tales are instead the essentially repressive fan-tasies of the sort we can begin to intuit already in Acts' early narrative of Christian origins. Harsher but much more illuminating than such fanta-sies is the story in which, at a moment of Roman colonial and ideological counterrevolutionary suppression (which included and led to the spread of anti-Jewish pogroms throughout the empire and the rise of new forms of stereotyped suspicion against "the Jews"), there begin to appear new forms of self-protective sociological distancing among those also under the diverse umbrella of the Jews who are interested in distinguishing themselves from a (disavowed) version of the same. Thus it seems to be painfully ironic—brutally comical, perhaps—that the author of Acts, with his beneficent Romans always defending the innocence of Jesus's follow-ers against "Jews," that the famous Gamaliel is imagined retroactively as declaring:

> Men of Israel, consider carefully what you are going to do to these men, for before these days arose Theudas claiming to be somebody, with whom about four hundred men joined up. He was killed, and all those who were persuaded by him were scattered, so it all came to nothing! After him in the days of the census arose Judas the Galilean who led people in revolt. That one was was killed also, and all those who believed him were scattered. So, in the present case [i.e., with Jesus's followers] I advise you: Leave these men alone! Let them go! For if their purpose or activity is of the order of the human [*ex anthrōpōn*], it will be destroyed [*kataluthēsetai*]. But if it is of God, you will not be able to destroy these men; you will only find yourselves fighting against God [*theomachoi*].
>
> *(Acts 5:35–39)*

How perfectly such a little speech works in Acts, the wise one among the otherwise jealously violent leadership of Jerusalem voicing the same unanimous verdict as audiences of this text are always hearing from the wise juridical leaders of Rome: Leave these men alone! Let them go! Gama-liel, now wisened more than ever, is here the retroactive voice of a newly proposed theodicy, a justification of the ways of Rome before the eyes of Acts' readers. After all, while it is not spelled out in Acts, *who was it* who rounded up and suppressed the serially emerging messianic and rebellious movements in Judea and Galilee? It was of course the Roman military who sifted the difference between "human" and "divine" collective will and action in this way, making Acts' ideological gamble here blisteringly clear: God's will is made manifest in the suppressive or katechontic power of Rome itself. Military suppression is here the "miracle" which determines the very openness of the movement in question. The little speech, fit for Acts' retrospective purpose, operates as a kind of Christian whitewashing of the murder and enslavement of "Jews" around 70 c.e., and its placement in the mouth of the sage Gamaliel is a crucial thread for the ideological fabric of the larger narrative. Recall, after all, that the larger narrative will conclude with Paul's declaration that "the Jews" are hardened, judged, and left behind for the sake of an expansionistic movement to "the gentiles" (Acts 28). Read this way, Gamaliel's speech becomes a kind of performative utterance—a kind of a prayer—before the eyes of Rome or at least before the eyes of gentiles very anxious about Rome (and who wouldn't be?). The prayer is a kind of desiring machine, a machine which *wants it* to be the case that, after the horrors of Roman-Judean interaction, there is in fact an indemnifying *sōtēria* of God which has actually gone over the outsider nations (see Acts 28:17, 19, 22, 28!). If the "Jews" are beginning to be disavowed, it is for the sake of an apotropaic desire of other quasi-Jewish gentiles to find *security* before the military and juridical face of Rome.

Famously, of course, Josephus once led Galilean revolutionary forces against Roman armies only later to take a job, effectively, within the Flavian imperial court in Rome. Josephus retroactively presents his revolutionary activities, therefore, as an earlier and naive concession to the "bad" Jewish revolutionaries, insurrectionists, and upstarts whose subversive political activities indicated a clear lack—he assures his audience— of philosophical virtue.[44] The essential theoretical point to keep in mind perhaps is not simply that such shrewd retroactive self-descriptions were opportunistic or cynical. The essential point is rather that the very multiplicity of Jewish ethnicities, practices, ideas, and forms of solidarity made it possible for *others potentially under the same representational umbrella* to elude the concretely exclusionary effects of Roman counterrevolutionary or suppressive power.[45] Judaism was never ever just one thing, but nor was the *significance* of its own internal differentiation ever something generally agreed upon or agreed upon without dissonance between various parties. Said differently, these differences were real, constitutive, difference and division integral for every level of our historical description. And, with every gesture or bid of one community or writer to stand in *as* the exemplary indication of the significance in question, there was a new shuffling of the open-ended rules of naming, self-presentation, and recognition constituting the totality we might name early Judaism. With every contest the very identities in question changed, shifted, *became* something new. Such is our relationality in a world of difference. Nevertheless, the difference between the collaborationist opportunism (so to speak) of Josephus and the same in the author of Acts is that the latter begins to invent a more brutal machinery to hide away altogether the identity-defining struggle for hegemony. Instead of Josephus referring to ignoble, moribund, mad, foolhardy, or violent alternatives *within* a given identitarian nomenclature, Acts begins (though perhaps just that) to refer simply to "Jews" in a way that naturalizes and reifies the self-indemnifying gesture all at one go.

A great deal of modern scholarship on texts like Acts can be categorized according to whether the scholars understand that the rhetoric of a book like this one is not just representational—simply repeating or expressive of an identity that exists stably somewhere offstage—but rather processual, performatively, or protreptically *becoming* the very structures it projects. As I say, Nietzsche's Platonism for the masses inhabits most effectively the forms of narration of Christian origins, and if we shift our own thinking in relation to these forms the very politics of the machinery or apparatus begins to shift before our eyes. In this case, for example, some predominantly Gentile branches of the Jesus movement began to imagine more and more essential, representational, or ideal distinctions between themselves and the group that becomes, retroactively, "the Jews" as a suspicious name for what they themselves are not or with which they (self-protectively) do not want to be identified. The drama of Acts remains haunting, of course, and the eventual function of this canonized Western theologico-political history will end up having everything to do with the fact that "Christianity" emerges here through an agreement to participate in an economy of imagined identities within which "the Jewish question" under Roman imperial sovereignty was always *really about someone else*. Indeed, we might say that it was the desire for this "question" to be about "someone else" which drove an investment in newly invented names which immediately started to generate new histories, all these the little machineries, little organizational apparatuses, indelicate little clichés repeating themselves until they would become monstrously lumbering narrative and cultural archetypes. In the inflation or expansion of the intitial gestures we have begun to discuss, however, all the latter-day variations of the same ethical (and eventually ontological) problematic are repetitions made possible by such early Christian gestures of collaborationism, gestures that amount to the manufacture of identity premised on the disavowal of a "rebellious" Jewish element worthy of katechontic reprisal.

Jacob Taubes's fragments on Paul could be more clear (or perhaps more effectively staged), but one can see already how my genealogy remains true to one of Taubes's basic desires for the inversion of the conservatively authoritarian nature of Schmittian exceptionalism into a transformative exceptionalism of partisanship "from below." To accomplish Taubes's genealogical intervention more effectively, one must press the Pauline legacy back into and against the emerging narratives of an early Christian historiographical apologetic that was itself the most effective means of baptizing, or placing a halo above, a profound submission to the brutalities of Roman imperial management. Christian origins as a story in Acts (and even more so as time moved forward) was *itself* this halo and, as I keep repeating, was itself the invention of those imagined stable identities that Nietzsche presents as a Platonism for the masses.

At the same time, my shift in focus from Nietzsche's is both subtle and yet profoundly important, effectively reading Nietzsche through dynamics that are clearer in Freud than in the philosopher. On my reading, imagined stable identities around "Paul" emerged as retroactive justifications for the self-protective, even self-distancing or reflective behaviors of some in what was unquestionably a very awkward, even dangerous, political moment. Nietzsche was not wrong about the way a Platonism for the masses subtracted itself from the immanent economies of everyday life and its effective machinations. But he missed the crucial element of retroactive co-optation that I am trying to make clear by reference to Acts, the way that this reactive subtraction was not *against* the effective history of Roman power but was precisely a *collaborationist identification with effective history*. This attempt at identification was itself governed by a desire to distance itself, rather, from the subversive weakness of a counterimperial rebellion. In missing, as it were, the Freudian dynamics of the founding of this biblical touchstone, Nietzsche's story of resentment has the truth—but the truth rather precisely backward.

QUASI-TRANSCENDENTAL: AFTERWORD ON A NARRATIVE PLATONISM FOR THE MASSES

Already with these basics we have moved far from a story in which Christianity was an invention appearing in light of an ideal "event" or a straightforward theological "break" from, say, Jewish conceptions of ethnicity or law. The force of the new, the real (counter?) "revolution" of Christianity appears in the desire of predominantly Gentile members of a complexly diffuse Jewish collective to distance themselves from the more problematically anti-imperial elements of the movement itself. *Christianity*, as the designation of a founding of a new and more universal "religion," has its point of origin in this political turmoil and social crisis, an effect of the carefully managed pressure to participate in the imperial economy. The key point here, *one* of the lasting cultural effects of this moment emerges in the way this questionable or not so heroic "origin" was so profoundly mirrored as a *form of theological orientation indistinguishable from a form of historical narration*. Roman violence against the anticolonial uprisings of Judea and Galilee became understood—again, already in Acts—as retributive divine judgment against the recalcitrance of the Jews, the necessary displacement and scapegoating that made way for an imagination of the "original" and ever expanding "way" of the "Christians."[46]

As the early centuries dragged on, such implicitly theologico-political narrative machinery would develop in scope, sophistication, and organizational effectiveness. Clichés become archetypes. In fact, as should be clear already, I think it is essential to read *these narrative machineries* as the real essence of what Nietzsche—in dialogue with the scholar of early Christianity Franz Overbeck—designated as a popularized Platonism, that massively influential phenomenon which constituted a more easily consumable, and thereby all the more effective, form of idealist justification of a life that was actually maneuvering in a decidedly different theater of operations. Nietzsche and Freud (not to mention more recent disciples) liked to read the significance of "Paul" directly off the dogmata they imagined themselves to be getting from the Pauline texts, but in doing so they failed to construe or contest the massive apparatus of capture of the name Paul within an early Christian *form of narrative political theology* emerging already in a history like Acts or, differently and more developed, in Eusebius's later tale of Christian origins.

There is, of course, a great deal of tragicomic irony in this suspicious sublimation of origins, which even Freud seemed not to have recognized. As I keep saying, the genealogical implications of the canonization within cultural memory of this tragicomedy have still not been registered or worked through in its ongoing philosophical effects. Philo of Alexandria spent his first-century days "translating" Jewish Scriptures into Platonic ones—and vice versa—occasionally forgetting (in one of those sublime moments of archive fever) which is the one and which the other.[47] Other early Christians would perform a similar operation, tinkering together biblical traditions and Platonic traditions with great ingenuity (cf. already the reflections on dualism in 1 Corinthians 15, which Paul counters with Stoic immanence).[48]

But, unlike Nietzsche's gloss on the otherworldly dimensions of the cultural afterlives of Paulinism, for me it was actually the turn to *historical narration* in texts like Acts that became the most effective and influential mechanism for the transformation of an eclectic and diverse montage of ethnicities, obsessively repeated or deeply invested practices, and transformative ideas of history and solidarity into something else, something capable of being glossed as a stable or ideal identity. That this imagined stable entity emerged by placing itself outside both Jewish diversity *and* an effectively repressed anti-imperialism was just more icing on the cake in question. Indeed, this ideal entity very quickly became powerful enough, *present* enough, we might say, to begin to exist *behind* "Jewish" texts and histories, rendering their actuality a mere "shadow" of themselves, allegories pointing toward "Christian" actuality. And *that* remarkable phenomenon of shadow making, this machinery's retroactive manufacture of *mere* ghosts, is the capacity of what Gilles Deleuze (in dialogue with Foucault) named an *apparatus*, the emergence of a quasi-transcendental recursivity within a complex multiplicity of historical actuality.

Apparatuses are not new to us, who sense every day the fact that some discourses are, as it were, more alive than we are, more real than we are, as if we have become their ghosts, as if mere instances of their capacity to continue to replicate themselves despite all our protests.[49] The sometimes traumatic force of these repetitions is considerable, which is why I keep pointing out that—despite themselves—important philosophers continue to repeat them. In the ancient instance, the projection of distinct, ideal types coupled wonderfully with the brutalities of effective history in the first centuries C.E., as if this violence afforded the all-important teleological supplement (or clear interpellating experience) by which to drive forward the self-protective, self-constituting self-differentiation from "the Jews." As the repetition of *self* here implies, it was with historical narration, in other words, that a populist Platonism came into its own as a force in the Christian world, one so remarkably powerful as soon to attempt to render the Jews into the Christians' own recalcitrant shadow. The fact that Rome murdered and stole Jews en masse during the sixties and early seventies—just decades before the production of Acts, perhaps—simply provoked and bolstered the investment in an imagined ideal distinction between what would soon be referred to as two "religions." The wisened phantasm of Gamaliel was perfectly correct: in the illuminated clearing afforded by the *apparatus* of a Christian origins story, Roman violence appears as both solicited by and soliciting the *factum* of an ideal distinction between "Jews" and "Christians."

All of which returns us to Freud, but with a fresh thought.

MOSES THE EGYPTIAN, MEET PAUL THE JEWISH PARTISAN

It should be clear by now why I think it is so important that Nietzschean genealogy move beyond the limits of Nietzsche's (nevertheless brilliant) readings of the Pauline texts themselves or why I think it is so important that we realize that Paul only became the "original" Christian retroactively within this larger discursive development. Nietzsche was perfectly correct to see in the emergence and spread of Christianity a kind of pop Platonism (and, like Freud, sometimes a vindictively perverse or sacrificial one at that). What Nietzsche does not recognize sufficiently, on my reading, is that it is not so much Paul as *Paul's place* within an emerging Christian narrative Platonizing intervention that constitutes him as the purveyor of this, as it were, ideal or conceptual stance. In one of his remarkable analyses of Paul (which always need to be pushed just a little further to get where we need to be), this one from *Daybreak*, the genealogist of the material soul of the West concludes: "This [Paul] is the *first Christian*, the inventor of Christianness! Before him there were only a few Jewish sectarians."[50] It should be obvious by now why I think this is an astonishingly important insight that must be pressed much further than

Nietzsche seemed to have realized one could press it. Without the Christian origins story, without an ideal or imagined Christianness as a *cause* of Christianity's *not* being Jewish, our analyses of these texts must take into account partisan diversity without the capacity of being reclaimed, guaranteed, or justified by the teleologies of effective history. Nietzsche is here perfectly correct, but the shrewd genealogist of perspectivism, multiplicity, and irreducibly agonistic relations of power still fails to distinguish between Paul and the place of the inscription of this name within a discursive machinery that would come to dominate the effective history and cultural memory of Christian origins.

Interestingly, sticking with stories of the partisan within the irreducible multiplicity of the material world would constitute a kind of helpful affirmation of Nietzsche's usual readings of early Christianity that *also* find in the figure of Paul an oddly depoliticizing economy, depoliticizing precisely because it focuses on another world which is really, Nietzsche tells us, a phantasmatic negation of the effective political history of *this* world. In my understanding of the relation between Paul and Paul's reception in Acts, however, the Nietzschean tale is transformed in an important way that moves it out of this resentment/sublimation model. Above all, the basically stable presentation of "Christians" in Acts elides the fact that this name was proposing to identify an often unmanageable and diffuse constellation of events, ethnicities, and interests, and in this sense was itself already an elision of multiplicity (or open-endedness). This elision effectively functions in an effort to imagine itself—and to present itself to others—as a stable given *outside* the struggle of partisan potentialities, a bid for hegemony and exclusion which would—rather than "Paul" in any simple sense—become the keystone of a narrative Platonism for the masses.

Unlike Freud's apostle in *Moses and Monotheism*, Nietzsche's Paul was himself not already *split*, ambivalent, or stranded within effective history in a way that signals the potential for a *real* transvaluation of the value or function of the figure in question. Nietzsche therefore seems to me *not* to do with Paul what he obviously knew one *must* do in relation to modern Europe's Platonism for the masses, namely, to submit it to a properly *genealogical* critique. Instead Nietzsche reifies Paul, leaving his *place in the archive of Western ontotheology* unscathed, forcing the philosopher only to disavow, rather than to transform, the effective Pauline legacy.

Nietzsche saw the important modern issues, but failed to see that the *conflicting* forces of mastery and slavery were *already* completely intertwined in the figure of Paul, in Paul's *place* within the archive of the West.

Put differently, Paul was not the first Christian, but was made so and for very questionable ends. Before he was made the founder (indeed, perhaps, the founder of a commitment to foundationalism *tout court*) Paul was, as Nietzsche rightly asserts of the moment generally, *just another Jewish sectarian*, a deeply invested difference, as it were, trying to make a difference. My diagnosis is that it will be our task for some years to come—at historical, philosophical, and psychoanalytic levels—to configure this name, Paul, and the cultural tradition he organized *outside the guarantees or justifications of the "Christian origins" story*, which is to say as one among a multitude of different identities that do not naturally tend to organize themselves into received tables of stable entities and types. To pursue this task, one must begin (just for a start) to see that there is nothing re-presentational about Acts' emerging Platonism for the masses, a Platonism constituted by its effectively teleological projections of ideal entities distinguishable as the Jews and the Christians.

With the reappearance, against these Platonic idealisms, of *singularities* which the emerging theologico-political narrative machinery does not account for, however, we find ourselves within a very different story. In this tale the multiplicity of mere sectarians or partisans are observable in their sublimation/co-optation as the New Start, a new foundation, indeed, as the "original" of a new religion and the simultaneous fossilization of an "old" version of the same. Such events of beatification, such transformations of Paul into the shining "original Christian" were both paid for and demanded by a radical repression of Pauline actuality as one of a multitude of types of sectarianisms, but also, for the same reason, a radical repression (paradoxically) of ancient Jewish solidarity. Giving up this solidarity was itself the price, the sacrifice, that enabled the transformation of one form of organized multiplicity (sectarian movements of the ancient Mediterranean world) into a different one (of moments along the teleological Way of a separate or sublimated Christianity). It is this simultaneous repression and beatification that I present here, Freud alongside Eusebius, we might say, as the "concrete shoes" with which Paul the apostle has been so expertly fitted, leaden weights necessary to sink the apostle down, down to where all foundations lay. I will return to the scene in the conclusion of this book, but note for now that Eusebius is the expert witness here: Paul has become the original Christian, but only because he was so effectively done away with, as it were buried there in the "foundations" of an emerging church longing to become a darling of empire. What remains of the mere sectarian—and of a history of a multiplicity of sectarians—in the Platonic or metaphysically guaranteed institution is, precisely, the "sacred corpse" of Paul, his sublimated old bones the very "trophies of the apostles" buried away in and as the foundations of a new religion.

Repressed and sublimated all at one go.

Moses the Egyptian, meet Paul the Jewish partisan.

1

CONTINGENCY; OR, COVENANTAL COMEDY

In Praise of Strange Paulinist Federations

If development is entirely animated by accident, by the obstacle of the *tuché*, it is in so far as the *tuché* brings us back to the same point at which pre-Socratic philosophy sought to motivate the world itself. It required a *clinamen*, an inclination, at some point. When Democritus tried to designate it, presenting himself as already the adversary of a pure function of negativity in order to introduce thought into it, he says, *It is not the μηδεν that is essential*, and adds—thus showing you that from what one of my pupils called the archaic stage of philosophy, the manipulation of words was used just as in the time of Heidegger—*it is not a μηδεν, but a δεν*, which, in Greek, is a coined word. He did not say *έν*, let alone *ον*. What, then, did he say? He said, answering the question I asked today, that of idealism, *Nothing, perhaps?*—not *perhaps nothing*, but *not nothing*.

   —Jacques Lacan, *The Four Fundamental Concepts of Psychoanalysis*

And thereby that in which I live is not itself—in the flesh—present; and yet, it is not nothing, otherwise I could not say anything at all about it.
   —Martin Heidegger, *The Phenomenology of Religious Life*

For Heidegger, what remains unexplained in the conception of the intentionality as a relation between a subject and object is precisely what is in need of explanation, that is, the relation itself:
   The vagueness of the relation falls back on the vagueness of that
   which stands in relation. . . . The most recent attempts conceive the

subject-object relation as a "being relation" [*Seinsbeziehung*]. . . .
Nothing is gained by the phrase "being relation," as long as it is not
stated what sort of being is meant, and as long as there is vagueness
about the sort of being [*Seinsart*] of the beings between which this
relation is supposed to obtain. . . . Being, even with Nicolai
Hartmann and Max Scheler, is taken to mean being-on-hand
[*Vorhandensein*]. This relation is not nothing, but is still not being as
something on hand. . . . One of the main preparatory tasks of *Being
and Time* is to bring this "relation" radically to light in its primordial
essence and to do so with full intent.

—Giorgio Agamben, *Potentialities* (citing Heidegger)

We testify to messiah executed, which is only scandal and stupidity
except for those interpellated by this testimony. Those so interpellated
should look at their emergence as things which do not exist now
assembling together for the destruction of what is.

—Gloss of Paul (cf. 1 Corinthians 1:18–28)

WE SHOULD REVIVE THE EARLY CHRISTIAN PRACTICE OF PRODUCING
testimonia collections, little assemblages that effect the solicitation, repetition, and dissemination of new communal formulae, so many virtual
constitutions of questionably political bodies. With the little collection
above I want to flag some ways that to discover Paul floating within an
underground current of a new materialism is to read in him an exemplary case of that perplexingly obtrusive enjoyment which constitutes our
being—unsaved and unsafe—in the world. This enjoyment (Agamben will
press the topos toward the word *love*) is obtrusive in the sense that it is
constitutive, preceding or itself soliciting the emergence of subject and
object. To say this, moreover, implies that it is an obtrusiveness also in the
sense that, despite this enjoyment, this love, or this interpellation being
the scene within which everything about the oriented subject-object relation plays out, for that reason it remains a kind of provocation or incitement emerging, as it were, from offstage. Cagey as we might be, we cannot quite lure this scene-making lure itself onto the actual stage of our
performance. This is—to say the least—not a little perplexing, particularly
in a world where it seems that explicable reality simply *is* an organizational, perfectly managerial, relation between means and ends. For a little

testimonia book to conjure up such drama, replete with the indirection of an offstage directorial voice, we find ourselves naming a constitutive gap in self-ownership, the impossibility of properly, simply, *intending* ourselves. As the early Heidegger might have put it, eccentric actors such as these lose the capacity of ownership over themselves and their actions, all those capacities by which they might *mean* themselves. That which is closest to us is farthest away. Yet another witness to scribble into our archaic collection: "Wo Es war, soll Ich werden." Where it was, I shall become.

It is in two senses that I say to situate Paul within an underground current of a new materialism is to find in him an exemplary case of that perplexingly obtrusive enjoyment which constitutes our being. On the one hand, I think that Nietzschean readings of Paul miss this crucial element when they read *as if* we might find in Paul a means-ends calculation machine, all those debts and payoffs constitutive of a "higher swindle." Here—as I will explore in chapter 3 in relation to Foucault—Nietzsche always reads like the most traditional church theologian, never mind that they *valued* this reading in diametrically opposed fashions. But why would we ever allow the apostle to escape the odd revelation of an obtrusive facticity and its intensely invested symptoms, as if Paul were just what a triumphalist Christian tradition wanted him to be, namely, the sequestered founding father who transcends the logics that bind the rest of us? It is not enough to value the story of exceptionalism differently; we need to work it over entirely. On the other hand, if we consider Paulinism as another tale for our archive of subject-forming enjoyments, then there is no way around the comparative implication that we will discover to this same degree a Pauline stripe within our new materialist explorations of religion or of subjectivity. It is in this sense that I find the real forcefulness of the young Albert Schweitzer's comment (which I described in the introduction) that Nietzsche failed to capitalize on the radicality of his critique of Paulinism precisely to the degree that he *failed to become Paul*. We should take the comparative problematic seriously. Mutually displaced by the elusive solicitations of an underground current of materialism, Paul and ourselves would participate in an oddly secret sharing that needs to be made clearer.

As I have already begun to suggest with my little *testimonia* book, one way to unfold this tale is to consider Pauline *klēsis* or calling as a mode of Epicurean *parenklisis*, translated by Lucretius into Latin as *clinamen*, a tilt or swerve that is intimately linked to important recent efforts to imagine both the materiality of our being in the world and also the peculiarly open or contingent ground of our emancipatory hope. As the quotation of Lacan here indicates, his psychoanalytic reception of ancient philosophy situates, precisely, an obtrusive or decentering desire at the place of a *clinamen* or swerve within the otherwise smooth functioning of organized functional systems, which Lacan sometimes describes as "homeostatic": the swerve as a founding, and therefore fateful, accident of *tūchē*. Elsewhere Lacan will describe the decentering effect of *clinamen* as the essence of transferential love, the very ground of our forms of knowing.[1] Nor should we miss the way that on both occasions Lacan subtly links his story to the early Heidegger's, a move some may at first find surprising.[2] Following this trajectory, Slavoj Žižek has gone further in his own early developments of these genealogical points into a political category wherein *clinamen* as the swerve of "enjoyment" operates as a "constitutive ontological excess," a "pure excess" in the sense that it has "no presupposed normality."[3] We are bordering now on a discussion of a kind of excess constitutive of identity, a topic which will designate an important comparative exploration of Paul among the new materialists. Finally, and closely related, Derrida's psychoanalytic commentary on Lucretius's need for a declination, swerve, or *clinamen* within the otherwise orderly falling of atoms in the void could be an enlightening commentary on all of Žižek's Lacanian work on political enjoyment:

> Without this declension, "nature would never have produced anything." Only this deviation can change the course of an imperturbable destination and an inflexible order. Such erring (I have called it elsewhere "destinerring") can contravene the laws of destiny, conventions or contracts, agreements of *fatum* (*fati foedera* [2.254]). I emphasize the word "contract" for reasons that will become clear later. Allow me here a brief digression toward a classical philological problem concerning the indeterminate reading of the word *voluptas* or *voluntas* (2.257). The mere difference of a letter introduces a *clinamen* precisely at the point where Lucretius is explaining why the *clinamen is* the condition of freedom, of the will (*voluntas*) or the voluptuous pleasure (*voluptas*) wrested away from destiny (*fatis avolsa*). But in any case, the context leaves no doubt as to the link between *clinamen*, freedom, and pleasure. The *clinamen* of the elementary principle—that is, the atom, the law of the atom—would be the pleasure principle.[4]

In terms of political life, then, the unconscionable or unconscious swerve—the invariant declination from the untilted according to

Lucretius—would become a peculiar analytic category that would, by definition, not be transparent to or functional for itself, perhaps *precisely* because it would rest in itself as *clinamen!* This constituting or *grounding* pleasure, as a swerve, would therefore be a peculiar and peculiarly intransigent *resistance* to all such transparencies or functionalities, a structural oddness that has come to be nicely evoked—consider a young Heidegger's discussion of Pauline temporality—by a biblical archive of "calling" and "expectancy." Finally, with a tip of the hat to the reception of these tropes in Giorgio Agamben, the *clinamen* could thus become another name for the oddly paradoxical force of a *performance* of political power. As performance, power could just as well name a *lack* of power inasmuch as performance relies only on the spectacular *aura* or specular *enjoyment* of its own repetitions. In keeping with these other articulations, the identity of power is split, haunted by a spectral doubling which it itself is not. Initially and briefly, then, these *testimonia* indicate some of the paradoxes of performance, paradoxes of immanence, or paradoxes of singular phenomena that may all find their repetition or isomorphic indication in Pauline discussions of *klēsis*. In every case there is an excess, a kind of nonbeing shadowing the singular being in question, which is from the outside only a kind of comically weak foolishness—save for the identities precisely driven by it, constituted by it.

In order to press the genealogical point, we could assert that one could go further here without straying at all from the basic cluster of mutually reinforcing concepts, from the "absent cause" of the late Louis Althusser's materialist philosophy to the development, in the work of Chantal Mouffe and Ernesto Laclau, of the singular emergences of hegemony.[5] For my purposes I want to mention only two further genealogical interventions importantly related to my own efforts in this chapter to situate Paul within an underground current of materialism. Note that in an important archival development of these conversations, Eric Santner explores the topic of obtrusive, excessive, or self-grounding enjoyment as a key for unlocking a contemporary political theology, as it were, of (the unconscious) God.[6] One could even say, perhaps, that a genealogy of the (unconscious) love of God, the history of singular loves constituting a knowledge beyond what God "knows," is not unrelated to the project of releasing Paulinism from the calculations and certainties imagined to go hand in hand with most inherited Christian origins stories. Or, in yet another echo of Lacan, Giorgio Agamben finds in Heideggerian "facticity" a kind of "love" which itself excessively opens up the appearance of our lives as such.[7] The ecstatic (dis)placement which is "facticity" becomes the swerve constitutive of worldhood, and another important genealogical counterpoint to the Pauline *klēsis*, as the early Heidegger himself already recognized.[8]

Note that my little *testimonia* book weaves together all these interrelated tropes with a Pauline gloss whereby a genuinely surprising "federation" or covenanted collective emerges from "the nothings" or "the nonbeings" (*ta mē onta*), disparate nothings knitted together into a social experience. To say that it is only in the "weakness" of a witness believed that unites them is to say that their evental emergence or consolidation differs in no respect from the self-grounding or performative strength of what we will soon hear described as interpellation. In the *clinamen* or *parenklisis* of *klēsis* something emerges from nothing, and Paul's call indicates only the mysterious *forcefulness* of the, as it were, uncalled for organization of new community.

In each instance of the *testimonia* book, therefore, it is the resolute difficulty of maintaining oneself as a singularity that solicits the "return" of the archive of Paulinism. This is important to make clear in the sense that it is not incidentally but rather *precisely, specifically* that the new materialism invites a genealogical association between Pauline *klēsis* and Epicurean *parenklisis* or Lucretian *clinamen*. The issue is already the staple through these disparate quotations, and it is essential for the larger thrust of this book. Fastening these texts together (by staple or nail) will have been ultimately a political *problem of existential—which is to say singularized and immanent—enjoyment*, the topos becomingly increasingly, obsessively haunted by visions of Paul, law, desire, and emancipation.[9] In a way, this entire book draws on those multiple comparative and genealogical threads linking texts of an ancient apostle to this decidedly modern effort of thought to stay with the immanent. Forget what everyone is saying about the "surprising" philosophical turn to Paul: the issue is to unpack the long-standing, deeply ingrained genealogical links between Paulinist discussions of call, excessive life, community formation, and decidedly modern emphases on immanent, singularized swerve as the very ground of existence. The links are not surprising, just daunting and—in the current state of academic formations—dauntingly "multidisciplinary." So we begin by pointing out, simply, that this link is already true of Heidegger, Lacan, Žižek, Agamben, Santner (we should mention Alain Badiou, of course), as if the apostle were the site through which to construe power's relation to the phenomena of the everyday. An "underground current" of a Paulinist new materialism, we might say, is already down there, waiting only for the otherwise assumed ground beneath our feet (which is also to say Paul's feet) to tremble, perhaps to quake, but in any case to give way so

that a new form of thinking—about "materialism" and about "religion"—
may take the plunge.

Amidst tremors of this approaching turmoil, this chapter articulates
a moment in earlier materialist philosophy which marked an important
transition relevant to each of the turns to Paul mentioned above, namely,
Louis Althusser's step toward an "aleatory materialism." I want to go on
from there to suggest—by way of the Paulinism of Althusser's intellectual ally Stanislas Breton—initial ways we could understand Paul and the
vexing political problem of singular, immanent enjoyment, which I take
to be the nail piercing the disparate texts in the epigraphs to this chapter. In placing Pauline *klēsis* at the center of the "underground current" of
materialism, I also want to point out several moments in which Jacques
Derrida, despite being such a good detective of the "material soul" and its
symptoms, sometimes failed to see what I am trying to make clear here.
On those occasions, I will suggest, it was Nietzsche who misled him. In
Derrida's peculiarly dogmatic repetition of Nietzsche on several occasions, Derrida makes of Paul the first Christian and the worst kind of pop
Platonist. As I have already started to explain, as ironic as it may be, a new
materialism must learn to *read religion like the postfoundational materialists we claim to be* rather than looking to it for indications of an idealism
we want to designate as an enemy. In repeating Nietzsche, Derrida effectively leaves the real issue—the excess of phenomenal immanence that
disturbs everyday life—outside his readerly frame. This, in turn, causes
him to repeat tales of a mistakenly imagined two-tiered metaphysics or
ontotheological Paulinism, which helps neither a "religion" that remains
undisturbed in an imagined world of private, identitarian ownership nor
a new materialism which continues to imagine that the archive of "religion" must be proscribed, prohibited as off limits to the life of thought.
To repeat the odd line of Schweitzer: new analysis of the archival figure of
Paul can show the way here; but only if we materialists are willing, in some
sense, *to become him* by way of an analysis that reads Paul as, like the
rest of us, subjected to the aleatory displacements and oddly enthusiastic
movements of a material soul.

PREPARING THE WAY FOR A PAULINIST MATERIALISM: ALTHUSSER'S TURN TO THE ALEATORY

Just for the moment, let us turn away from my *testimonia* collection to
the quotations with which this book begins. As we read there, late in his

career Louis Althusser began to articulate a profound "turn" in his thinking about Marxism, about philosophy and the critique of ideology, and about the freedom of emancipatory political movements.[10] In keeping with his earlier reading strategies of these traditions, Althusser described this transformation as the recognition of an "underground current" within a philosophical tradition he identified as "materialism." As if to spice up the detective story—which at this point in his life and career was not at all simply relegated to questions of philosophy—Althusser describes this underground current as a shock of insight that was repeatedly "contested and repressed [in the philosophical tradition] as soon as it was stated" (167).

The subterranean insight, ever articulated and always immediately forgotten, Althusser understands as a countermaterialism, a "completely different mode of thought" to the "various materialisms on record," including (he tells us) that of Marx, Engels, and Lenin as these tend to be understood (167). In fact, Althusser finds the renewal and liberation of this subterranean materialism also in Heidegger, so it is no surprise that Althusser claims that this materialism eludes "the classical criteria of every materialism" and that, in this respect, "We continue to talk about a *materialism* of the encounter only for the sake of convenience" (171, my emphasis). More interesting still, in unearthing this countermaterialism from a repressive oblivion of forgetfulness, Althusser sees himself as subverting a "Western" mode of philosophy, that mode being a "destiny" which is ours as participants in a "logocentric" being in the world. We are the ones, after all, who are predisposed to think, talk, and act as if we could assume there is a "priority of Meaning over all reality."

Althusser's subversive genealogy of a philosophy of the encounter, written in the early eighties, situates the critique of logocentrism and the future of materialist analysis in important ways that invite several immediate questions. How, or from where, will a subterranean power arise that has the potential to transform a practical and theoretical "destiny" of Western thought? Similarly, how does one emancipate nonsense and nonmeaning, not simply as random and ephemeral moments of anarchic freedom but as an integral quality of communal invention, the formation of new communal forms? Finally, and to evoke Paul's Corinthian echoes more explicitly, how would we describe that community afforded by disruptive mechanisms of a "materialism of the encounter" without repeating philosophical traditions of community founded on logos and the assumption of the priority of meaning and sense? Althusser's late excavations attempt to expose the sheltering ground of community to an ungrounding or destabilizing encounter that cannot be fixed (or managed) either by "idealism" or, we might add, by a discourse ethics like that of Habermas. On what decentering event of rupture with meaning, then, will this serially repressed but nevertheless coming community be thus (un)grounded? And, if not by a discourse ethics in the usual sense, how would the organizing communications of this community testify to a community-forming encounter that itself must be subtracted from the tallies of logocentric system or the repetitions of identity constitutive of "idealism"? In a word, and to repeat the lines of Paul directly, what is it to have one's communal subsistence consist in a nothing *except* a subtraction from preexisting structures?

THE NEED TO "PROCLAIM OBSTRUCTION (*SKANDALON*) AND STUPIDITY (*MŌRIA*)" AGAINST THE WISDOM OF ALTHUSSER'S DEFINITION OF RELIGION (CF. 1 CORINTHIANS 1.23)

As bearers and heralds of this subversive and subterranean "current" of thought, Althusser mentions Lucretius, Spinoza, Machiavelli, Hobbes, Rousseau, Marx, Heidegger, and Derrida. Althusser does not mention someone whom his life-long friend and interlocutor, the philosopher and Passionist priest Stanislas Breton, would no doubt have included in this list of bearers of an "underground current of the materialism of the encounter": the ancient apostle Paul.[11] I want to develop in the next chapter several contributions of Breton's reading of Paul for my own very different political project. But I want to argue, even more, that an underground vein of Paulinist materialism of the encounter is indeed buried away, even if a little deeper—which is to say more surprisingly—than that indicated by Althusser's reference to Lucretius, Spinoza, or Heidegger. Without question, the most important stated reason the apostolic exemplar of Althusser's "secret tradition" of philosophy would not be mentioned here is because *Althusser is repeatedly at pains to suggest that "religion" is precisely the mode of thought which is rendered inoperable by a materialism of the encounter.*[12] The gesture is typical enough, completely clichéd in fact, both in its association of "religion" with Western logocentrism and also in its abandonment of a figure like Paul to the hegemony of the same. As should be clear by now, everything I do is a refusal of these paths. It is the conservatism of the Nietzschean gesture that leaves "religion" on the imagined shore of an idealized life not subject to the material pressure of the absent cause operating behind the back of thought and political action. "Wo Es war, soll Ich werden." One either believes it or not, one sticks to it as an analytic agenda or not: where It was, there Paul (too) shall be.

For his part—and I think this is important—that obsessive Paulinist, Stanislas Breton, first added himself and his Paulinism of the crucified to the list of "aleatory materialists" only in a private letter. In this way, Breton operated as a kind of ecclesiastical obverse of the post-Christian Althusser, as if Breton, too, were reticent to let loose a destabilizing effect which might emerge from his association of "religion" with the "underground current of materialism." Whatever the specifics, that Breton first kept the underground (as it were) under his hat is intriguing to me given the way the connections, links, and implications for Breton's oddly postmodern and postfoundational neo-Platonism—not to mention Althusser's "materialism of the encounter"—are all readily perceived once stated openly. Or, to put it with the focus and force the point deserves, these *isomorphisms* are all readily visible *once one lives as if one does not know* either what "religion" is, why a materialism of the encounter should not subsume religion more radically into its purview, or why—it would always amount to the same thing—"religion" should ever be allowed to save itself as an insulated "idealism."[13] In this light, Althusser and Breton alike (not to mention Derrida after them) are in my story still indications of the refusal of a Paulinist materialism which is peering at them through the very fault line and fissure of the clichéd and reified distinction between "religion" and "materialism."

To refuse what amounts to an idealist distinction (we should not forget) between these two categories is to refuse docility before a massive genealogy and its carefully sequestered and policed archives. It is no small task to incite others to remain intentionally "stupid" in relation to the established wisdom about the inside and outside of religion or material phenomena. I understand more than most that this strategic *mōria* is usually taken to constitute a calculating effort (read: infuriating *skandalon*) to subsume either religion or materialism into its preestablished opponent. But the issue is to begin to articulate a Paulinist materialism of the encounter that opens up when we, Bartleby-like perhaps, prefer not to do the usual labor to render stable the ready-made accounts. Here I point only to the repetition of the word *religion* in the lines of the initially private letter of Breton to a slightly paranoid ecclesiastical friend about Althusser, a friend who had with evident annoyance questioned Breton's relationship to the famously materialist Althusser. Breton responded with a repetition of the word *religion* that I read like a symptom of an underground current which will not remain forever repressed. Breton wrote: "To those who ask me about the religion of Althusser in his last moments, I respond that he had nothing to say except that (*sinon que*) I discussed with him what he called *aleatory materialism*."[14]

Strange scene, the Passionist priest speaking with Althusser as he lay dying. Perhaps like Paul, who preferred to speak about "nothing but" the cross and the crossed out (cf. 1 Corinthians 2:2), Althusser determined with Breton to know nothing but an aleatory materialism. Breton's letter goes on to describe how he understands that this late Althusserian "aleatory materialism" could be read next to certain aspects of the theology of John of the Cross, adding—intriguingly—that Breton's own neo-Platonic philosophical theology and Althusser's aleatory materialism were rather intimately related.[15] I will return shortly to some of the comparisons to be discerned between Breton's Paul and the late Althusser. But, for the moment I want to repeat very directly that it *is a materialism of the encounter itself which, on its own terms, cannot allow either "religion" or Paulinism to remain unscathed* or self-enclosed as the idealism they might even think themselves to be. One imagines the inverse discovery to the one I found in Breton's archives, this one the (imagined) private letter of a dogmatic adherent of the underground current of materialism hoping—honestly and unabashedly hoping—that his priestly friend, in those final moments, hit upon the deep consolation and illumination of the singular *pressure* or excess of life that they were attempting to articulate and theorize. I imagine the question, "In that moment, did you discuss the vibrancy of a new materialism?" with the answer: "I can say that, in that final moment, we talked always of an apostle."

Fantasies of virtual letters notwithstanding, it is this underground current of "materialism" *itself* that must refuse the very distinction whereby this enemy, "religion," would remain—safely and unscathed—an antagonistic opposite. The unfinished project of modern Epicureanism, so to speak, this is a pressure that a new materialism must engage, namely, the question whether or not it can encounter and account for religion without rehearsing the same fantasies about that entity which religion itself (sometimes, at least) peddles. With that specific pressure in mind, I begin not yet on the similarity between the late Althusser and the philosophical Paulinist, but between the late Althusser and the young Jacques Derrida.

WHO IS REFUSING PSYCHIC SYMPTOMS OF SWERVED COVENANT COMMUNITIES? READING DERRIDA, PAUL, AND EPICURUS

> This only do I want to know: were you interpellated when you lived like the Jerusalem community or when we lived as we do in Galatia where we heard and believed? We the believing, we're the real kids of Abraham.
>
> —cf. Paul to the Galatians (3:2, 7)

One of the important things about Derrida's genealogy of Epicurean *clinamen* in "My Chances/Mes Chances: A Rendezvous with Some Epicurean Stereophonies" is the way it inflects and avows the *materialism* of his early and career-making doctrines about writing and dissemination.[16] Indeed, in this essay the young Derrida situates himself in a way very closely related to Althusser's late "Underground Current" essay, and we should not forget that in that essay Althusser lists Derrida among the exemplars of this "secret" tradition. The respective essays of Althusser and Derrida share important characteristsics, in fact: Derrida presents us with a similar cast of repressed characters from Epicurus to Heidegger; a similar exposition of chance, encounter, and event; and a similar naming of this assemblage of characters, ideas, and overlaps as a *repressed materialism*. By the same token, the "materialism" of both essays will echo very forcefully psychoanalytic traditions of the decentring and transformative effects of the unconscious. Strikingly, one of Derrida's suggestions (to a group of psychoanalysts in fact) is that it is the materialist who refuses to exclude from her analysis the aleatory, material marks that Derrida takes in turn to have been integral as well to ancient Epicurean considerations of the *stoicheia* or elements. Derrida's genealogy therefore solicits a kind of community over time of materialist analysts, including in this virtual guild some Epicureans, some psychoanalysts, and the great detective Dupin of Edgar Allen Poe's wonderful short story "The Murders in the Rue Morgue" (1841).

This diverse assemblage of ages, actions and personae are linked together to constitute a countergenealogy, all becoming exemplars of those for whom mediatic slips, misfires, and unintended affectations are essential, an analytic interest in what Derrida glosses as materiality. "Wo Es war, soll Ich werden." The philosopher even links the analytics of materiality strategically with the Epicurean teaching of a material soul. Against imagined self-enclosures of identities and idealisms, the material soul names a research project in which these ideal entities are incapable of remaining self-enclosedly preserved from slips of the pen, tears in parchment, or other marks of the material history of communicative media (352). That we tell the history of philosophy (or religion) as the history of ideas rather than the intimate imposition of these materialities, however, is not incidental: "But never forget this: the Democritian tradition, in which the names of Epicurus and his disciples are inscribed, has been subjected since its origin, and first of all under the violent authority of Plato, to a powerful repression throughout the history of Western culture. One can now follow its symptomatology, which begins with the erasure of the name of Democritus in the writings of Plato" (362). The an-archic and aleatory effects of these unconscious material agencies operate (as Gilles Deleuze might have put it) on a plane of immanence, in the precise sense that ideal entities and self-enclosed identities are not immune to their mutually transformative capacities. As Clayton Crockett explains in his excellent book on Deleuze and Badiou, Deleuze sometimes interchanged nominations of this deterritorialized territory, speaking of a "plane of consistency," a "dark precursor," and a "plane of immanence."[17] Indeed, with his own nomination of "materiality" here, Derrida is primarily interested in designating the mutual affectation, the constitutive co-agitation, of strata we tend to take as distinct: the realm of *techne* and the apparatus with all their merely contingent or senseless imbrications within historical worlds (on the one hand) and the realm of meaning, internalized sensibility or selfhood (on the other). The question of mediated, material souls articulates Derrida's fascination in the essay with Epicurus's ancient rejection of Herodotus's dualistically split soul and body in favor of an analysis that tracks phenomena by focusing *peri tēn psuchēn ta sumptōmata*, a phrase Derrida glosses (for an audience of Freudian analysts) as "psychic symptoms" (352).

There will be a strange kind of freedom here—we might echo Althusser—which idealism cannot recuperate to itself, but to which idealisms of any sort will always remain exposed. Derrida's text is generally much less oriented by modes in which the vicissitudes of the dice throw of chance turn up as unforeseen and unplanned emancipation, the very issue driving Althusser's texts on "aleatory materialism." But Derrida does explore the way Epicurean *clinamen* or swerve is precisely that an-archic force capable of scrambling, rendering inoperative, or setting on a different footing what the ancient philosopher already described as so many *federations*, but which we might just as well render *covenants*, a term I do not want to forget in the context of our virtual community of analysts of the material soul.

DERRIDA'S (NIETZSCHEAN) OBFUSCATION OF PAULINIST MATERIALISM

To say it bluntly, I hardly know why Paul should be the better trafficker in psychic symptoms of covenant federation than we are. That is, I hardly know why we would allow *ourselves* to imagine "religion" as a space of immunity to or refusal of aleatory or stochastic powers of material immanence. It is in this light that I very much miss Derrida's earlier detective work—that eye and that ear for contingent clues, that inestimable and unruly passion to see where they lead—in a later text in which Derrida engages explicitly with Pauline texts. This missing, his and mine, is all the more striking inasmuch as that text, "A Silkworm of One's Own" (1996), repeats an interest precisely in outdoing Paul on the topic of life. Derrida's piece even concludes by linking precisely this worthy fantasy—the outdoing of Paul on resurrection or the creation of unexpected life—with another one, the final overcoming of a philosophical history of truth as veiling and unveiling. Saving Paulinism (or, which is to say the same, doing it one better) and being saved from the ontotheological cycles of Western thought: it's not a bad day's work. It will also always have been the question of how to negotiate Nietzsche's tale of the West as the global expansion of Platonism by way of Pauline Christianity. Derrida writes: "Of course, I still dream of resurrection. But the resurrection I dream of, for my part, at the ends of the verdict, the resurrection I'm stretched out toward, would no longer have to be a miracle, but the reality of the real, quite simply, if it's possible, ordinary reality finally rendered, beyond fantasy or hallucination" (87). The beatific conjuring of the final act of this dialogue, then, is one in which the textual persona of the philosopher, so wearied with the weaving and unweaving of discourses of truth as unveiling (cf. 39f.), finds

himself happy in the everyday, not tormented by desire either to veil or
to unveil but contented in the everyday as a *"new finitude"* (87, emphasis added). Here, too, he continues with a language whose psychoanalytic
echoes are unmistakable: "What luck, this verdict, what feared chance: yes,
now, there will be for me worse than death, I would never have believed
it, and the enjoyment here nicknamed 'resurrection,' that is, the price to
pay for the extraordinarily ordinary life toward which I should like to turn,
without conversion, for some time still—such an enjoyment will be worth
more than life itself" (87). To hit upon, and to remain with, an everyday
enjoyment worth more than life itself will save miracle itself by redeeming
it as the "extraordinarily ordinary." That longing set, however, our detective on the plane of immanence confronts us with few surprises: no real
intrigues of conspiratorial contingencies in the texts of Paul (of all people,
what a media history, what a history of coverup, co-optation, contingent
elisions and afterlives!); no new modes of analysis of those post-Pauline
apparatuses (so many geological formations) which apprehend, lay bear,
or give significance to the name of this apostle over time. On this occasion
Derrida veers closer to Althusser's "religion," while Paul will be left alone,
simply, as a version of the pop-Platonic self-same that confuses the real
work of thought, as if thought, too, does not also want to work Paul over,
to show him, as it were, how resurrection is done. Importantly, Derrida's
text leans on Nietzsche as an important figure in this escape from, waking
up from, or (another of its nicknames) resurrection from the very dream
of an escape from the everyday, a weaving together of names and philosophical issues which is not at all incidental. Indeed, we are told: "what I
admire most in Nietzsche is his lucidity about Paul" (41). In other words,
one of the tactics of the essay which seems fully operational, to the point
that it is almost tritely repetitive, is precisely the deployment of a Nietzschean Paul in the great Nietzschean genealogy of Western thinking about
truth. "What I admire most about Nietzsche is his lucidity about Paul."

True to the master, in Derrida's text Paul appears as the "first Christian"
and proponent of a concomitant pop Platonism, adding to Nietzsche's
basic story only a sensitivity to potential anti-Jewish or misogynistic
elements in Paul (to say the least, two issues that did not seem to keep
Nietzsche awake at night): "The one who wanted to veil the heads of the
women and unveil those of men, that very one denounced Moses and
the children of Israel" (77). Paul functions in Derrida's essay as the perfect touchstone in the standard Nietzschean tale of a dominant Western
discourse about truth: denigrating the everyday; promising a revelatory

vision which circumvents the veil of everyday life and language. Derrida's is without question the Paul of a "higher swindle" that is the functional dualization of a more immanent form of excessive "enjoyment" within the everyday.

One needs to be precise about the nature of my criticism here. My unease at Derrida's engagement emerges not from a sense that Nietzsche was incorrect to argue that Paulinism had come to function as an exemplary "Platonism for the masses" in Western discourses about truth—anyone who does not agree with Nietzsche should speak more to those participating in dominant contemporary forms of Christianity. But neither does my criticism emerge from the fact that, here, Derrida follows a master rather directly and unsurprisingly. At one level, the arguments as such are all fair enough: for Nietzsche, for the Paulinism Nietzsche imagined to be nameable also as modern Christendom, and for the ancient apostle. The pressing issue for me at the moment, the real pressure *we* should feel when reading this piece, emerges from elsewhere. In a word, what is happening here to that *contretemps* to which Derrida also claims to want to witness, that accident and that contingency that is the primary mode in which the other will speak in and through—even despite—us? Put differently, where is the enjoyment that both subvents and subverts the everyday, all every days? The significance of the issue is easy to see: what happens, in relation to the analysis of the Pauline texts, to the basic structures of the Derridean promise, that heraldic opening to transformations and transvaluations which the structure of the promise harbors like so many fugitives from and of justice? Put differently, why is Derrida's essay so docile in the face of Paul's texts, even if this docility functions in the service of criticizing Paulinism as a discourse of (both) veiling and unveiling which—precisely—must be eluded as part the old epoch of "truth as onto-logical revelation" (83)? Derrida's is here the same laziness or dogmatism we noted in Althusser's text, a laziness or dogmatism—we should never forget—which is simply the obverse of the (initially) self-protective gesture of Breton as ecclesiastical gatekeeper of Paulinism.

Where, in other words, is the (psychoanalytic) detective who tracks so shrewdly the contrapuntal agency of the unconscious, all those hazards, happenstances, and accidents that would constitute—let's say it—the "material soul" of our otherwise rather flatfootedly Western, veiling/unveiling, or ontotheological apostle? Derrida's Paul is here too simply given, and readers are essentially left with a Pauline soul which has no traffic *peri tēn psuchēn ta sumptōmata*—the apostle has become a great man if ever there were one, patriarch of a Western idealistic soul, exemplary guarantor of ontotheology, apparently free of "psychic symptoms." There is something misleadingly polemical about a piece that would leave Paul—even as antagonist—as the great exception of all the analytic characteristics for which an earlier Derridean detective of material immanence had us cheering. The issue is not simply what has been, whether Paul was or was not an idealist or a veiling and unveiling dualist, is it?[18] At one level, that question is simply so much the better or worse for a deceased apostle. But it seems an altogether different point in relation to our own thinking, or of Derrida's, a matter of, precisely, an immanent material world of "souls" all bearing the marks and spurs of "psychic symptoms." The issue is, in other words, not the Paul who was or who thought himself to be but rather the Paul—as it were—who must be, the one who will have been once diagnosed and analyzed. The point is that *we* cannot escape the encounter or the Paul who emerges once we name and track all those psychic symptoms by which the Pauline identity of even Nietzsche's (or Derrida's) anti-Paulinism becomes interrupted or run through an analytic ringer of a future from which Paul's resurrections will have become otherwise and—why not cast our dice this way?—even redeemed.[19] All of this, we might say, is primarily a problem for us, analysts of the material soul, rather than for Paul.

We should refuse, therefore, to participate in Derrida's well-meaning apostolic exceptionalism which subtracts the name Paul from analysis, just as we should refuse every analysis which so easily forgets the magical and transformative quality of aleatory contingency, as if the Pauline soul—providentially or miraculously, perhaps—had no psychic symptoms. We should refuse both, and particularly so when the central philosophical persona of this piece presents himself, in both biographical and dialogical terms, as the very one who wants *to save* resurrection and its absurd performatives, all those as-if's of being-dead and being-alive (25). Paul is here rather simply—without careful attention to texts, contexts, mediatic stagings, and therefore without much surprise—dispatched as the exemplary patriarch of onto(theo)logical authority, even as Derrida's authorial persona presents himself rather eagerly as the one hoping to think of a pure site of revelation, as the teacher of an experience of a resurrection which is the manifestation of the "extraordinarily ordinary"? Far from a problematic "turn" to (or within) "religion," the problem here is a lack of the very gamble on aleatory materialism that makes possible the early Derrida's opening onto a future at all.

In this regard, I want to suggest that Michel Serres's discussion of *clinamen* in *The Birth of Physics* is better attuned to the stakes of a Pauline future. Like the late Althusser and the early Derrida, Serres wonders about the modes in which we can think an "intelligent materialism" (again, on an immanent rather than dualistic plane). Serres wants to think an immanence within which differences of agencies, territories, strata, and informational processes are imagined as recursive, so many refrains that repeat themselves and each other just as they affect and are constituted by multiple outsides.[20] In light of Serres's later reflection on Paulinist *Angels*, I would like to propose an Epicurean question for my fellow materialist philosophers of difference.

WHY ARE THERE CORPORATE CELEBRATIONS OF A DEAD HERO RATHER THAN NOTHING? (IDEOLOGY AS MATERIAL SWERVE)

> Why is it that he [Epicurus, in his will] makes such precise and careful provision and stipulation [*tam accurate tamque diligenter caveat et sanciat*] that his heirs, Amynochus and Timocrates, shall after consultation with Hermarchus assign a sufficient sum to celebrate his birthday every year in the month of Gamelion, and also on the twentieth day of every month shall assign a sum for a banquet to his fellow-students of philosophy [*itemque omnibus mensibus vicesimo die lunae dent ad eorum epulas qui una secum philosophati sint*], in order to keep alive the memory of himself and of Metrodorus? That these are the words of as amiable and kindly a man a you like, I cannot deny; but what business has a philosopher, especially a natural philosopher, which Epicurus claims to be, to think that any day can be anybody's birthday? What, can the identical day that has once occurred recur again and again [*Quid? idemne potest esse dies saepius qui semel fuit?*]? It is definitely not possible [*Certe non potest*]. . . . Is a person's birthday to be observed when he is dead [*etiamne post mortem coletur*]? Such a provision ill became one whose "intellect had roamed" over unnumbered worlds and realms of infinite space, without shores or circumference [*innumerabiles mundos infinitasque regiones, quarum nulla esset ora, nulla extremitas*].
>
> —Cicero, *On Ends*, 101 (II.xxxi)

From this perspective, the meals of early Christians (and other Hellenistic groups) appear as a series of bold social and spiritual experiments. They allowed early Christians [*sic*] (and other Hellenistic groups) to try out new behaviors in dialogue with their social visions. On one level, these social visions were described at meals as participating in "the realm of God," "the body of Christ," "koinonia with God," "the heavenly court," or "the heavenly city." On another level, as noted in this chapter's close assessment of meal gestures and constituencies, the meals became a laboratory in which a range of expressive nonverbal "vocabularies" explored alternative social visions. The vocabularies consisted of alternative social relationships at the meals, complex ritual gestures, body postures, and actual food elements.

These meals need to be conceived as spiritual experiments as well. By this is not meant that they were occasions for mystification of real-life issues, retreat from social realities or intellectual quests, or some kind of prototype for later Christian liturgy. Rather, the meals enacted new social alternatives so vividly that the meal participants experienced themselves as actually a part of a new social order. Both as groups and as individuals, many of those at the meal felt as if they were living in a different world.

—Hal Taussig, *In the Beginning Was the Meal*[21]

I confess I love these two textual witnesses, that I have wanted to mention them both—and side by side—for some time now. On the one hand, our essential Roman, Cicero, playing the polemicist on behalf of his school and in a philosophical treatise on functional ends expressing that not even for a second would he tolerate a community that does not understand that *memorializing* must be controlled, reasoned, delimited. Note here what becomes the interchangeability of spaces and times, Cicero's anxiety about calendars becoming a philosophical anxiety about proper limits, appropriate borders. How much better if Epicurus would die, stay dead, that his death would *not* become a kind of unplaceable banquet of philosophical friendship. My God, as if *any* day could be your birthday? Even worse, do the *dead* have celebrations of birth? One is, above all, struck—dumbstruck even—by the way Cicero's evidently sarcastic remark begins to look, in the context of such anxieties, like a frank admission of a world—its spaces and times—reduced to single measurements, measurements without unconscious declination for a new comedy of covenantal federations of rogue friendships. Cicero's philosophical slip of the tongue, therefore: could someone who so confuses the finality of death and the finitude of ongoing life be one whose "'intellect had roamed' over unnumbered worlds and realms of infinite space, without shores or circumference"? Indeed! And is it not the interest to control the impudently roguish *afterlives* of Epicurus which here spurs a philosophical slur against the processual infinity of an Epicurean universe? That very Roman philosopher here gives us an important clue: we should consider the genealogical link between philosophical immanence, philosophy without a stabilizing "outside" to guarantee or judge its relational phenomena, and the perversely destabilizing capacities of swerved communities to inhibit the measurable or operative distinctions between life and death, atoms and communities.

This oddly undying life—life's unexpectedly free participation in death—this life without shores or circumference, here solicits comparison with the equally obtrusive calendrical misfires and banquet performances of a life that is undead, living on as a communion of and in the absent founder who is nevertheless not *not* present either.[22] Further echoes of our *testimonia* book from the beginning of the chapter. Or we should consider that these two tales of illicit sharing of meals in the name of the undead are part of the repression of an underground current of a new materialism, a repression that—on all sides, it seems—seems to legitimize itself by reference to a founding functional dualism between "religion" and "material" philosophy. Along that track it is fun also to see in Cicero's measurements and judgments of the good in relation to an end some early echoes or foreshadowings of the anxieties that the imperial governor of colonial Bithynia, Pliny, would pose to Trajan almost seventy years later. *Of what sort of guilt* is an association which does not observe the proper boundary between death of a hero and the ongoing communal life of the participants in his ideas? "I do not know," Pliny writes, "what is customarily punished."[23] How to measure deviation? It's the really vexing political problem for most, and after an examination Pliny trots out virtual Christians who swore that "the sum of their guilt or error (*summam vel culpae suae vel erroris*) amounted to this, that they used to gather on a stated day before dawn and sing to Christ as if he were a god." The same might-be-Christians further assured Pliny that in doing so they were *not* committing themselves to the performance of crime, but rather only to some perfectly acceptable Roman virtues. As if not to be easily duped, you might recall, Pliny claims to have tortured two slaves (who held church office, apparently, perhaps another confusion of proprietorial social limit) to see if he could learn otherwise.[24] Once the deviating rift or transgressive decline comes to be read as declination or transgression, suddenly "anonymous" lists of potential deviants start to circulate, neighbors naming neighbors as potential Christians.

Not inclined to remain deviants, of course, Christianity would eventually learn the lessons of Roman philosophy, the tactics of its governance, and it would soon enough forget the peculiar instability of boundaries which *constituted* the vibrancy of its Paulinist precursors. As if summarizing our genealogical tale, Aquinas speaks perfectly in an imaginary dialogue that perhaps should have struck him as being more hauntingly odd than it seemed to have done:

Q: What human action is right?

A: I answer that evil is more comprehensive than sin, as also is good than right. For every privation of good, in whatever subject, is an evil: whereas sin consists properly in an action done for a certain end, and lacking due order to that end. Now the due order to an end is measured by some rule. In things that act according to nature, this rule is the natural force that inclines them to that end. When therefore an action proceeds from a natural force, in accord with the natural inclination to an end, then the action is said to be right: since the mean does not exceed its limits, viz. the action does not swerve from the order of its active principle to the end. But when an action strays from this rectitude, it comes under the notion of sin (*Summa Theologica* 1).

Cicero could not have said it better. Ruled. Human action, above all, as ruled, judged, submitted to the measurement, and this hierarchizing relation fantasized as the very force of force and nature of nature as such. Christianity has, very decidedly, learned a particular sort of philosophy, and from no uncertain cultural source and with no uncertain political consequences. What is forgotten in the new constellation, perhaps, is the way Hal Taussig's work invites us to read the way the Pauline *theologoumena*, all those antitheses of "good and evil" (to borrow from Cicero and Aquinas alike), were conjured in order to blow a bubble of protection around what was essentially an experimental (re)enactment of decidedly swerved "federations" (to borrow from Epicurus) or "covenants" (to borrow from Paul) for a risky politics of friendship that seems to be indistinguishable from a kind of forgetting of specific instances of death. In order to keep pace with the phenomenon in its enactment, Taussig finds himself speaking of a utopian "social laboratory," with the banquets themselves becoming the testy testing ground whereby a deviation from the cultural norms was able to emerge, to come to a sense of itself, and to be memorialized as a federation without inherited ends and means (cf. 20, 35).

As a kind of genealogical counter to Aquinas's foreclosure of such a reading, we might mention a young Marx—that stalwart of our underground

current—puzzling over the difference between Democritean and Epicurean structures of materialism and causality. As you may recall, in a foreshadowing of Pierre Hadot, the later Michel Foucault, and Peter Sloterdijk, the young Marx takes up Hellenistic philosophy for its significance
as an indication of the "subjective form" (rather than "metaphysical content") of the philosophical enterprise. For Marx, as for the later thinkers,
this period of philosophy becomes important, above all, for its indications
of—one might say—spiritual exercises. Marx finds in the philosophical
archive pointers about the possibility of thought as a disciplined "way" of
life in practice, practicing at life. Indeed, it is this aspect of the practice of
philosophy that, Marx argues, constitutes the often elided chasm of difference between the philosophical systems of Democritus and Epicurus. In
Marx's genealogy, Democritus thinks that subjective appearance is *mere*
appearance, a *merely* subjective effect of causal structures that constitute
a systematic whole in their own right. Radically different, according to
Marx, is the Epicurean view that the subjective is itself *grounded* without
reserve in the movement of atoms in a way that precludes any dualism of
the phenomena, quilting together more primordially natural ground and
phenomenal perspective on the same.

With this distinction, Marx concludes, appears the distinction between
a Democritean fall into dualism and an accompanying Democritean
empiricism, which heralds in turn a docile passivity of thought excluded from a reified natural reality. For Marx, Democritus is thus no longer
capable of theorizing the affective, empassioned, or phenomenal links
between the objective and subjective spheres. Small wonder, Marx jokes,
that Democritus traveled obsessively, as if desperate to hit upon more
and more external facts that might offer some form of escape, whereas Epicurus scorned such a way of life, preferring instead to live—and
write—"unknown," free of the desire to quest about for guarantors and
guarantees of phenomenal causality as such. Marx intuits here overall a
profound difference in *modes* of thought which are not themselves reducible to distinctions in content, pointing to the concepts "necessity" and
"luck" (*anangkē* and *tūchē*) as fissured right down the middle of a parting
of the ways between these two philosophers.

In siding with Epicurus against Democritus, Marx wants to remain
faithful to a thought of contingency, read as subjective openness to being
otherwise, as itself *internal* to the system of causality itself. In doing so,
Marx argues, we remain faithful to a strange thought of freedom *in causal
relations themselves*. Indeed, by thinking in a more immanent mode of

relationality what Democritus wanted to imagine as an external or dualistic relation of causality, we hit upon the possibility of thinking, Marx writes, "the chance of thought itself," the eventalness we might say in which our contingent freedom participates.[25]

Moreover, as if himself sitting down at the Epicurean or Pauline table of contrafactual enactments of undead teachers and illicit philosophical solidarities, the young Marx writes: "*Lucretius* therefore is correct when he maintains that the swerve breaks the *fati foedera*, [bonds of fate] and, since he applies this immediately to consciousness, it can be said of the atom that the declination is that something in its breast that can fight back and resist."[26] Internal to immanent, causal realities from which we will not be saved by another world or outside agency, there is nevertheless a chance, the very chance of thought itself, which is indicative of a minor freedom, a minimal swerve, a line around which we might spin ourselves in a *metanoia* that will itself feed back into the otherwise ironclad ground from which it emerged.

PAUL AMONG THE VORTICISTS

It may be, therefore, that to cut against the grain of traditions (which are never merely philosophical, political, or theological) toward a Paulinist materiality will demand of us intensive reworking of inherited models of myth and ideology. Forget Nietzsche's imagined Paulinism, vacuous tricks as promises of a life by and by for those who will agree to sacrifice their trying or risky freedom in the present, the entire panoply of Nietzsche's Platonic/Paulinist "higher swindle." For the moment, forget too Nietzsche's flat-footed readings of resentment or what the young Marx liked to call repulsion. We need rather to stage a virtual encounter and mutual explication of the celebratory conjurings of Paul and Epicurus to come to grips with the Pauline *klisis* toward an undead messianic figure, this obtrusive tilting toward some third space of life and death that sets off a paroxysm of new oppositions, uncharted territorialities, and—we should remember Lucretius's fascinations as much as Paul's—strange "federations" as so many queer contracts and covenants. Even in posing the comparative situation this way one begins immediately to see the significance of the fact that Nietzsche read Paul always already as caught up in a virtual encounter between Paul and Plato. But the appropriation of, the *Auseindandersetzung* with, another philosophical tradition, indeed with the "underground current of materialism," sets our thinking in very different directions. At this level, in fact, Nietzsche was always a fairly docile repeater of strategic and intentional early church receptions of Paul within a clunkily Platonic framework. The Platonic glasses Nietzsche borrowed from the ecclesiasts of the second century onward enabled him only ever to see Pauline topics—like Paul's irruptive "future" in the "now," Paul's undead among (and now dwelling in and as) the living, refracted ethnic inheritances, and so on—as stable entities functioning as guarantors of empty promises and sacrificial (or, if you prefer, idealist) economies. How unfortunate that Nietzsche did not rather cut against the grain of the Platonic machinery which, despite so many loose threads, tried to weave the apostle into the same pattern Nietzsche later discovered as if ready-made: the first Christian and Platonic popularizer. One cannot be too hard on Nietzsche, of course. After all, how telling of the sheer power of the ontotheological tradition that it has taken so long to read the apostle with Epicurus in hand, that it would take so long to name a Paul of the "underground current" in order to explore his topoi in light of those ancient thinkers of flux, vortex, and the true as the off-kilter![27] Again, the problem is not how one ought to be polite to "religion." The pressure or more pressing issue emerges from whether we do or do not think there are "psychic symptoms" in that paradigmatic "soul" of the Western tradition. Is *our* thinking faithful to the Epicurean legacy (better yet, the legacy of the "underground current"), and does the *clinamen* of our immanent vision see how our truth is true in the transformed inscription of the apostolic name?

Even that thinker of *parenklisis* and ecstatic projection who was the young Heidegger rightly corrected Nietzschean readings of Paul only to come to another version of a Christian origins story whereby Paul was read as yielding some kind of extralegal advance beyond Judaism.[28] In Heidegger, after all, the rupture of temporality and ecstatic facticity with which the young philosopher was so obsessed was still the owned material of an explicit Christian origins story—and to that degree still a version of the Christian exceptionalism story which really does not at all escape the fundamental operation rightly uncovered by Nietzsche's diagnosis of the "higher swindle." As I say, it may be that the underground current will be most significant when it starts by reflecting further on the materiality of myths and movements of resurrection. Neither Nietzschean lies and false promises nor even Heidegger's much better intrusions of a break with time, we would intuit rather the effects, the representations, of a Paulinist vortex giving rise to a *pressure*, a declination or tilt that revalues an instance of death or catastrophe, and which itself consolidates—for a while, always only and ever a while—a new bestiary of divine and human or (ambiguously, curiously) divine and human bodies of political or social solidarity.

Nietzsche tried to convince himself that the emergence of new mystico-political bodies in Paul should be read as fully bonded and secured (and therefore impossibly obfuscating mythologies, guarantors of docility). But should we not count Paul among the producers of a kind of thinking Michel Serres refers to as "statics"? Could we not say of the proliferation of divine, human, and animal bodies in and around Paul what Serres could say of the "concept of deviation" in Archimedes, namely, that it is a kind of "theorem of statics"? Note that Serres is not far here from our aleatory materialism, not to mention our evocation of a Lacanian Democritus at the beginning of the chapter:

> The idea goes to the heart of philosophy, that is, metaphysics. If we had only the principle of identity, we would be mute, motionless, passive, and the world would have no existence: nothing new under the sun of sameness. We call it the principle of reason that there exists something rather than nothing. From which it follows that the world is present, that we work here and that we speak. Now this principle is never explained or taken up except in terms of substantives; the thing, being and nothingness, the void. For it says: *exist rather than.* Which is almost a pleonasm, since existence denotes a stability, plus a deviation from the fixed position. *To exist rather than* is to be in deviation from equilibrium. Exist rather. And the principle of reason is, strictly speaking, a theorem of statics. If things exist and if there is a world, they are displaced in relation to zero. And if there is a reason, it is this inclined proportion. If there is a science, it is its evaluation. If there is a discourse, it speaks of inclination. If there is a practice, it is its tool. We do not exist, do not speak and do not work, with reason, science or hands, except through and by this deviation from equilibrium. Everything is deviation from equilibrium, except Nothing. That is to say, Identity.[29]

No wonder that Nietzsche's critique of Paul needed to be so hysterically repetitive about Paul's calculating intentions in the manufacture and broadcasting of his promises. That is, Nietzsche needed to forget, at the very moment of his critique, his own version of Spinozist *conatus*, the way egos are not in charge, in control, lucid because detached calculators, but rather ecstatically swept up and carried off by *forces* working through them. Nietzsche had to become what he himself rejected in order to see it in Paulinism. In order to banish the imagined origin of the bourgeois ego and its calculating values, Nietzsche had to think like one, as if sacrificing himself to redeem us from the sin of an imagined calculatingly bourgeois Paul. And once the iconoclast agrees to have such lenses fitted, Nietzsche himself became part of what Derrida describes as the "powerful repression" that governs the destiny of erstwhile thinkers of "statics."[30] To the psychiatrists, Derrida spoke: "By exaggerating only slightly, one could say that Freud simultaneously identifies and transfers a symptom that could be called: the disciple of Epicurus and the forgetting of his name. I leave it to you to pursue this further. But never forget this: the Democritean tradition, in which the names of Epicurus and his disciples are inscribed, has been subjected since its origin, and first of all under the violent authority of Plato, to a powerful repression throughout the history of Western culture."[31]

In a world of contingent vortices contracting multiplicities in a void or—it amounts to the same—a swerving world without end, there are no stable subjects and objects, leaving us therefore with experiences or perceptions which could only elude the standard measurements of the deviations of "ideology." The point, ultimately the point of the early Marx, is critical. The irreality of ghosts, for example those indwelling spooks of the lowborn in Corinth, cannot be made in the vorticist universe to testify *against* their reality, as if by answering to a stable judgment. Cicero and Aquinas alike must not be given Roman instrumental control over these celebratory sessions. Serres summarizes the point by reference to the *simulacra numinum* of Lucretius, those simulations or images which cut across vectors of space and time like so many nomads, rogue wanderers (recall, precisely, Cicero's joking sarcasm about Epicurus's mind) along fragments of time.[32] Such ghosts, such simulacra, are as real, as material, as anything (and everything).

As our inclinations, our little tilts, are always already playing themselves out in unexpected ways (or as the repressed is always returning in surprising ways to elude our intentions), what do we find in Nietzsche except a materialist Paulinism on its way, pointing to the liberation of free spirits, but this time with only a change of name and identity card: Zarathustra. My concern here is not that Nietzsche attempts to subvert Christianity by way of a repetition and immanent intensification of a Lutheran Paulinism: cast out the calculating laborers in order to herald the freedom of the uncalculating! In the larger political trajectory of the higher swindle

Nietzsche just replaces Luther's "Jews" for the upwardly mobile classes of modern capitalist economies. That is a different tale, but what needs to be pointed out at the moment is the way the difference between a philosophy of identity and a philosophy of "statics" and stochastic emergence of ungrounded difference insinuates itself not in Nietzsche's *rejection* of Paulinism, but in his reception of it *as* already a form of Platonic guarantee.

We need to attune ourselves to a new model of myth production, one where religion is not (apparently) always guarantee, pop metaphysics, Platonism for the masses. As Serres writes in a line we will need to learn to take seriously at the level of our understanding of religion: "The beam no longer has a balance point. Here or there, yesterday or tomorrow, deviations appear stochastically. Or differential angles of inclination. Here is something rather than nothing, here is existence, here are vortices, spirals, volutes, all models out of equilibrium."[33] Why are there celebratory banquets for the undead rather than nothing? To understand, we will need a new model of myth that will have nothing to do with the need of the critics of "ontotheology" always and ever to imagine religion as wanting to be thought of as a stable doubling structure of the world in another one. Rather, as Serres writes, these stochastic emergences "are brought back to zero by deterioration, ruin and death. But, temporarily, they form" (22). Indeed, and so did Paulinism, for a while until its expectations and desires faded and his curators therefore pretended as though he had been teaching the stabilities of a pop Platonic universe.

As Hanjo Berressem points out, Serres's Lucretian physics of fluxes, declinations, vortices, and flows are essential for Serres's entire corpus of writing.[34] Most importantly for our purposes, Serres leads the way when, in *Angels: A Modern Myth*, he presents Pia and Pantope, those wonderful Roissy transients, discussing Lucretius as the conduit of an aleatory materialism for the information age. As a moment of the repetitive short-circuiting of science and myth that this virtual conversation enacts, it is worth noting that Paul as "apostle" appears in the text alongside Serres's "angel" as a figural instance of, precisely, the short-circuiting of these two practices of thought. Paul comes back once the conversation turns to the aleatory materialism of matter and mind: "I find that the process of thought is rather like a large, unitary, fortuitous moment of being carried away, which is broken down in to little squalls and flurries which have no particular relation to each other but which all come together in a greater overriding movement. At a level above the myriad angels, puffing away with their chubby cheeks and creating chaos and confusion, a great archangel advances, flying with the wind behind him, and it is his will that pushes me in the direction in which I wish to go."[35]

A force emerging from what Marx might have called the "chance of thought"—or from what Gilles Deleuze might call the "disjunctive synthesis" of multiple or aleatory fields of forces—thinking this mythical power of enunciation behind thought frightens Pantope who prefers to imagine "that we're the only intelligent beings in this world" or, at the very least, that our wishes remain our own. Pantope responds accordingly, as if anxious that he is becoming, in Pia's discourse—and by way of Serres's Lucretius—an apostle: "I'm rather alarmed at the idea that thinking might end up being like the destructive seizure that had St Paul falling off his horse. In the same way that a sudden gust of wind and the pitching of a boat can send us sprawling on the deck. A slap in the face, a sharp, heavy blow, exactly applied, which makes the body unsettled, makes it lose its balance, and draws our attention to the proximity of death" (33).

What, then, is this material thinking? It is the *après coup* loss of balance and the overwhelming fascination of a new thought, a new life, that is indistinguishable from our lack of resistance to it. There are echoes here, as we will see in the next chapter, of the "passion" of Heidegger's "facticity" and the potential importance of phenomenology for the question of a critique of ideology. Serres summarizes with utter clarity his discussions of Lucretius and the *singularizing* encounter that is the swerve or *clinamen*, such moments of giving up our lives to have them back new, when he describes them, perfectly, as a threshold at which "something other" begins. The movement of thought and things, thought-things, evokes once more the apostolic burden: "the emergence of something new . . . of life, of good tidings" (34). Early ecclesiasts eager to conjure a superiority of Christianity over Judaism, and to save a fading Paulinist ethnic experimentation with undead solidarities by way of Plato, are not the only ones anxious about *everyone* being able to be a true Paulinist. Serres is too, but his is a more useful comparative game of borrowed naming than the endless repetition of the same old story about the exceptionalism and stable metaphysical identities of Plato and that saintly Paul who was retrofitted with the concrete shoes of a foundational ontotheology. With Michel Serres's disconcerting good news in our ears, in the following chapter we will expand on the emerging comparative Paulinisms of Louis Althusser and Stanislas Breton.

2

ON BEING CALLED DEAD

Splitting the Imperative of Being

I have been crucified with Christ and I live no longer. The life I am living . . .

—Galatians 2:19

IN THE LAST CHAPTER WE BEGAN TO DISCUSS THE SECRET SHARING of the Paulinism of Stanislas Breton and the aleatory materialism of Louis Althusser, tabling initially several ways in which such sharing indicates new ways to understand an apostle in the "underground current of materialism." I want now to focus on the issue more directly by showing just what was the Paulinism of Stanislas Breton in relation to the implicit turn toward aleatory materialism in the late Althusser. My own work on both figures takes seriously something Breton once said about Christianity, something I think we should affirm in relationship to materialism as well: "We consequently relinquish the image of a simple body that the dream of a new alchemy would disengage under the sign of critique at the end of its effort. Authentic Christianity [sic] is not behind us: it is in front of us."[1] We should perhaps risk a fidelity to the project, gather round its table, particularly as to do otherwise is implicitly to give way to those inherited proprieties and property rights which continue to control most reflection on "religion" and "materialism" alike. As we have always said, to find Paul swimming in the underground current of materialism is to resist a tendency to place Paul otherwise. Moreover, I have also been making it clear that, in keeping with a radical reformulation, such resistance would need to be exerted against Paul's critics as well as his curatorial friends. I have been particularly keen, for example, to point out that Nietzsche's general diagnosis of Paulinism as a kind of "Platonism for the masses" (which hamstrings the affirmative, creative force of European culture) is missing a more radical way in this regard. Nietzsche was of course no idiot—and one of his roommates was a renowned historian of the early church—so he was aware that to place Paul among the materialists would be to go against an otherworldly and calculating apparatus of capture which overdetermined the Pauline legacy almost from the very start. So, perhaps—given that the second century "fathers" were relying on Plato rather than Lucretius in order to make Paul appear as an appropriate founder of a significant cultural movement—one needs to stick here with Breton in affirming two programmatic points. First, there is no alchemical process which effects the retrieval of a "simple body" in the past, as if we would uncover the past in order to invest it with fantasies of pristination. Rather, we found ourselves to have agreed to a genealogical struggle with which where we are going, where Paul is going, where Plato and the materialists are going all seem, strangely, "in front of us," as if on the way by virtue of the strategies of thought that constitute our labors. Secondly, a wild openness within these recursitivies, all these intertwined and therefore displaced temporalities, appears as a kind of *kairos* or chance timeliness. In both respects, there will have been a kind of Paulinist messianism in the very way in which we *think*, what Marx in the last chapter referred to as the "chance of thought" itself or what he imagined as the subjective openness *within* material causality as such. Breton, as we will see, articulates an isomorphic ontological structure which he refers to as a form of swerve he imagines as a "wink."

In any case, at a moment like ours, when forms of thought, modes of life, or readily defined identity groups defining the inside and outside of religion seem to be in flux, as if perplexed by an inheritance that has become too constrictive or predictable, Breton's lectures on Paul become a significant interlocutor. Above all, for our purposes, Breton—among many other things a lifelong friend and intellectual ally in important respects of one of the great Marxist thinkers of the twentieth century, Louis Althusser—presents us with a Paul, described in relation to Western philosophical, theological, and political history, that helps us to understand the fundamental paradox of recent readings of Paul: that the self-proclaimed apostle of a resurrected Christ would stand in as perhaps the best indication, the shortest pathway, to a theory of subjectivity that is avowedly *materialist*.[2] If we are witnessing today a short-circuiting of distinctions between the "religious" and the "secular"—and how else would we understand the phenomenon of Paul returning as the great guarantor of an effort to think, to ground a contemporary philosophical materialism?—then why has Paulinism reappeared as a particularly forceful index of this scrambling of received codes?

Breton's own reading of Paul and Paulinism, I should point out, is decidedly singular, eclectic, variously philosophical, political, theological, and not always something I myself find useful to repeat. Just to mention something about the latter issue, it seems to me that Breton generally has no inkling about the way it is possible to historicize Paul more radically than Lutheran interpretations did for centuries, a historicization which could never escape variations of the "first Christian" or "Christian origins" stories. A more radical historicization would, as I argue in the introduction and elsewhere, subtract Paul from that great theological and, subsequently, modernist discursive machine we generally gloss as the quest for "Christian origins" in which Paul criticizes "Judaism," universalizes it, and—by this gesture—founds Christianity on the ruin of a (now) hidebound, localist, ethnocentric Judaism.[3] Put differently, Breton does not—despite himself—see how, *at this level*, his engagement with Paulinism might refuse or defuse or rewire the mechanics of the machinery of the Platonism for the masses. While Breton is alternately alarmed, mournful, and critical of the political implications of this well-worn theologico-modern machine, he does not yet realize the tools historical reconstruction affords him to participate (again, at that level) in its transformation.[4] On my reading, Breton's Paul is—like the Paul of Alain Badiou's universalism book or (if I may say so) Daniel Boyarin's earlier writings on Paul—one of the more importantly radicalized and politically significant in a largely Lutheran tradition of interpretation. (Just note the presence of Rudolf Bultmann in Breton and Badiou). More to the point (and as a spur for other fellow biblical scholars), while important indications of a genuinely post-Lutheran historical interpretation of Paul might be now appearing in pockets within academic biblical studies (this book not the least of them I like to think), philosophically and politically significant adventures with this new and post-Lutheran Paul have barely begun to see the light of day. In Breton, to be sure, one does not learn what the best recent historiography can tell us about the historical Paul. But one *does* begin to catch significant modes of reading a radicalized Lutheran Paul with Aristotle, with Aquinas, and with Platonic traditions, all of which are more "with" us, in us, constructing our modes of thinking (historical or otherwise), the more we fail to process them, slowly, carefully, patiently. So, perhaps, until recent historiography finds forceful and interdisciplinary modes of articulation, Breton's Paul remains unique and uniquely illuminating for an encounter between Paul and the philosophers.

In keeping with Breton's own model of approaching Paul, we could perhaps also approach Breton's own reading laterally, by setting up intersections or multiple modes of encounter between thoughts whose comparability may not seem obvious, prefabricated, or culturally ready-made. Paulinism for Breton stood in for a kind of effective history of the Pauline legacy, a shifting, developing, and contested or ruptured legacy that, for all these reasons, affords an archive which, for the thinker (in both senses mentioned earlier), opens up a multiplicity of territories for expansive conceptual exploration and inventive affirmation. Breton of course knew very well that his is not an interpretive game emerging from strict historical method or history in the usual positivistic sense.[5] This is not simply a point about Breton's affinity for certain aspects of hermeneutics as a kind of fundamental philosophy, but also a simple statement about the concrete approach of Breton's engagement with the apostle. When he speaks of Paul and allegory, for example, Breton uses two texts (from Ephesians and Hebrews respectively) that are, he fully acknowledges, not generally imagined by contemporary biblical scholars to be written by Paul himself.[6] Nevertheless, he invites, can they not "seem to form a kind of preface to any introduction to the allegorical method"?[7]

By the same token, Breton's reading of Paulinism is focused on the cross—he was a true Passionist after all—by way of both pre- and postmodern ontologies. Breton's Paul is a kind of thinker of the cross as a productive subtraction at the origin of things. In the case of Paulinist allegory, for example, Breton's caveats about historical authorship are immediately followed by a striking discussion of time plunging into eternity, of the Christ of Ephesians—caught up in such a plunge of the contingently historical into the permanency of the structural—becoming the "copula of the universe," that originary mediation which scrambles both subjects and predicates in a rhapsodic movement of cosmic reconciliation which Breton calls (in the words of the letter to the Ephesians 1:23) the "all in all." Breton's philosophical reading of this passage solicits our consideration of the Christ of Ephesians in philosophical modes we might have otherwise missed. Of course, by wiring ancient metaphysical (and, I must repeat, sometimes anti- or postmetaphysical) axioms into the apocalyptic and mystical world of Paulinist insurgency, metaphysics (as well as the limits of metaphysical reasoning) lights up with a strangely Paulinist hew as well.

As Breton writes of the Christ of the letter to the Ephesians becoming the copula of a universal philosophical system: it is the energy of a circuit or "loop-like construction" of action that—narrative time plunging into structures of eternity—"mimes . . . the aseity of self-sufficiency of the Absolute," as if the narration itself were positing its own presuppositions, retroactively "looping" into reality that from which it came.[8] This fundamental operation of the "construction" of reality will be important for Breton, and here we should read Breton's particular focus on the ontology of Paulinism alongside more recent efforts to rethink ontology in a hypercapitalist era under the rubric of "quasi-causality" (Gilles Deleuze) or the *objet petit a* (Jacques Lacan) as a kind of surplus investment which itself *produces* the background economy it claims to serve, as if the "effect" had retroactively posited its cause. There are echoes here already, not only of Marx's or Serres's break with a subject-object dualism or the dualism of material causes and phenomenal effects which we considered in the last chapter. There are also echoes of that intellectual moment burbling up through the cultural economy in the late sixties and early seventies, evident in the writing of Althusser or in Breton's philosophical interest in Lacan. As Slavoj Žižek writes: "The quasi-cause is not an illusory theatre of shadows, like that of the child who thinks he is magically making a toy move, unaware of the mechanical causality which actually does the work—on the contrary, the quasi-cause *fills in the gap of corporeal causality*. In this strict sense, and insofar as the Event is the Sense-Event, the quasi-cause is non-sense as inherent to Sense."[9] The background economy, if you will, does not itself exist without being posited by, precisely, the fetishistic, swerved, or ungrounded investments in "pieces" of it. In a world which continues to be dominated by finance capital and the fetishistic utopias of "little" consumerist investments, Žižek's diagnosis is both compelling and an important supplement to the kind of (late) Althusserian Paulinism I describe in Breton.

In a description that is very much in keeping with what Breton does with allegory, Žižek brilliantly suggests that the very reversal of temporal or mechanical causality is what keeps pace with a contemporary ontology within a world of hypercapitalist economies of life, but also what makes us need to reverse simplistic reversals of Hegelian assumed idealism into a certain type of Marxist materialism:

From his early writings (the once famous "Economic and Philosophical Manuscripts" of 1844), Marx succumbs to the Feuerbachian temptation of formulating "alienation" and class society in terms of a mirror-reversal of the "proper" relation of causality: in capitalism, the subject is enslaved to its own product, "dead labor" (capital) rules over "living labor" (the workers' productivity), the predicate becomes the subject of its own true subject, the effect becomes the cause of its own cause. What if, however, this "capitalist reversal" (the effect retroactively subsumes its cause, the process that generates capital appears as its own subordinated movement) is grounded in a more fundamental "reversal" constitutive of subjectivity as such? What if subjectivity *is* an effect which retroactively posits its cause, a "predicate reversed into subject"?[10]

Žižek's Marx-become-a-Hegelian-Lacan is here very close to the scene I am constructing between Breton and the "underground current of materialism." In his discussion of Ephesians 1:9–12, Breton imagines a teleological movement of divine intention, planning, and effective carrying through of an action to gather into God, by way of a cosmic Christ (Breton's "copula of the universe"), *ta panta* (all things). As is typical of him, however, here we see Breton squeezing together mystical and philosophical texts tighter still, forcing each, as it were, to bleed into the other. Compressing his religio-philosophical construction further, Breton adds the all-important final twist: when religious narrative mimics ancient philosophical structure (and vice versa), readers are, Breton writes, confronted with a play of gestures in which a teleological reading of the structure of the universe explodes to life, precisely, as a "semantic order," as if the "meaning of Being," or the structures of ontology itself, could be read in the forceful imperative of a speech performance like "let there be light!"[11] The narrative loop here is one in which power is produced immanently or retroactively in the spectacular doubling or affirmation of power itself. Power exists only in its subjective affirmation, a purely superficial or surfacy phenomenological space that is only "caused" by power after the excessive fact of its affirmation, a story that increasingly began to dominate Althusser's rewiring of Marxist traditions of ideology.

I am unpacking this moment in Breton's reading as it exemplifies an intensity of interpretive juxtaposition and mutual explication of intellectual traditions that characterizes Breton's book on Paul generally. To keep up with Breton, readers must endeavor to be agile, for in forging such connections, quickly and schematically, this philosophical Paulinist takes us from statements of a Pauline disciple (say, the author of Ephesians), back into Paul (Romans), and then out again into classical Greek philosophy (Aristotle) and its mystical interpreters (Meister Eckhart), finally arriving at a subtle commentary not only on Martin Heidegger ("the meaning of Being") but also on Louis Althusser (for whom emergence into being and subjection to the performative speech act of sovereign power occur simultaneously). To think with the Pauline legacy, Breton's reader finds, is to grapple also with ontologies and theories of power and subjection in which a *being* in the world emerges only *in, with, and through* a yes-saying to a substance best understood in terms of a *performative speech act*—"Let there be light!"—or, as in Louis Althusser's famous example of the policeman addressing someone in the street, "You there!" When the light switches on, or when that someone turns to the authority to answer, "You mean me?" then reality starts to appear *as* summoned (in Althusser's terminology, interpellated) by the call that is itself the movement of self-reinforcing power.

At the instigation of Breton and Žižek, now listen to an Althusserian depiction of power's revelatory function in the "call" of ideology, this time keeping predestinarian Pauline texts in mind. In an interview with Mexican philosopher Fernando Navarro, for example, Althusser describes:

> There is a paradox here. It is as if, when I believe in a notion . . . I were not the one who recognizes it and, confronted by it, could say: "That's it, there it is, and it's true." On the contrary, it is "as if," when I believe in an idea, it were the idea that dominated me and obliged me to recognize its existence and truth, through its presence. It is "as if"—the roles having been reversed—it were the idea that interpellated me, in person, and obliged me to recognize its truth. This is how the ideas that make up an ideology impose themselves violently, abruptly, on the "free consciousness" of men [*sic*]: *by interpellating* individuals in such a way that they find themselves compelled "freely" to recognize that these ideas are *true—compelled* to constitute themselves as "free" "subjects" who are capable of recognizing the true wherever it is present, and of *saying so*, inwardly or outwardly, in the very form and content of the ideas constitutive of the ideology in question. . . . That is the basic mechanism that transforms individuals into subjects. *Individuals are always-already subjects, that is to say, always-already-subject to an ideology* [emphasis added].[12]

As Breton is pointing out so clearly by way of the discussions of Pauline "predestination," the basic circuitry of Althusser's construal of subjects as effects of power issuing as a call to individuals is comparable to the surprising Pauline move in Ephesians or Romans 9 to imagine the individuality and qualities of individuals as *effects* or machinations of sovereign power. Breton's reading allows us to feel the rhythms of Althusserian notions of ideology in Paulinist conceptions of predestination. By the same token, of course, and perhaps more surprisingly, Breton invites us to intuit a form of Pauline sovereignty and Paulinist allegory (with their respective visions of the aseity of the divine) in Althusserian notions of ideology. Wiring all these links back into his construction of Paul, readers of Paulinist texts of predestination and mysticism are therefore led to the heart of a logic in which, as Meister Eckhart had it, "the being (of things) is the verb by which God speaks all things in speaking to them," or, even, "(the creatures) are the adverb of the Verb" (59). Ontology shifts entirely into the space of Paulinist predestination and discussions of "calling," part of a larger mode of thinking about the world in which performative speech act, the call and response of power, constitute the world as it is. Paul the apostle now converses with Althusser, the great inventor of an aleatory materialism in which "ideology" is no longer simple "false consciousness" (which would imply the existence of a world *without* summoning interpellation) but rather *the mode in which worldhood exists*, namely, as emerging from the practices of interpellated subjects. In keeping with our discussions of the previous chapter, Breton's Paul, we might say, will be tailor-made for the society of the spectacle.

As Paul Ricouer could still lecture in the 1975, it is perhaps surprising in light of some of Althusser's earlier writings to see how Heideggerian his later reworking of materialism seems.[13] Perhaps so. However, we should not miss the way in which, already in earlier statements about ideology like this one, Althusser was fascinated to think the relationship between economic base and superstructure—the former still providing "determination in the last instance" to the latter—in a way that was not merely "descriptive." And, with this passing beyond analysis that is mere "description" of a state of affairs, Althusser's thinking begins to be lured away from the noun to the verb (as it were), to the question of the *modes of relation* between these related structures, to an actively and essentially relational sphere in which related structures solicit and respond to one another. Consider Ricoeur, who misses very precisely the affinities I am diagnosing here: "Althusser reminds us of Heidegger in the hermeneutic circle, though I doubt he had that at all in mind. (Althusser hardly seems very much Heideggerian; Heidegger must be the worst of all ideologists for someone like Althusser.)"[14] Ricoeur did not see the significance, precisely, of what seemed a kind of category mistake to the hermeneut, Althusser mistakenly presenting his work on ideology as a form of Heideggerian facticity. As noted previously, Giorgio Agamben reads Heideggerian "facticity," or the thereness of the everyday, as a form of "passion," which I further explicated in light of the "swerve" of *clinamen*, links that will mean a great deal to Breton.

Even in these earlier writings of Althusser, we should note, the sphere of a "mode" of production was better accessible to a mode of phenomenological description than to mechanistic or topological metaphors. Descriptive modes open up ways of matching effects (Althusser mentions censorious bans on cultural works as an example) to causes (a repressive state apparatus operating to maintain the status quo). But this possibility of matching layers or instances of the self-reproduction of the society is, strictly speaking, distinguishable from the emergence of what Althusser calls "a very special kind of obviousness," that phenomenological space in which one declares, "Yes, that's how it is, that's really true!"[15] To say the same thing somewhat differently, this move toward the "special kind of obviousness" inhering in new subjective forms can also be read as part of what Étienne Balibar describes as Althusser's "conceptual break with any expressive causality, the decisive step towards *materialism*" or toward a kind of immanence in relation to the self-reproductive force of the social itself rather than to second order *descriptions* of it.[16] Warren Montag describes similarly a movement in Althusser toward immanent critique and immanent description by showing Althusser's deployment of Spinozist immanence against the *hermeneutical* tradition.[17] Ironically (given the frequent hand-wringing and criticism about Althusser's panoply of mechanistic, functional, or process metaphors), it is the move away from expressivist hermeneutics (in which ideology would be a symbol of structures appearing or existing elsewhere) that allows Althusser to afford a material density to ideology itself. This is the very density, I am suggesting, that Žižek wants to analyze as the retroactive positing of subjectivity as the quasi-cause or the *objet petit a*.

Or, put differently, do we not see here the exemplary way in which power as exteriority or transcendence is collapsing into something else, a society of the spectacle that works via immanent forms of *prestige*? The umbilical link between a society of the spectacle and the Spinozistic

making-immanent of a God function occurs in the paradoxical intensification of the religious archive of the call and response of a "revelatory
encounter." The immanent cause becomes all the more blisteringly present in its (traditionally understood) causal absence, forcing us into a general reduction or epoché of causes under the name of their effects. As
Althusser would write after his turn to an aleatory materialism: "No Cause
that precedes its effects is to be found in it [i.e., aleatory materialism],
no Principle of morality or theology (as in the whole Aristotelian political tradition: the good and bad forms of government, the degeneration
of the good into the bad). One reasons here not in terms of the Necessity
of the accomplished fact, but in terms of the contingency of the fact to
be accomplished."[18] In light of Breton's invitation to think Althusser with
Paul, we should note the fundamental sense in which an exploration of
the "obviousness of obviousness" is integrally related to Althusser's desire
to move from "descriptive theory to theory as such," as if entering into
the life of power rather than picturing it from the outside. The "return"
of Paulinism here is, therefore, rather *precisely* in keeping with an effort
to stay with the ungrounded or aleatory investments constituting the new
"underground" materialism itself, something we must reflect on increasingly. For the moment, recall that the earlier Althusser himself referred to
the Paul imagined in the New Testament book of Acts:

> As St. Paul admirably put it, it is in the "Logos," meaning in ideology, that
> we "live, move and have our being." It follows that, for you and for me, the
> category of the subject is a primary "obviousness" (obviousnesses are always
> primary): it is clear that you and I are subjects (free, ethical, etc.). Like all
> obviousness, including those that make a word "name a thing" or "have
> a meaning" (therefore including the obviousness of the "transparency" of
> language), the "obviousness" that you and I are subjects—and that that does
> not cause any problems—is an ideological effect, the elementary ideological
> effect. It is indeed a peculiarity of ideology that it imposes (without appear-
> ing to do so, since these are "obviousnesses") obviousness as obviousness,
> which we cannot *fail to recognize* and before which we have the inevitable
> and natural reaction of crying aloud (aloud or in the "still, small voice of
> consciousness"): "That's obvious! That's right! That's true!"[19]

Like Heidegger's efforts in his early *Phenomenology of Religious Life* to
think everyday temporality as such apart from extraneous metaphysical

models, Althusser also is led back to the religious archive for images able to keep pace with the machinations of immanent, everyday obviousness and the fetishistic or ungrounded investments constituting the economy of life. Contingency, the necessity of the "as if" which guards all everyday experiences of reality, begin to blur into a kind of Stoically or Spinozistically immanentized repetition of earlier tales of revelatory encounter, an encounter with radically exterior sovereignty which functions as a touchstone all the more dramatically for its having become immanent, as if democratized or universalized in the experience of the everyday. While they sometimes seem skittish about using the Pauline archive themselves, the basic paradox here is just what Gianni Vattimo and Santiago Zabala explore as a form of (to mention the title of their book) *Hermeneutical Communism*. Heidegger, they write, "noticed how every statement, whether true or false, valid or invalid, good or evil, is always a derivative one, since the 'apophantic as' is only possible within the 'hermeneutic' as." Generally preceded by, and therefore repeating, a disclosive or founding revelatory event, most of our oriented thinking operates as an effect of a (hidden or absent) cause.[20]

Just to fill out the sketch, this is of course the same dynamic that leads Giorgio Agamben, too, to explore a kind of phenomenology of the spectacle, which he construes in terms of ancient theologies of "glory." In light of the mention of Althusser and Heidegger, Agamben's framing of his own project needs to be cited:

> Let us begin this investigation with an attempt to reconstruct the genealogy of a paradigm that has exercised a decisive influence on the development and the global arrangement of Western society, although it has rarely been thematized as such outside the strictly theological field. One of the theses that we shall try to demonstrate is that two broadly speaking political paradigms, antinomical but functionally related to one another, derive from Christian theology: political theology, which founds the transcendence of sovereign power on the single God, and economic theology, which replaces this transcendence with the idea of an *oikonomia*, conceived as an immanent ordering—domestic and not political in the strict sense—of both divine and human life. Political philosophy and the modern theory of sovereignty derive from the first paradigm; modern biopolitics up to the current triumph of economy and government over every other aspect of social life derive from the second period.[21]

As Agamben is quick to point out, not to be missed here are the echoes of Foucault's project from *Discipline and Punish* onward, the effort to think power beyond the hegemony of sovereigns and states, power displaced into more immanent, if diffuse and dispersed, forms. Playing off of Kantorowicz's classic study of *The King's Two Bodies*, Santner shows how, as it were, the society of the spectacle—in which power is diffuse, dispersed, decentralized—seems to solicit repetitions of Paulinism. Importantly—and unlike Badiou, Žižek, and Breton alike—Santner does not locate this repetition so much in visions of a Lutheran Paul overcoming or universalizing inherited Jewish *nomos* discourse but rather in visions of a Paul who appropriates and subverts Roman discourses of the political body.[22] Santner's siding with Taubes here would, of course, be important to me as someone who argues that the imagined anti-Jewish founder of a new religion was precisely an early and epoch-making interpretive dispatching or repression of Paul (fitting him with the concrete shoes of a pop Platonism), a dispatching which, among other things, both functioned and continues to function to *depoliticize* Paul. Reading Paul against the backdrop of Roman imperial discourse with Santner is a task which remains to be carried through, and Santner's work should be paired with Dale Martin's *The Corinthian Body*, as perhaps theoretical and historical readings which would mutually electrify.

For our present purposes, note the way that Santner's reading of Paul in a moment of biopolitical immanence does two things that may, despite their differences, also be found here in Althusser and Breton. The pairing of Paulinism and immanence democratizes or (perhaps better?) universalizes Paulinist tropes, thus politicizing Paul for a society of the spectacle. On the other hand, and just as importantly, the society of the spectacle receives from the religious archive something of the utmost necessity: a comparative name for the obsessive persistence or stuckness of everyday life in its fractured certainties, its stupidly everyday (though perhaps ignored) facticities or as if's. In Santner's language the society of power via spectacle, immanence, or the "special kind of obviousness" receives from Paul a notion of "the flesh." For Paul, he writes, *"the flesh is the thorn in the body*, the dimension of embodied subjectivity that registers an excess of the normative pressures that inform and potentially 'deform' a life lived in relation to agencies of authority and authorization."[23] Just to repeat the point about immanence of self-grounding swerve I have been pointing out in Althusser, note that Santner goes on to write (by way of a Paulinist tradition in Ephesians) that the problem of deformation as "the flesh" is precisely this: "The complex symbolic dynamic of the constitution of kingship itself comes 'to a head' precisely when the *body* of the king is posited as the *head* of the body politic." Put differently, once the "special kind of obviousness" will become increasingly detached from mechanically causal institutional functions, the question of *autonomia* becomes all the more strangely opaque, soliciting a return of comparative tropes, metaphors, and structures of thinking which are able to keep pace with the peculiar repetitive intensity, aporia, and alterity endemic to self-grounding identity as such. Santner will name the set of issues as the problem of "a surplus of immanence within immanence."[24]

A great deal remains to be said about Santner's attempt to rewire discussions of Paul and the disclosive "event" to a history of the body and its excessive ticks and quirks and desires, all those "thorns in the flesh."[25] For the moment it is worth noting that it is precisely in the context of *this* juxtaposition of Paul and Althusser that Breton's central reflections on the kenotic, emptying, or hollowing "call" that is a Pauline proclamation of a crucified messiah become significant as a mode of subverting the otherwise always already effective link between power and facticity. In Breton's philosophical appropriation of Paul is the scandalously unsettling, even "stupid" (cf. *mōria* in 1 Corinthians 1) identification with the crucified messiah that names a potential detachment, unhinging, or bracketing of the "special kind of obviousness" by which our world, or any world, solicits our participation, incites affirmation, thereby becoming what it is.[26]

FOUNDING RUPTURE: PAULINISM AND VOID-TALK[27]

When I spoke above about Breton's distance from the (academic) authorities on Paulinism and the Pauline legacies, I was not merely making evaluative claims. On the contrary, such an authorial stance was Breton's effort *not* to play the docile philosophical transmitter of the authoritative word of experts from abroad, whether the theologians, the historicist biblical scholars, or pious ecclesiasts who also lurk here and there within Breton's books, often to be subverted by way of a deft wiring of Pauline writings into various schemata of philosophical logic. Breton is almost always aware of the expert writings, but his singular encounter with Paul remains much more than the purveying of expert knowledge, and this because of a structural necessity. Breton's own Paulinism is, after all, nothing less than an attempt to resituate thought itself—to question what counts as thought—by installing Paul as a figure and indication of some of those *aporiae* or deadlocks of theory that Breton found always and everywhere.

In this precise respect, we need to move to the topos of the crucified, which drove Breton's lifelong philosophical Paulinism, in order to consider how Breton's philosophy *participates with* Paulinist proclamations of the crucified messiah in indicating a peculiarly unpredictable *gap* or *void* in all knowledge, all identity, and all forms of cultural or political power. By trafficking in this radical image of stark *dispossession* within the heart of all possessive identity—a messiah dead on an apparatus of imperial control—Breton wants to bore a hole through the completion of all projects of expert knowledge. In this respect we may say of Breton's oeuvre what he liked to say of Paul's, namely, that, *rather* than the certainties of knowledge, his writing burns as a testimony to a "founding rupture (*'rupture instauratrice'*)."[28]

Those accustomed to the usual platitudes about religion or theology being the last hope for modernity's escape from an otherwise soul-searing nihilism will be surprised to see the way Breton finds in the apostle an exemplary thinker of "the nothing," of all those hollows or voidances that creep into or magically appear within otherwise internally coherent structures of thought and cultural practice, all those modes of the "very special kind of obviousness" which makes worldhood and subjects. This category of the irrepressible void, however, was an integral part of Breton's work throughout his career, and it is precisely as a participant in thinking through this category that Paul remained an obsession for the philosopher. Always interested in mathematics and set theory, for example, Breton's early *Theory of Ideologies* orients a thinking for structures of thought around the way all countable elements within any given ensemble or category must necessarily participate in a kind of zero degree, an "empty part" that is inseparable from "the totality" of the set.[29] The zero degree or empty part is "in the grammar of ensembles an indispensable sign for our operations."[30] Breton sometimes described this null, empty, or zero degree element within the ensemble as a kind of in-difference within the identity of the system, neither integrated inside nor safely outside of the system and yet utterly indispensable, a sine qua non of the countable ensemble in its hanging together *as* a system. The "neuter" or "neutral" part in the establishment of identity, this nullity forever disturbs all totalizing self-enclosure or self-grounding of identity as such.[31]

In a different context and much later, Breton summarized the same issues as a fundamental problem for any metaphysics oriented around *identity*. Indeed, the problem of the impossible but structurally necessary moment in the construction of identity is described by Breton as an "evil genius" within the system of identity:

> What would be the logical formula for a statement as banal as the following: "There are French philosophers"? Retranslated into simple language, this equivalence would take the following form: "a determinate set," described by the quality "French philosopher," is not empty, or distinguishable from the set "zero." Thus one has to pass through zero in order to arrive at an existential judgment. The zero set, however, is defined by the entire number of objects which, not being identical to themselves, can only be contradictory. Ontological difference [between Being and beings] only seems thinkable through this detour which confronts us with sheer nothingness. The impossible becomes a necessary condition. These strange propositions, which I will allow to develop freely here, join the by no means less strange metaphysics that controls the access to Being through its opposition to "nothing(ness)," which means its opposition to the absolutely absurd.[32]

Significantly, however, it is not simply that Breton reads set theory or that he finds the self-grounding of all countable sets, like "humanity is humanity," to be perennially haunted by the supplementary assertion, "and nothing else."[33] There is in this haunting of or voidance within the ensemble "a minimum of division" in its very identity, and Breton suggests the haunting *sense* of this "minimal" gap in the identity of a given cultural setup can produce extraordinary effects. There can emerge, for example, an obsessive passion to purify "humanity" as if by way of a violent extension of this imperative to "nothing else," identity becoming resolved only by way of a violent exclusion of what will count as "not" humanity. As Breton describes it, one way to cope with the ineluctable "empty part (*la partie vide*)," the "indispensable void (*la vide indispensable*)" within every system is to find in it a kind of intolerable "limit" internal to the ensemble.[34] Ideology, or simply a representable ensemble or cultural setup, finds within itself an irreparable desire to *pierce through* appearances, the fragile stability of the ensemble's identity, and this in order to encounter this "void" directly. As Breton puts it, this impulse can result in the demand to sacrifice the ensemble itself for the sake of a pure encounter with the excess "beyond" its limits, and in such instances those within the cultural ensemble may be driven to acts of profound "enthusiasm" in their desire to rid themselves of this minimal voidance within the ensemble, within the heart of their collective project. This "lucid folly" (whose status as either "satanic or divine is of little importance," as Breton liked to say) is itself "incompatible with life" in the sense that the "enthusiasm" to rid oneself of this minimal gap in identity may well drive our lucid fools to a point of intransigence at which point "a diplomacy wearied with youth" may simply "nail them to the cross."[35] Whether or not this "lucid folly" drives one to acts of martyrdom or profoundly violent exclusion, Breton's approach suggests that one is always or structurally liable to the lure of ecstatic, impossible moments.

These last lines already begin to suggest the relevance of Breton's engagement with set theory as a theory of violence for his understanding of Paul. The relevance hinges on the way Breton's *own* way of responding to the structural possibility of voidance is different from reactionary or revolutionary violence (both reactions to the same threat or lure of the directly encounterable void or the void as substratum). Crucially, Breton goes on in his theory of ideologies to propose that the "pale substratum," the void both sustaining and haunting the ensemble, "does not exist."[36] This way of reading "nothing" here is critical, as it implies that all efforts to pierce *through* the identity of an ensemble, the appearance of a cultural form, in order to achieve the serenely self-subsisting essence of the beyond, are doomed to failure.[37] There is no direct encounter with the *nihil* for the would-be revolutionary or reactionary sacrifice, as neither active nor passive sacrifice can *save* identity—past, present, or future—from this haunting void. It is not possible, for example, to *eliminate* the haunting of cultural mode or ensemble by the "nothing else" that lures cultural conservatives to supreme acts of suppressive violence in their efforts to fill the gap that seems constitutively to endanger the given cultural identity. The void into which one may throw threatening terrorists of all sorts is an abyss that can never be filled, as the constitutive *threat* of the negation of an ensemble is a wound that can never be healed. In this respect, Breton's work is very close to the discussions of ideology in Slavoj Žižek, as both imagine that what the limit to identity prohibits—the access this limit also forecloses (to the new, the beyond, the purified, unscathed, or saved)—is reflective or *internal* to the system itself.[38] Breton will suggest, therefore, that the martyrological or persecutorial passion of enthusiasm—the obsession with finally solving or grounding the ensemble in question, with finally conjuring it into full presence—is itself merely a form of the "death instinct," a longing for the release of cultural life from its limits, in death or in a way that is (as Breton suggests above) "incompatible with life."

MAD RHAPSODIES OF THE PAULINIST GOD

How then do we cut through ideology, once we read ideology as the very substance of subjectivity and that "very special kind of obviousness" we enjoy so much? Crucially, at pivotal moments in his early discussion of such structural models Breton's theoretical structures elide themselves into a Paulinist narrative, and this as Breton proceeds with his elucidation of a theory of ideologies. (Of course, to return to my earlier point about the inability of the historical, narrative "Paul" to remain safe against the tides of philosophical thought, this is *also* to say, vice versa, that the religious narrative begins to slide into a theory of ensembles and their reliance on a "zero" level!). Moving somewhat closer to his full disclosure of a *Paulinist* critique of ideology, Breton writes that, within Paulinism, the cross signifies the pale void that renders inoperative the fullness of any ensemble or cultural form, that is, of all ideology *tout court*. In this respect, Breton's emptying or kenotic function of the Paulinist cross functions in a similar way to the ineluctable "remainder" or remnant Giorgio Agamben finds in Paul, a topic that becomes operationalized in Agamben's Paul through the messianic "call" that hollows, renders inoperative, or (following the Paul of 1 Corinthians 7) "as if it were not" (*hōs mē*).[39]

Given these underpinnings, it is no surprise that Breton's Paulinism usually brings with it sharp critiques of triumphalist and repressive Christian institutions and culture, with the philosopher adding on this occasion that the void-function likewise renders inoperative both the all-consuming and self-enriching God of "integrative theologies" and the cultural tectonics of a Christian "hermeneutics" that has repressed "the poverty of its origin."[40] Those who would be faithful to the Paulinist logic of the cross, he asserts, must remain faithful to thinking all beings, and indeed being itself, in a way that is "meontological," that is *not* (*me-ontological*) science of self-grounding *identity*.[41] With this move from harmonious self-possession to the "founding rupture" (*rupture instauratrice*), Breton begins to make clear the ontological revolution or "turning" involved in a Paulinist appropriation of the cross, as well as to make clear how it is that this Paulinism affords an inexhaustible source for the *critique of ideologies.* Ever deferring and subverting the ontological identity that could provide justification or warrant for the triumphalist "evolutions of the city of God" or the legitimizing ideologies of the state, the meontological cross will be for Breton the unsettling thought that is at once a Pauline story of the crucified messiah and also the indication of an immanent, universalizable voidance that plagues all identity. And it is perhaps the indeterminacy of the mutual affectation of this isomorphism that names something essential about reading Paul with the philosophers.[42]

More should be said about the critical function of Breton's Paul, however. Notice the way Breton's reading of the cross bleeds over into an Althusserian statement about the permanency of an ideological state's "zero level" of repression and exclusion. Althusser once declared in relation to Heidegger that the zero level of an ideological state is the Heideggerian "there is" of factical being, always already thrown, specified, organized *as* a singular state of affairs which, for this very reason, seems to solicit a *destruktion*, a deconstruction, a revolution.[43] And, just between these echoes, Breton insinuates the Pauline story of the crucified messiah, a kind of permanency of the crucified and a kind of eternity of that moment whereby, through identification with the crucified, the "nothings" would become "something," thus "destroying" the *paradeigmata* of the world that first deprived them of their being in the first place (I am borrowing the Pauline language of 1 Corinthians 1 and Romans 12).[44] Making similar connections, Breton writes:

> At origin, and I have no doubt that it is a question of origin, "there is" (*il y a*) the judgment of the Cross. This judgment divides humanity in what would be, according to the etymology of *Krisis* translated again by the German *Ur-teil*, a decision-separation: on the one hand, those who exist according to the noble values of wisdom and power; on the other the anonymous and undifferentiated ensemble of those who, by reason of constraint and not of essence, do not accept those values. But Christ [*sic*: actually the argument works much better from Breton's beloved 1 Corinthians 1] pronounced himself without equivocation for what does not exist. The God he evokes tolerates no wavering; this God can be spoken of or affirmed through neither classical philosophic categories nor in the traditional attributes discerned by a religion.[45]

One does not encounter the divine precipitate of this crisis, in other words, either by deduction from generalities or from the induction of particulars. Indeed, none of the "justifications," so many niceties, of power's knowledge and wisdom, will lead you to the (as it were, revelatory) encounter or stabilize you once you are there. What then? This is the encounter open only to the partisan, *those who side with the "nothings"* in a struggle against those wisdoms and powers which constitute themselves on the exclusion of these (now named, particularized, emerging) nothings. Two further aspects of Breton's Paulinist critique of ideology should be pointed out here, as what has been said so far may suggest that it is a simple, formal paradox that implies (even as it disavows) a zero level within all cultural acts of counting as. Worse, such an easygoing formalism lends itself to a sense that the paradoxes in view are (just as simply) useful tools available for those already disposed to criticize formations of power. But this is to miss the almost anarchic and free forcefulness of cultural transformation Breton has in mind, a forcefulness he articulates in different ways on different occasions with depictions that are decidedly more visceral, gut-wrenching, and dark than mere formalisms might suggest. In this respect, we should not miss the way Breton's darker modes (wherein, for example, "Christianity" has its original inspiration in a nightmare and where freedom is largely an illusory obfuscation of our real function within relations of power) are more decidedly Pauline modes (on the one hand) and hovering at the deep level of ontological commitments (on the other).[46]

Consider, for example, a kind of introspective self-examination and summary of his work that appeared in 1990, when Breton drew an explicit link between "meontology" and the (Heideggerian) "ontological difference," that philosophy of thinking the difference between being and beings as, precisely, *difference*, a *gap* from which representable beings *cannot be saved*.[47] Here Breton goes one step further in his theory of these pluriform "signs" of the "cross," reading Paulinism in light of the work of Rudolf Bultmann, early twentieth-century biblical studies colleague of philosopher Martin Heidegger. For Breton, the important thing about Bultmann is the way he suggests that the voidance of the Paulinist cross is that which makes possible a critique of reification, fetishization, or the "magical instrumentalization" (through "ritual technique") of all representations of the Absolute. The cross, as Breton explains Bultmann, is that which renders the Absolute inoperative, unavailable for all such economic gestures, and this because of its own "subtraction" from all determinate contexts.[48] As such, the cross is the name of that which escapes a modern system where, increasingly, the only mode in which anything can exist is by way

of effective production, an activity modernity accomplishes by organizing ends through measured means, this being the modern mode of being
Breton glosses as the "will to power." Repeating his earlier definition of
both cross and set theory, and this in his own book about ideology and the
critique of power, Breton summarizes these ideas as Bultmann's "heroic
meontology." As we will see, one of the reasons it is "heroic" for Breton is
because Bultmann was (theoretically at least) willing to sacrifice for this
thought of the Paulinist cross a "possessive instinct," a rendering inoperative of the culture of private property that Breton takes very seriously in
all his writings.[49]

Breton is clear about such a dynamic throughout his own expansive
and diverse "meontological" writings. On the one hand, the cross annuls
sacrifice. He already suggested as much in his discussions of the lure of
the metaphyisical "pale substratum," for which adherence to ideological
formations will sacrifice either the formation itself (in revolutionary violence) or all those who seem to threaten it (in an endless conservative sacrifice of "terrorists"). In either case, one is only attempting to localize and
annihilate the specter of the void that haunts the formation, thus making fully present and fully safe the identity of the system as such, finally
avoiding its void. In this respect, Breton's Paul explores similar political
logics as does Alain Badiou's remarkable work of theater, *The Incident at
Antioch*.[50] Thus, in a striking repetition of the haunting early Christian
line, whoever *saves* life in this (sacrificial) way only loses it: one finds that
the kingdom or revolutionary utopia does *not* arrive, despite the execution of all those "obstructions" thought to have blocked it, or one finds
that the systemic *place* of the executable "terrorist" is *itself* never sacri-
ficable, despite the sacrificial execution of countless terrorists. To put it
differently, the placeless and unrepresentable *nihil* that haunts a structure cannot be exorcised by any effort to *localize* this threat, to place this
placeless space in Guantánamo Bay or to concretize its unrepresentable
trauma by filling it with unrepresented—and it still seems, (legally) unrepresentable—human beings.

At the same time, however, the unsacrificeable sacrifice *does* make
difficult demands of a different sort for Breton. He speaks frequently of
the gapping or "distancing" effects of the voidance of "the cross" in all its
guises. Following an aged philosophical tradition of "training for death,"
Breton's "nothing" urges us to see beyond the "reification" of subjects and
objects as they have come to exist in our time or that of others.[51] This
necessarily ascetic openness to seeing our world "negated" in this way,

this form of losing of our lives for the sake of the inaugural rupture, how-ever, is *also* a way of gaining a sense of a *creative* pulsation of life yet to come, indeed a pulsation Breton describes as "the auto-construction of the spirit, the specific autonomy of the [world] soul and of the birth of the world."[52]

This is important to say, as this productive movement, this dispos-sessed life, is what Breton sometimes calls "the rigor of the negative," the paradoxes of which (between loss and excess, death and life) are unavoid-able.[53] In ways reminiscent of Walter Benjamin's "messianic" figures, in Breton the minimal difference indicated by reference to a "void" within the field of the visible may be read as a kind of wink, a slight alteration in appearance that *is also* an indication that the world of appearances is or could yet be otherwise. Like Benjamin's messianic time, the revolution-ary transvaluation of all values, the changing of *everything*, is a potential of a minimal, evanescent tweak of appearance.[54] In the thinker's (and, more aptly, as it is the figure Breton almost always has in mind, the *cul-tural critic's*) openness to the messageless message of the wink, however, a truly excessive being may yet donate what Breton often designates as "that which it neither is nor owns." To return to the issue of the "peculiar kind of obviousness" that is our more or less prescripted place within a given world, here we see Breton exploring modes of thinking "cross" as that which insinuates—weakly, with a mere wink or even as only a form of dreamy madness—a solicitation to a world in which everything will be changed.

But we must say more still here in order to make the depth of Breton's commitment to a Paulinist ontology of the crucified clear. For Breton, in other words, the *scandal* and *stupidity* of the failed messiah in the first two chapters of 1 Corinthians (which organized Breton's thinking so pro-foundly) was not simply a tactical inversion of worldly categories, with apparent or reified wisdom being brought low by way of the excluded. It was, more profoundly for Breton, how divinity, or how truth, appears as such. And, with that simple gesture of intensification or generalization of the Pauline statements about the crucified in 1 Corinthians 1, 2, we open up the door to an ontology (and perhaps a meontology) from which no one remains unscathed. One must say emphatically, for example, that for Breton the Paulinist divinity does not remain *outside* such assertions or the wrenching exertions of paradoxical inversions of value. The identifica-tion of the divine with the crucified for Breton then names the crossing of multiple intersections. In its pathological attachment to the moment of a crucified messiah, divinity finds itself inflicted with the most hair-raising case of what Breton sometimes calls "mad love," impassioned attachment that unhinges the coordinates of preestablished identity. At the same moment of this intensely erotic investment, however, there is for Breton an uncanny distancing effect that settles into the otherwise personal attachment, this dual and paradoxical movement summarized perfectly by Breton as a "shadow cast by a personal relation converted into the *a priori* of generalized perception." There is thus a strange, simultaneous dual movement: a "mad love" that distends and transforms the desiring self in relation to the beloved; and—at the same time—a settling back of this singular love into a "distanced" or formal structure. Breton goes on to further elaborate this strange double movement constitutive of his philosophical reading of Paulinism by adding: "The paradox, if there is one, is the coincidence of a mad love and *another folly*, also divine, which strips that love of its too-human resonances or consolations" (emphasis added). Echoing Paul's peculiarly paradoxical pronouncement that "I no longer live but Christ lives in me," Breton generalizes the Paulinist cross and its crossing or dispossessing of identities as that "sublime point where man [*sic*] ceases in some way to be man" and "where God in some way ceases to be the God common to religions."

Existing at the intersection of two forms of madness, at this crossing of a dual movement in the Paulinist cross God is no more a coherent identity than the human. This is an important point, as, unlike a long history of Christian theologizing, for Breton's Paulinist faith in the crucified divinity is not a realm of security against the dispossessing movements of mad love, an inflection of a metaphysical tradition with serious political implications. Representing neither the transient human nor the stable ground of metaphysical structure—but rather caught between two forms of madness—for the Paulinist there remains only a lived surging of a transformative insurgency into the *paradeigmata* of a cultural setup. Not (predictably, safely) representational, with the Paulinist there is rather a singular process of cultural transformation that is a riskier, if freer, kind of gamble. Pressing these aspects of Paulinist narrative back into the philosophical structures of the unavoidable void of the neutral, Breton brings together all the strands of our discussion by summarizing Paul's argument in 1 Corinthians 1 this way:

> To press the Greek text, which uses two substantive adjectives in the neuter, it would be helpful to translate the passage in the following way: "under-

neath the Apollonian face we give God [i.e., "wisdom"], there is a nocturnal passion putting him 'outside himself' by madness (*to moron tou theou*) and impelling him toward the 'infirmity' of an abasement (*to asthenēs tou theou*). Under these dramatic images there breaks through a free energy separating them from all our thoughts of divinity, whether common or learned. The faith whose infirmity participates in that of the Crucified puts the sign of the Cross over all our too-facile beliefs. Yet Paul declares without a little enthusiasm that that infirmity and that madness liberate a power that is stronger than that of men and a wisdom wiser than their wisdom. He could have added that 'she who has ears to hear' will wonder about her capacity for understanding."

The dispossessing madness of love within Paulinist divinity—that which, Breton tells us, names the cessation of a sort of God—finds an answer to its own echo in the Paulinist believer who measures the neutrally unhinged and therefore unmeasurable expression of God in the only way possible: intensive, self-forgetful enthusiasm. If there is a freedom of a decidedly Pauline thought of the cross, a freedom in the impossible naming of the execution of a messiah as a revelation of the strength of the divine, it is in the explosion of this space of a void, the dispossessed, unmeasured, or unjustified nature of which does not temper its forceful emergence. This moment of freedom is inextricable, therefore, from that writhing tangle of limbs and identities Breton will, throughout his work, name only the "nocturnal passion" or "nocturnal upsurge" of God, nights and movements from which no one in the Paulinist universe emerges unchanged.

And is not the most important issue in Breton's philosophical encounter with Paul the intersection of these two aspects of his work? On the one hand we have the formal-structural models of ideology and its exploitable gaps and also a neo-Platonic ontology whereby the One unfolds itself always and already by way of negation and self-othering. On the other hand, we have the texts of Paul, whereby Paul organizes a movement of those who will look upon the abject failure of an imperially executed messiah and find therein a sign of the movement's own triumph. The real forcefulness of Breton's reading of Paul *only* emerges when these two aspects of Breton's work are viewed as the same moment, and particularly when one reads 1 Corinthians 1 and 2 not as doctrinal or rhetorical representation of an event of dispossessing identification but as this act of "mad love" itself.[55]

Once such an interpretive move is made, however, the entire archive of Paul and the philosophers leeches out into another sphere entirely. The pressing question, in this sense, is never really one of the universal validity of notions of resurrection, first-century christological or pneumatological conviction, or the Jewish orthodoxy (or otherwise) of Paulinism. The real trial of Paulinism as explicated by Breton is the simple question with which it faces us: are similarly dispossessing, value-inverting moments— in short, a radical and effective critique of ideology—possible? Can the catastrophic wreck of liberatory hopes be subsumed by a fierce enthusiasm in which the very matrix of the play of identities is transformed, whether of the remaining or newly faithful, the named catastrophe, the divine, or that "world" in which all alike find their space of a no longer atomized encounter? Is there a reality, a hope for, irruptions of freedom as "nocturnal passion," sovereignly opaque because ungrounding the very ground of all judgments about them? In that respect (we could summarize self-consciously in a Bultmannian vein) the *krisis* that was Paul's own is no different from our own. Is there, for us (and that with or without this name of an apostle), the possibility that we can avail ourselves of the freedom of the unsurveilled? One is tempted to repeat the lines of Jacob Taubes, that great defender of a Paulinist *skandalon*: "The horns of the dilemma cannot be escaped. Either messianism is nonsense, and dangerous nonsense at that, but the historic study of messianism is a scientific pursuit . . . or messianism, and not only the historic research of the 'messianic idea,' is meaningful inasmuch as it discloses a significant facet of human experience."[56]

DISPOSSESSING PRIVATE PROPERTY

The subterranean surprise and promising forcefulness of Breton's philosophical Paulinism now begin to peer through the ideological fault lines constitutive of culture. Several summary ideas—critical punch lines in Breton's critique of power and ideology—should be stated outright at this point, all the more so as they situate a critical space for Paulinism that seems all but foreclosed by Christendom's current function to baptize capitalism and neoliberal empire. First, it is clear that the Paulinist stance constitutes a *critique of Christian identity*. Breton's term for this tends to be that there is an "originary poverty" about the founding of Paulinist identity, rooted as it is in the crossed out messiah or murdered divinity. This is particularly important to remember when it comes to Breton's grandiose *inflation* of the Pauline story of the cross as *another name* or similar "sign" of that drama to which *all* ideological forms or countable sets *must* be subject. In other words, it is a very peculiar universalizing of Paulinism that is being advocated here, as Breton's generalization or globalization of the cross universalizes a particular thought of the *dispossession and failure of identity*. Put bluntly, and directly to the contrary of that hegemonic ethos which continues to dominate both popular and academic discussions of "religion," Christian identity is *not* imagined by Breton to be private property (or, to put it differently, as *either* private *or* property). Remarkably, the resources afforded by Breton's Paulinism are free for all because they dispossess everyone. It is in this respect that Breton speaks frequently of the meontological cross as the name of a constitutive possibility of *exodus* from self-enclosed or self-grounding identity, and this structure of voidance is Breton's central challenge to any leveraging of identitarian habitations against the "outsider." In this case, Breton's communism, as it were, the universal ownership of this "sign" of dispossession, necessarily condemns the history of all those attempts to designate oneself as the border guard (and, invariably, the toll collector) of the identity in question. The triumphalism of the ecclesiasts or hermeneuts collapses into the void of the cross.

No doubt, such language of a universalizable *dispossession*, rather than an occidentally governed identity, was poignant in recent decades even as it remains so today amid a frightening paroxysm of *identitarian* bids to power in the name of this or that religious identity. Finding a profound similarity in the seventies critiques of philosophy as ideology and modern humanism's assertion that all must overcome theology, Breton declares that the "colonial empire" of earlier metaphysics and the worldly practices that undergirded them "had crumbled," leaving the "disciplines" this empire once made mandatory "emancipated."[57] This emancipation of formerly ordered hierarchies of discipline must, therefore (and in another striking repetition of his reading of early Christianity), attempt to think through this *kenosis* of the imagined self-enclosed system of authority. This kenotic emptying of a former mode of cultural power invites a rethinking of the Paulinist cross, and Breton's effort to create a postcolonial critique of ideologies was indistinguishable from his efforts to think of that strange "nothingness" or "null element" that was, for him, also Paul's crucified messiah (116f).

DISPOSSESSING BEAUTY: THE "CRITICAL INSTANCE"

Second, Breton notes with admiration here and elsewhere the absence of "humanism" in the Paulinism of Bultmann. The crucifixion of the messianic figure heralds the impossibility of closing off onto a purely immanent, identitarian sphere, the cosmos or humanity, as if to reduce such things to their recognizable theoretical or practical role (in Heideggerian terms, of the *Vorhanden* and *Zuhanden* of a culture). Without affording new definitions, and even without "declaring war" against the specific everyday routines undergirding such recognitions (as if to counter one routine with a specified other), Breton's Bultmann presents a cross that nevertheless, and universally, declares a "judgment" against the constituted or everyday world (95).

Finally, and in the third twist of the single screw that is the null part, Breton presents Bultmann in a favorable light inasmuch as the biblical scholar opposed the cross to "private property" as a variation of the humanist egocentrism and its world of consumable (or, readily available) identities and actions. This entire ensemble of subjects and objects Breton, following Bultmann, designates as a "possessive humanism" (cf. 94–98). In a world where will to power projects its measurements on the being of everything, Breton praises Bultmann's "heroic 'meontology'" and its "subtractive" intervention for making thinkable diverse bands of "all those who resemble the four winds of heaven" in their ephemeral refusals of the "idol" of that which is. The philosopher discovers a collective of all those possessing no power besides "this null element, without density or prestige, which the Christians symbolize by the sign of contradiction, the sign *par excellence*: that of the cross" (95).

Here again is Breton's intensification or universalization of the Pauline story of the cross, and its political qualities should not be missed (particularly when articulated by way of Bultmann). In Breton's inflation of the story, the story itself loses its own identity as the name or form of political critique that may just as reasonably be symbolized by set theory or neo-Platonic reflections on the accursed share of the "pale substratum." As Breton goes on to say, the null part is "secreted" with every delimitable ensemble, unnameable, unowned (or, rather, dispossessed and dispossessing), and therefore always liable to found those who without "density or prestige" sweep through a fixed ensemble or state with the powerless power of the "null part." *As such* it is a potential that does not exist in any way within any localizable, repeatable cultural sphere—indeed, one should not really say it *exists* in any way at all—so much as it is strangely "secreted" by any ensemble or cultural set. For this very reason, however, Breton states that it is "universal or omnipresent" (98). For Breton, therefore, the Pauline cross is a part of a much larger, indeed universal, archive of which he dreams, a massive study "of the concrete forms taken by this *operator of transcendence*" (my emphasis). This "systematic" archiving of world culture would search "in every system of thought or action" for "a critical instance," a moment which perhaps could never become a rule for further critique but that, nevertheless, signifies lacunae, lacks, or questions attending the operativity of the given system. This "neuter" space within all ideologies Breton calls an "element so strange that we reserve the name 'operator of transcendence'" for it (96). Adding nothing, neither a positive nor a negative determination, this operator appears, as a wink, as a gap, as a "critical instance," the extreme preciousness of which is not verifiable or calculable. Here again the Paulinist cross is universalized as "the signification of the neuter element or of the empty ensemble on the interior of ideologies" (48).

In his 1989 *Philosophie Buisonniere* (Truant philosophy), Breton offers a reflection on his visit to the Turner exhibition at the Grand Palais in Paris. The essay, "Portrait de rien" (Portrait of nothing) elaborates Breton's negative anthropology, offering the audience thoughts about the ontology of spectatorship by playing on questions of "event" and "visitation" in terms of the museum and art industry.[58] (What is it that inclines us to visit a museum? What do we expect to find there?) Breton likewise offers not unsurprising renderings of the work of art as the appearance of a "singular" value which establishes itself as a new standard for a new category. Thus, it would be ridiculous to try to quantify and measure the beauty of one work of art against another, as such an enterprise could only operate successfully were there to be a uniform table of comparable beauties. If, however, the work of art appears as that which has a kind of unknown beauty that nevertheless demands respect, then things are otherwise. Breton's standard reading here is spiced throughout with intriguing (and rhetorically shrewd, given the audience) jabs at the museum industry by comparing it to the institutionalization and "sainting" operations of the Catholic Church. For the moment, however, what is important to notice is the way Breton concludes the reflection on the nature of the work of art with a gesture to those aspects of Paulinism that obsessed Breton in every sphere of his work. "The 'portrait of nothing' reminds me (and how would I be able to forget it), of this otherwise than wisdom and power that inspires us, in the face of the cross, in the infirmity of madness and weakness, the new sign of the divine."[59] Like the work of art, the cross would therefore "subtract" itself from preexisting categories, thereby refusing (or simply not needing) the justification they could afford. As such, cross and work of art both solicit an exodus from "our measures and estimations" that constitute the current economies of life, inasmuch as they testify to a nonsurveilled, nonincorporated "excess" of being that testifies to an "otherwise" than the reigning wisdom and power.[60] Without guarantee or justification for its existence, therefore, this "wink" (*clin d'oeil*) on the surface of the world's appearance says nothing because it speaks "by nothing" or *ex nihilo*, as if repeating only that *rupture instauratrice* or chaotic excess "before the world was formed."[61] The whimsical gesture of the wink, moreover, is not accidental, inasmuch as the indication of an "otherwise" is not *only* the mortality of the age or the solicitation to go beyond the limits of the age's modes of action and recognition. With the wink, we catch a sense of the *rien par excess* (a nothing by way of excess [rather than lack]), not a negation of limit so much as an excess of alterity from which the present order emerges and toward which it may yet be propelled in further creation.

One should perhaps be clear here, as the "excess" in this case does not point back to the world "before the creation" in any temporal sense, as if there is a static fund of excessive white noise out there from which and into which all creation or all orders of words and things must flow. Rather, the excess of the wink is here immanent to the order itself. As Breton likes to say at points, *the order itself* "secretes" a "gap" in its own smooth functioning from which the order cannot be saved, a kind of irredeemable wound to self-identity as such.[62] A wink, we might say, is always insinuated *into* some particular conversation.

And here, with a wink, is the appropriate place to break off from our discussion of Breton's philosophical encounter with Paul, an encounter that gives rise to a particularly forceful negative anthropology. It is easy to see why I consider him an important interlocutor for my project to reconfigure Paul as part of the "underground current of materialism," and this perhaps as the only way to escape his co-optation (and all this represents) back into the tale of ontotheology, with Paul as (always both) the supersessionist "first Christian" and the instigator of the "higher swindle" of pop Platonism that Nietzsche rightly criticized. For me, Breton becomes rather an invitation to think for ourselves about the Pauline texts and those philosophical traditions with which they have been, are, or may yet become intertwined. With this concluding wink, Breton's work invites us to think about Paul and the philosophers in the light of a poverty of origin that cuts against the grain of two thousand years of Western valorization of Paul, that proverbial "man-mountain" who becomes a "classic" sufficient to ground, found, and set the agenda for a West that follows.[63] The significant political question invited by the wink, however is not: what does Paul found? What does he ground? Is the man-mountain a worthy founding figure? (and on such questions go). It is rather an invitation to wonder about what, in relation to these texts or under the repetition of this name—in (or out of) our own time—might *subtract* itself, *absent* itself from the economies within which words and things are what they are for us. And, having subtracted themselves from these cultural ensembles, what might be the forcefulness of an event in which such nothings might appear, so many "four winds" sweeping through the world, heralding very specifically scandalous modes of an impossibly unscripted, unsurveilled, and therefore risky newness? This dispossessed and dispossessing wind, this new life, is the unpredictable and unmeasurable measure around which Breton's reading of Paul invites a necessarily vertiginous form of meditation. At a moment when variously prescribed and ready-made identities claim to determine theory or always already to have oriented freedom like so many safely gated communities, Breton's philosophical encounter with Paul invites us to think otherwise and, in thinking otherwise, to find ourselves living "a more difficult freedom."

3

INSURRECTIONIST RISK
(PAUL AMONG THE PARRHESIASTS)

We must cease once for all to describe the effects of power in negative terms: it "excludes," it "represses," it "censors," it "abstracts," it "masks," it "conceals." In fact, power produces; it produces reality.
—Michel Foucault, Discipline and Punish

You also died to the law . . . that you might belong to another.
—Romans 7:4

But at the same time, in this doctrine that [Foucault] professes to his own cost, a sceptic may seek a depersonalization, a living death. Such a depersonalization—or personality-split—involves a high-voltage spiritual exercise that is as demanding as a religion. . . . "By splitting myself in order to speak the truth," Foucault wrote, "I abolish all interiority in this outside world that is so indifferent to my life and so *neutral* that it makes no distinction between my life and my death."
—Paul Veyne, *Foucault*

Consider yourselves dead . . . but alive.
—Romans 6:11

PHILOSOPHY HAS ALWAYS BEEN EXEMPLARY IN ITS CAPACITIES TO conjure a feeling of being stuck between a necessity and an impossibility of articulating responsibility for the common, for a communal life this collective would itself call good. In recent years the very delicate—and sometimes hesitating or ironic—resurgence of communism as a topic for political theory remains within the orbit of this aspect of the genius, that juicy little *daimōn*, constituting the ongoing vibrancy of philosophy. As is made clear by the awkward efforts to say the name of the common without repeating inherited and readily recognizable philosophico-political disasters, any associational logics by which we are—or might be—networked and incorporated in any other way than by the *mythoi* of today's capitalist astrologers seems extraordinarily unclear. Boris Groys, in fact, suggests looking to the (ancient and modern) paradox, the self-obstruction of political speech, as itself indicating something like a philosopheme to which we must remain committed: "paradox, by which Socrates describes his own situation, should not be eliminated or transcended, nor should it be deconstructed. Instead, this paradox provides the basis for the philosopher's political claim to power."[1]

Philosophy is returning again to rewired ancient spiritual exercises, little practices of remaining stuck, tarrying with the stuckness itself as the only site from which a properly *philosophical logos* of self-obstructing totality might be—must be—enunciated.[2] Read this way, philosophy is that enterprise which neither overcomes nor compromises with paradox by obscuring it or making it profitably manageable. Quirky spiritual exercises, we might say, are not therefore sophisms but rather the effort to overcome the otherwise ineluctable sophisms which dominate the management of our lives. In those singularly odd performances of stuckness, philosophers fold and hold and speak themselves along paradoxes for which there is no originally unparadoxical state or for which there cannot be a clean formalization. One lives, learns to live, practices at living a life that is not distinguishable from a relation to the very limits the philosopher will not explain away or render "merely" incidental the life in question. As such, one strategically inhabits the hollow of power, taking up residence in what was no doubt originally an "unfortunate exception" or inexplicably forced intervention of state power in relation to that authority of life or naturalized sovereignty which—because mere life or naturalized power—is normally praised as given, simple, the way things are. And in the exceptionalism of intervention and control wherein the state, any states, must manage themselves, one takes up a collective residence, folding suppression over into an odd form of collective shelter within otherwise unspeakable scandal. In a Paulinist mode, *we* are the messiah otherwise effectively repressed by Roman colonial functionaries in Jerusalem . . .

The gesture, through and through resourced and resourcing only the immanence of life always and ever remains materially soulish, a spiritual practice of exceptional, paradoxical, or biopolitical bodies. Here, along-side projects like those of Friedrich Nietzsche or Didier Franck, Paul seems useful as an inventor and organizer of community forms under Nietzsche's Spinozist axiom and provocative challenge: "we do not yet know what a body can do."[3] Or, perhaps, as Deleuze articulates Spinoza by a citation of Nietzsche: "'Perhaps the body is the only factor in all spiritual development.'"[4] Or, as Franco "Bifo" Berardi glosses the quest for a materialist spirituality, "I want to discuss the soul in a materialistic way. What the body can do, that is its soul, as Spinoza said."[5] Best of all for my interest in the fundamental status of a relational vibrancy, perhaps, is what the late Michel Foucault said of Plato's Alcibiades: "You have to worry about your soul—that is the principal activity of caring for yourself. The care of the self is the care of the activity and not the care of the soul-as-substance."[6] The soul as an immanent, ecological, or relational vibrancy of *care* which constitutes self and others: thus found ready-made, Pauline texts are an invitation to construe new thoughts of simultaneously creative or inventive bodies that are imagined *as* material. Of course, to think simultaneously both poles of inventive newness *and* materiality is not the usual operation whereby materialisms are usually reductive, repetitive, representational even as spiritualisms tend to think newness only in stably idealist or otherworldly modes.

One way to develop such a project would be to pick up on Foucault's later writings in which Hellenistic *askēsis*, an instance of "technologies of the self," and risk as a type of public speech on the political emerged as central preoccupations for the thinker. It is difficult to overestimate the significance of Foucault's genealogical explorations, with technology, experimentation, and risk being named as the essential modes of thinking a complex and therefore multiply open-ended or processual space of political life. Foucault here seems very close to the agenda of Heidegger: as tropes, both "subject" and "self" are completely emptied out *into* the world, with no selfhood save for those immanent tactics and technics of "care" which act and react as a singular form of life. But, precisely because Foucault's fascination with the ancient Mediterranean world was an effort to think selfhood as immanent life without metaphysical guarantees, it has always seemed to me that Foucault missed an important opportunity to name, appropriate, and organize differently large swaths of a sedimented intellectual praxis this effort implicitly engaged. In a word, Foucault failed to come to grips with a figure he was in fact thinking about, a figure who guaranteed—in these ready-made or sedimented intellectual structures—the distinction between "religion" and "philosophy," as well as the difference between Greco-Roman aesthetics of self-fashioning and a later Christian/medieval apparatus of the guilty subject. Like Derrida (see chapter 1), I want to argue here that Foucault missed a chance for a subversive genealogical encounter with Paul.

Like Derrida's, Foucault's was not a merely incidental failure, on my reading, as his genealogical intervention could have constituted a crucial act of sacred or profane violence that would have expanded the discursive range and forcefulness of his critique of modern power, even as it would have afforded a new archive for a comparative, processual, experimental rethinking of subjectivation and political agency. There is nothing that constrains us to let matters remain where they were left off, however, and I want to begin to extend the focus of the earlier chapters into a meditation on the way Foucault could have included Paul in that late project to stay with the question of the singularity and immanence of life without a preconstituted subject.[7]

Once again, this labor is a matter of no longer reading like Nietzsche in the sense that we no longer imagine Paul to be the exemplary purveyor of metaphysical guarantees. Nietzsche, after all, reads Paul as much the "one who knows" as Christian ontotheology did, even if Nietzsche wants to fulminate against what Nietzsche thinks Paul knows. As I keep saying, there is no escape from the odd dialectical game being played in *our* situating of Paul within the organization of Western thought. Released from Nietzsche's particular constellation of mirrors, however, perhaps there is little need to police the borders between "religion" and "philosophy" as (I will argue) Foucault also does in relation to Paul. Paul will be every bit the parrhesiast of experimental finitude, every bit as emptied out into *forms* of care of the self, every bit as subtracted from that great epoch of Christian metaphysics as we will allow ourselves to be. In this mode a hermeneutical transformation that affects us as much as the apostle, Paul becomes much closer to the Greco-Roman philosophers, those peddlers of oddly paradoxical "spiritual exercises," than Foucault seemed to realize.

In this light it is crucial to point out an understandable—but nonetheless profound—historiographical traditionalism within Foucault's work at an important point, his failure to elucidate Paul in relation to the Hellenistic philosophers at the conclusion to the third volume of *The History of Sexuality*.[8] As I will argue, Foucault's unreflective traditionalism here consists in his assumption that the "religion" of Paulinism constitutes a difference that forecloses real comparative analysis, Paulinism being consigned to becoming—again, in a profoundly traditional form of organizing this material—the founder of a form of Christian moral system whose inventive machinations will engender a "self" constituted by its being turned against itself, at once constitutively guilty, fallen, and also profoundly normalized by the universalization of its underlying metaphysical narrative. Foucault's own *récit* at this point is simply, wholly, even unreflectively, Nietzschean, a fact leading to some peculiar consequences.[9] Foucault seems almost to stumble, as if by accident, on the archival question of Paul and Greco-Roman technologies of self-making at the end of the published studies of sexuality. The short space afforded to Paul, given his constant interest in debunking received narratives of the relationship between Greek, Hellenistic, and Christian models of sexual selfhood, is itself rather peculiar. The stakes of the encounter are remarkable, after all. Among these, the encounter constituted, as it were, Foucault's chance to break with a dominant Nietzschean story of Western culture, but Foucault fails to grasp the opportunity.

SUBJECTS OF SEXUALITY IN THE THEATER OF ATTENTION

This failure to step outside the Nietzschean story even as he criticizes standard stereotypes about distinctions between a tolerant Greece and a repressive Christianity bears along with it several paradoxical implications we should not miss. Consider the way Foucault repeats, at the end of the third volume of *The History of Sexuality*, a late nineteenth-century debate about the disciplinary arrangements whereby Paul should or should not be read next to Hellenistic philosophers. Paradoxically, Foucault's basic repetition of a Nietzschean story will cause him to inhabit essentially the same discursive position on this disciplinary and cultural question as the nineteenth-century antimodernist German churchman and biblical scholar Theodor Zahn. Zahn, I will show, assumes essentially the same stance as Foucault, though the conservative churchman *values* or invests each specific gesture in their shared stance in ways diametrically opposed to Foucault. The point to make, however, is that Foucault's failure to rethink a basic Nietzschean story renders him an enemy of Zahn, but only at the price of becoming ineffective in rethinking the very coordinates grounding their differing value judgments.

Here we hear echoes, once more, of the young Albert Schweitzer's odd diagnosis: the *problem* with Nietzsche's reading of Paul is, ultimately, that Nietzsche *refused to become Paul.* The ironies here are stark. For example, after elaborating ways in which he himself prefers *not* to see shared discursive modes at work between Paul and a Stoic like Epictetus, Zahn goes on to assert that a fidelity to the clear distinction between the two objects of academic labor enables one precisely to protect and valorize (an imagined) Pauline vision of human sinfulness and the divine pity of a transcendent God over against what Zahn also imagines as the more immanent thoughts of force, self, or agency in Epictetus's Stoicism. Remarkably—and here one longs for Foucault to question the fundamental orientations and implications of Zahn's genealogy—Zahn concludes by suggesting that only Paulinism, imagined as the proclamation of a universal slavery redeemed by divine pity, gives rise to the benevolent paternalism of modern European government. As always, divisions of academic labor repeat and inflect social hierarchies and arrangements of power. In this case, Zahn praises the benevolent transcendence of European power even while he imagines that critiques of tyranny in Epictetus (not to mention those modern philosophers with which Epictetus is in this text clearly interchangeable) would necessarily be hamstrung, precisely, by Stoic materialist immanence. You can see the point. If there were ever a moment to intervene in the ready-made machinations of a "Christian origins" story whereby the "Christian" element is safely subtracted from immanent analysis or thoroughly relational explication, this is it. Foucault will instead basically repeat Zahn's fundamental story, even if he does not (at the end of the third volume of *The History of Sexuality*) explore its implications or cultural afterlife within contemporary analyses of governmentality or modern "pastoral" power.

At one level, however, that Foucault—working through genealogies of the biopolitical and the necessity to radically reformulate agency and ethics—would allow Zahn to press him toward an equally standardized Nietzschean counterreading is understandable. After all, Zahn's story of redemption through the benevolent, transcendent (and would-be universal) paternalism of modern European government and religion, with a culturally unique Paul as the guarantor of this theologico-political setup, fits Nietzsche's symptomatological critique of the modern network of religion and authority to the letter. Indeed, reading Zahn one gets the feeling that he had been working on his costume and perfecting his dance steps for the Nietzschean masquerade ball his whole life long. Here, too, however, the Nietzschean story does not take us far enough, inasmuch as it only refuses, rather than resituates, Paul as the imaginary guarantor of the religio-political epoch that is a "Platonism for the masses," culminating in Zahn's Paul, decidedly *not* a Stoic philosopher, and this in order to be preserved or sublimated as the founding father of a benevolent European governmentality. Concrete shoes indeed, only this time it is Hellenistic philosophy rather than early Judaism from which Paul is sublimated or excepted. Here, however, Foucault's brilliant Nietzscheanism does him no favors, as Foucault's participation in a repetition of the tableau causes Foucault essentially to remain in the same fundamental orbit as Zahn, even if Foucault values every set figure in the tableau oppositely from the biblical theologian. Analytically, however, Zahn and Foucault are here perfect bedfellows, which is to say that Foucault's genealogy only works because it sinks back, with Zahn, into a peculiar, almost churchy, sleepiness about how we might configure a comparative mode of reading these figures that would have been relevant to Foucault's story. Foucault falls into the same trap we witnessed in the last chapter around Derrida's simple repetition of Nietzsche's anti-Paul story. Such things need to be made clear, as a more radical transformation of the archival network constituting the name Paul is integral to my own move beyond a Nietzschean critique for what seems to me a much more subversive rethinking of Paul and the immanent, material politics of contingency. It is a matter of being subversively faithful to the *eventalization* of the hackneyed stereotypes and tattered hierarchies whereby entities like Paul, philosophy, and beneficent modern governments look for genealogical reinforcement of their identities.

Recall that, at one level, Foucault's fundamental project in *The History of Sexuality* is constituted by a well-known move to place "sexuality" under an *epoché*, effectively to ignore it as a given or constant substratum existing as various modes of a coherent identity over time. To play on the work of Jonathan Crary and Peter Sloterdijk, this technique or spiritual practice of the "suspension of perception" begins to conjure alternative modes of attention or care by which we are (increasingly) constituted as subjects in the first place.[10] Foucault was searching particularly for modes of attention attuned to the historicity, singularity, or specificity of contexts within which, precisely, a care for "sexuality" or the recognition of ourselves as always already *being* subjects of sexuality both emerge and enforce themselves in that concern and recognition. Read this way, which is to say in light of his work on the disciplinary society, Foucault's *epoché* opens a history of sexuality by opening the question of a history of sexual *attention*, a history of the techniques and attentive apparatuses of the sexual observer. Foucault wants his fabulation of this archive to disclose various practices and modes of knowing as themselves participating in an umbilical or materially phenomenological linkage between contexts and experiences. As he states it in a later development of the project, he operates by way of a concern to grapple with all those "formation of disciplines [*saviors*]" which have installed within us an "'experience' that caused individuals to recognize themselves as subjects of a 'sexuality.'"[11] The sexual subject does not preexist or exist outside its emergence, appearance, or dramatic performance in and as *forms* of sexual attention, tactics, and techniques that orient attentive concern in the world.

One sees immediately how the project is closely related to our earlier unpacking of Breton's Althusser-inflected Paulinism as a mode of factical attention, itself always already a result of interpellation. Shaping context and experiential narrative are given in the same moment, with Foucault naming sexuality as that crystallization of a multiplicity of modes of knowing (*savoirs*), a crystallizing, grounding, or sedimentation of these fields that emerges by way of an "experience" or a "recognition of oneself" as a bearer of "sexuality." The becoming-a-subject-of-sexuality, in other words, is that performance wherein the techniques and tactics of knowing sexuality emerge alongside an otherwise ungrounded "yes, here am I" repeated on a large—almost geological—scale, a willingness to imagine "sexuality" as itself the operant skeleton key which can unpack an otherwise disparate multiplicity of material and ideational occurrences. Similarly, in a way of speaking that evokes Foucault's ally Gilles Deleuze and Foucault's readings of Heidegger, Foucault's project proceeds by naming "problematizations" of sexuality, by which he designates agonistic sites "through which being offers itself to be, necessarily, thought."[12] To speak of the *problēmata*, for Deleuze or for Foucault, is to draw out the life of *singular* questions, uniquely active and empassioned modes of expression within (and therefore of) complex adaptive systems. Indeed, Deleuze's refashioning of the old topos of philosophical *problēmata* for philosophies of difference occurred through an encounter with, precisely, notions of singularity, swerve, and *clinamen*. In terms comparable to those of Jacques Derrida, Deleuze sometimes explored the *question* about haecceity or singularity of a phenomenon usefully consolidated in the image of "the signature." That these sites would themselves again crystallize or intensify a disparate crisscrossing of "practices" implies that the emergence of *problēmata* are not simply explicable in terms of their being broken down into discrete elements. As Deleuze wrote already in *A Thousand Plateaus*,

Figures are considered only from the viewpoint of the *affections* that befall them: sections, ablations, adjunctions, projections. One does not go by specific differences from a genus to its species, or by deduction from a stable essence to the properties deriving from it, but rather from a problem to the accidents that condition and resolve it. This involves all kinds of deformations, transmutations, passages to the limit, operations in which each figure designates an "event" much more than an essence. . . . Whereas the theorem belongs to the rational order, the problem is affective and is inseparable from the metamorphoses, generations, and creations within science itself.[13]

In distinguishing a nonfoundational philosophy of difference from traditional metaphysics, Deleuze even asserts that the former treat "problems" as singularities in which answers and problems fold over into each other. The latter, traditional type of metaphysics imagines rather that problems are temporary obstructions in the revelation of a deeper truth, a fantasy of salvation Deleuze glosses as a form of philosophical "repentance."[14] This distinction between two economies of salvation, so to speak, is no doubt relevant to our larger story, particularly for Foucault's efforts to map the question of "modern" singularity *versus* traditional metaphysics onto an ancient (and generally "religious") distinction between Judaism, Christianity, and Hellenistic moral formations. For the moment, however, new forms of self-surveillance and stratagems of management provide useful hints about concurrent material practices of subjectivity given in the emergence of the "problem." As Foucault writes, "I would like to show how, in classical antiquity, sexual activity and sexual pleasures were problematized through practices of the self, bringing into play the criteria of an 'aesthetics of existence.'"[15]

Recalling these elements of the basic project in which Paul will appear (as both a pressing topic and strangely inconsequential addendum) highlights some reasons for my discomfort at what I have described as Foucault's failed encounter with Paulinism as an organizing node within the archive of Western material techniques of care constituting the self. In referring to the earlier debate within biblical studies and philosophy about the comparative location of Paul and the Greco-Roman moralists, for example, Foucault is thinking about just that nineteenth-century moment when, he recounts, "sexuality" became a hegemonic name of a subject emerging alongside—and as a historically singular crystallization of—specific disciplines, tactics, and apparatuses of knowing. That the emergence of this subject appeared forcefully enough to radiate its energies back through time, reformatting the past into a sexual archive, moreover, hardly even needs to be stated. One thinks of the way the medicalization of sexuality during this period so relied on writings of Sacher-Masoch, who, in turn, staged his ("masochistic") fantasies as a genealogy of ancient and modern, Hellenic and "Northern" European bodies, so many genealogies of sexual dominations or agencies (e.g., recall the initial conversations in *Venus in Furs*). One could point to a similar overlap between genealogies of religion and emerging categories of sexual normalization in relation to the work of a young Albert Schweitzer. Recall that Schweitzer's turn-of-the-century historical categorization of the ancient Jesus was as a mistaken apocalypticist from the ferment of "late Judaism"—a categorization which wrecked a century of questing for what Schweitzer described as a "modern" and "liberal" Jesus.[16] It is less remarked that one effect of Schweitzer's categorization was that his picture of Jesus was quickly taken up by Charles Binet-Sanglé, the "psychopathological" interpreter of quasi-criminal weaknesses in historical figures, as an indication of Jesus' "biological" and "sexual" disorders.[17] In every respect the invention of modern academic biblical scholarship occurred in a rather intimate relation to the emergence of a modern subject-of-sexuality, a quality of the Paulinist *problēmata* which Foucault, even at the end of the third volume of *The History of Sexuality*, somehow does not face directly.

Within and no doubt participating in this nineteenth-century reorientation of, as it were, the subjects and objects of knowledge, Foucault highlights an evident and open-ended crisis in the academic and cultural organization and control of modern modes of knowing in relation to erotically regulated bodies of the Hellenistic period. At the conclusion of the third volume of *The History of Sexuality*, Foucault *registers* the earlier hesitation or implicit openness within academic orientations that were themselves, Foucault reminds us, indissociable from the constitution of the modern sexual subject he wants to unearth, illumine, and contest. But somehow Foucault does not try to rearrange or scramble the links forged by that earlier moment of university agonism.

To expand the stakes of what I have called Foucault's failed encounter here, consider also that the genealogist's investigation of the Hellenistic period was itself part of a genealogical turn invested with hope of a possibility for rethinking the "subject of desire" that had become so prevalent within modern theories of culture.[18] Foucault was already glossing his investigative turn to the Greek and Hellenistic periods as a wonder about the formation and limits of the "Christian experience of the 'flesh,'" its specific techniques and technologies of focusing attention on desire.[19] These techniques and technologies, he suggests consistently, cleared the space for an interpellative "yes, here I am" of recognition, an affirmation that constitutes a kind of material substratum of the "subject of sexuality" *in modern culture, cultural theory, and psychoanalysis.*[20] Or, to turn up the volume of the Heideggerian echoes a bit further, in thinking about the Hellenistic period we are considering the regions or "areas of experience and the forms in which sexual behaviour was problematized, becoming an object of concern," and this as a way of rewiring, precisely, the emergence of the modern subject of desire.[21] And yet there he will stand at the end of the third volume of *The History of Sexuality*: Paul, a very ambiguous narrative bridge between (to borrow from his writings on pastoral power and spiritual direction) "Judaism" and the related "systems" of "Christian" morality and therefore as a potential monkey wrench in the narrative distinction between "traditional" and "modern" ethics of the self![22] More will be said, but for now we must simply repeat Foucault's own summarization of the nineteenth-century debates about Paul and the Hellenistic philosophers by declaring emphatically that "we can hardly let the matter rest here" where Foucault himself also left off.

BEATIFICATION AND THE CRISIS OF LEGITIMATION

We can hardly let the matter rest there inasmuch as the recuperation of significant space of analysis between Paul and the Hellenistic philosophers remains to become an essential element in a Foucauldian excavation of, as he called it, that "veritable golden age in the cultivation of the self" to be found in first- and second-century moralists.[23] More to the point, new types of interruption and reorientation of the *modern* subject of sexuality are possible if we attend to a reworking of what remained a general refusal of thinkers like Zahn to deeply explore the comparison of Paul and the Hellenistic philosophers, *particularly* at the level of practice and the competitive peddling of "spiritual exercises" for the overcoming of "passions."[24] To repeat uncontested the received archival distinctions or disciplinary divisions of labor between "religion" and "philosophy" is effectively to repeat the very ecclesiastical modes of historiography that have operated as the curators of Paulinism since Zahn's position effectively became the dominant path of English-speaking biblical research. To fail to contest this, particularly at that delicate moment within nineteenth-century constructions of the sexual subject, has a remarkably unhelpful effect to blunt the genealogical, comparative, or contestatory forcefulness of our excavations. To repeat the inherited coordinates—however we value them—is effectively to repeat (even if from "the other side") that self-protective hiving off of "religion" which operates through the beatification of Paulinism by someone like Zahn. There is, we must always repeat, a more thoughtful—which is always to say more rebellious and aggressive—mode of contesting this Platonism for the masses than simply declaring oneself not to be a fan of it. Here Foucault, too, must become caught up in our project more radically to contest the Paulinist Platonism for the masses than Nietzsche was able to configure.

To name one final stake, perhaps the most important, note how Foucault continues in the same section of the third volume of *The History of Sexuality* by suggesting that this "golden age" of the care of the self must be searched for treasures in light of a (welcome) modern crisis of legitimation, precisely, within Western, and largely Christian, moral systems.[25] Crucially, what appears in Foucault's text on sexuality as a distinction between religious morality and the flourishing techniques of the "care of the self" during the Hellenistic period will double, elsewhere in Foucault's work, as a distinction between a ubiquitous and *representational* ethics and ontology of the West and an ethics and ontology oriented around the thought of *singularity and difference*. Foucault's entire section resonates with his late concern with games or modes of truth telling, and one sees immediately why the incidental, even peripheral, figure of Paul must not be left unremarked in Foucault's text. Foucault's apostle here exists textually at the archival hub of a massive sketch of Western power, the manner and style of which his earlier micrological analyses of power and sexuality might not have prepared us for. As Gilles Deleuze remarked on the latter two volumes of *The History of Sexuality*, produced after a kind of hiatus following from the first: "[Foucault] seemed to still be working on the history of sexuality; but he was taking a completely different line, he was discovering long-term historical formations (down from the Greeks), whereas up to that point he'd restricted himself to short-term formations (in the eighteenth and nineteenth centuries); he was reorienting all his research in terms of what he called modes of subjectification."[26]

To return to my concern about the *eventalization* of an archive about religion, philosophy, and modern governmentality, the name of Paul at the end of the third volume of *The History of Sexuality* virtually joins the quest to think the self as technics and attention freed from representational categories. Paul is a name of the question about the limits or delegitimation of a mode of Western ethics and ontology and therefore a potentially evental turning point for a transformative experience of this same tradition. Put differently, Foucault's reflections at the end of the published volumes of sexuality reflect on Paul, situating these reflections in relation to what he describes as a collapse of Western ontotheological structures and the moralities they yield. This collapse, in turn, was of course (as Foucault's earlier work patiently described) indissociable from an immanent and technical shift in everyday life from practices in keeping with imagined stable and transcendental forms of "repressive power" to an epoch of power-as-incitement, power emptying itself into forms of immanence, a key feature of an emerging biopolitical, or perhaps consumerist, regime. And, in precisely such a context, several specific academic disciplines within this larger assemblage of discursive practices were asking themselves: why have we not been exploring what are striking similarities between the speech of Paul, ostensible founding father of Christianity and its moralities, and Epictetus, purveyor of spiritual exercises oriented by a Stoic materialist immanence? The issues are stark, and we simply must reflect on how the potential disciplinary scramble housed in this question from the late nineteenth century is not just *related* to Foucault's larger discursive concerns about the end of representational thought. We need to reflect more pointedly on whether it *is itself* precisely the indication of the larger shift Foucault's later work consistently flags up. If so, just as in the last chapters, here the need for problematization and eventalization presses itself in on us all the more forcefully.

Throwing in our lot with eventalization of this earlier problem of the biblical scholars, we find that the organization of the literary canons and academic disciplines would not mirror a shift in the form of sovereign power Foucault wanted to understand so much as *to be* that shift, played out as a (potential) transformation of academic *praxis*, noting that variations of the questions I have gathered here under the name Paul emerge at other moments in Foucault's work as well. As Mika Ojakangas has shown persuasively, for example, the Foucauldian genealogical distinction between juridico-institutional sovereignty and the productive solicitations of biopolitical immanence was sometimes mapped by Foucault onto a distinction between Hebraic and Christian forms of pastoral power.[27] In the former, Foucault argued, pastoral surveillance and governance of the individual was itself subservient to political forms of *law*. Christian modes of pastoral power were, by contrast, a result of a denigration of law, which translated into an interest in or attention to more immanent forms of life as generative mechanisms that must be surveilled and managed. The shift from Hebraic to Christian forms of pastoral power, in other words, is discursively organized by way of Pauline tropes of "law" versus "spirit," these tropes in turn being understood by way of a larger history of religion—indeed, a history (here again very traditionally) of *two* religions. More still, this archival tale obviously affords for Foucault an echo of a shift in modern power relations whereby exterior, repressive modes of power are increasingly supplanted by immanent, productivist solicitations of subjectivation. As Deleuze points out in the citation earlier, such conjurations of echoes—even epochs—in the late Foucault may be surprising, given earlier discussions of Nietzschean genealogy, difference, and memorial culture, but we should not fail to notice the way they play crucial roles within Foucault's late interventions in cultural history. Paulinism names at once a historical shift from one to another religious form, even as it indicates a shift in modern power from a repressive to a biopolitical model. And why not? Our problem is not how to remain faithful to multiplicity but how to conjure, by way of the archive, a transformative *turning*, at once a turning of our experience and of the coordinates whereby we imagine these to be related.

It is in precisely this respect that I find the situating of Paul among some of the peddlers of Stoic immanence and the self as technique of attention or processual form of care a much more explosive gesture than Foucault recognized explicitly. Foucault's genealogy, after all, follows a Nietzschean trajectory in the sense that it looks *outside* the discursive regime of Christianity, and perhaps Christian ontotheology, for indications of an alternative to its forms of representational or juridical selfhood (and the moralities which follow). How much more interesting to note the way Paul may constitute a powerfully repressed and co-opted "alternative," a figure like Freud's Moses, whose effective cultural force emerges from his disavowal, from the massive investment of energies in suppressing, controlling, memorializing him as he came to be? The problem of nonrepresentational singularities or the clefts in representation indicated by the cleft or gap of finitude itself were not *simply* historical paradigms of subjectivity emerging with the modern period. Nor were they simply Greek alternatives to Christian cultures of the self. Rather, they were there, always already managed, controlled, refused by a metaphysical or representational apparatus which existed in and through the energies released by this very refusal.

Genealogically speaking, there is an august cast of characters standing with Paul at the end of Foucault's third volume of *The History of Sexuality*. But the discursive scramble or eventalizing risk that Foucault *could* have insinuated into these massive discursive strata by way of the apostle remains in his text only a slight evocation, a rather quiescent and unactualized dream. It is no great difficulty to frame, unearth, or conjure a mutually explicating juxtaposition of Paulinism and Foucauldian genealogy that is significant for thought, however, provided we attend to the controversy about comparisons differently than did the nineteenth-century biblical scholars *and* differently from Foucault. As the strangely tragic event-thinker Paul put it: such an enactment is not far from us, hidden away in heaven or buried away in the earth (Romans 10). It is rather sitting right in front of us within the cleft of traditional disciplinary distinctions and the distinction between the classical, the modern, and an emerging society of diffuse mechanisms of control or of a biopolitical society. On this occasion, such traffic crisscrosses deeply hidden in a cleft before which Foucault tended to act in a rather sleepy and inoffensive fashion. For a more subversive genealogy, for a new Paulinism and a new materialist immanence, let's not "let the matter rest there."

REWIRING THE INCONSEQUENTIAL CONCLUSION OF FOUCAULT'S *HISTORY OF SEXUALITY*

Let us press the point by looking more carefully at the concluding reflection. At the end of Foucault's third volume in the unfinished *History of Sexuality*, the genealogist as cultural critic finds himself reflecting on a vexing "problematic" or driving question: how shall we understand early Christianity in relation to the philosophers and moralists of the Greco-Roman period?[28] Foucault highlights the importance of the question in light of his own narration of the way, compared with older Greek philosophical discussions of pleasure and sexuality, the "first two centuries of our era" were marked by a strengthening of the demand for austerity.[29] Physicians recommended abstinence, preferring "virginity over the use of pleasure," and philosophers of the period "condemn any sexual relation" outside monogamous marriage. In relation to this shift in moral exigency within discourses about sexuality, Foucault poses a critical, which is to say politically charged, question. Should one see in this phenomenological shift in bodily comportment a proleptic "sketch of a moral future"? More specifically: "Must one suppose that certain thinkers in the Greco-Roman world already had a presentiment of this model of sexual austerity which, in Christian societies, will be given a legal framework and an institutionalized support?"[30]

As Foucault understood very well, his genealogical distinction between forms of sexual existence was significant because of a long history of self-definition that constituted a massive cultural investment in the *differences* between the various figures on his genealogical stage at just this point (classical Greek thought, Hellenistic culture, early Christianity, and the age of developed Christian governmental systems). The modern theoretical "subject of desire" in fact is a discursive phenomenon that exists *precisely* by way of a complex refusal of similarity at work between, say, psychoanalysis as an imagined step outside "religion" and, precisely, certain Christian forms of subjectivation whose pastoral practices of observation and capture of a desiring subject paved the way for the modern enterprise. Assuring his readers only that the "question is important," what is particularly noteworthy for our purposes is how Foucault grounds this significance by reference to "a long tradition" of thought leading up to (and obviously including) his own concluding thoughts about the history of sexuality: *the question about how one is to articulate Paul in relation to his philosophical contemporaries.*

Foucault refers here to late nineteenth-century German scholarly debates within historical and theological biblical scholarship about the relationship between Paul and the philosopher Epictetus, a debate well known at the time but later generally forgotten. Far from an unimportant moment of forgetfulness, this lost debate forces itself into what is in some respects Foucault's very traditional history of the West (with its classical Greeks fading into Hellenistic culture as backdrop for the origin and rise of Christian culture). In the immediate context of this assertion of the seriousness of the genealogical issues at stake, some of Foucault's interest were fairly obvious. On the one hand, he was concerned to assert that there certainly *were* distinct lines of demarcation separating, first, Greco-Roman moralism from classical philosophical reflections about sexuality and, second, Greco-Roman moralism from more developed institutional Christianity. In the first case, Foucault summarizes, the transformation in talk about self-governance was marked by a heightened anxiety about the body in the Greco-Roman period, something that led to an intensification of attention to the body itself as the privileged site by which to comprehend sexuality.[31] There was also in the Greco-Roman period the emergence of a tendency to universalize the "form" of sexual embrace, thereby playing down the more local and contingent role of "status" in classical theorization of erotic liaison. This universalization or formalization of the pleasurable encounter emerged hand in hand with intensified *practices of reflective internalization* within the emerging subject of sexuality. As Foucault says with his usual material, phenomenological verve: "Problematization and apprehension go hand in hand; inquiry is joined to vigilance."[32] When sexual encounter becomes a generic form of relationship, individuals, he suggests brilliantly, increasingly become their own overseers, with the vigilant and conscious self appearing in order to maintain or guarantee adherence to the universal rule. These distinctions organize Foucault's summary of the difference between classical and Greco-Roman ethics of the body.

Secondly, however, Foucault is here particularly interested to point out as well that what he glosses as "Christianity" represented yet another qualitative shift along a longer trajectory of internalization and universalization. In this additional discursive transformation, the excessive nature of sexual desire and the potential dangers such excesses bring with them become, yet again, increasingly universalized and therefore detached from the contingent local specifics of encounter. With this transformation, "sexual activity is linked to evil" not only by its possible "form and effects, but in itself and substantially."[33] The analysis of the discursive logics is intriguing. Even more than with their Greco-Roman moralist contemporaries, therefore, in Christianity the mode of sexual individuation begins to appear *only by way of transgression of the universalized norm*, a phenomenological stance that demands new ideas of fall or (transgressive, guilty) finitude. Constituting a qualitatively different category from the Greco-Roman moralists, Christianity thus affords a "mode of subjection in the form of obedience to a general law," a law, we should add immediately, that—Foucault will suggest—likewise organizes the modern notion of a subject of sexual desire occluded by a repressive law, whether of divine law, the law of the father, or the law of the symbolic order.[34] To stay with Foucault's text about the ancient setting, excluded from the sphere of the universal or generic norm, individuals are subjects only inasmuch as they engage in "a type of work on oneself that implies a decipherment of the soul and a purificatory hermeneutics of the desires," which is to say practices of internalization and a thinking of individuality as that which can only transgress the generic nature of the universal.[35] Christianity produces those who look inward in order to become ever more completely split into masters (and therefore slaves) of themselves, providing us with the conclusion that this movement represents a qualitatively different "mode of ethical fulfillment that tends toward self-renunciation" when compared to Greco-Roman moralism.

One should hear echoes at this point not only of the Nietzsche story but also of Theodor Zahn's rather perfect enactment of its diagnoses. Affording individuation via abjection, this splitting of the self into a Christian subject wanting to incarnate the universal norm, but only able to do so through mechanisms of self-negation is a mode of subjectivation Foucault wants to keep separate from that Greco-Roman intensification of the austerity of classical Greek ethics. Its "arts of living" and its "care of the self" are, he suggests, of a qualitatively distinct order from the Greco-Roman moralists. In a way that leaves me haunted with visions of Zahn's own intervention into the question of comparison between Paul and the Greco-Roman moralists, Foucault even warns his readers that "*one should not be misled by the analogy*" one might otherwise see between Christianity and Greco-Roman moralism as two economies of pleasure, as if both were simply two more austere developments of the classical Greek model.[36] In this respect, Foucault's story—with its discrete periodization of classical, Hellenistic, and early Christian—is remarkably traditional, the only twist being that what usually functions as a Christian apologetic device and result of Christianity's beatification or exceptionalism of its own story (i.e., as unique, exceptional in relation to the discursive culture of its time) is here inverted by Foucault (with early Christianity representing a debilitating but nevertheless qualitative step beyond the already-austere Greco-Roman moralists). But, simple reversals of value aside, the fundamental narrative categories between Foucault and Zahn are remarkably stable, and Foucault's efforts to maintain them here by making taboo the allure of "misleading analogy" constitutes Foucault as the latest exemplar (and one of the most interesting) in what Jonathan Z. Smith once rightly described as a long history of the *politicized* refusal to fully process the "analogical enterprise" that is our understanding of the relationship between early Christianity and the Greco-Roman philosophies and religions of its time.[37]

One can see what Foucault is up to here. In the conclusion he corrects the biblical scholars Bonhöffer and Zahn by refusing their assumption that ethics in the Roman imperial period represented a stark break, in terms of austerity motifs, with the philosophical ethics of their Greek predecessors. Foucault, in other words, opposes a traditional tale in which Roman philosophy and, soon enough, early Christian theology, could be categorized as polarized and utterly distinct in relation to classical Greek culture. On the other hand, Foucault corrects, one genuine difference between the epochs is that the latter was marked by an increased medicalization of sexual acts, a more vibrant interest in the relation between bodily health and sexual activity. Interestingly, Foucault articulates this increased vibrancy in good phenomenological fashion, pointing out that this shift does not simply represent *more information* on the subject but is itself indicative of a *shift in mode of perception* toward a more suspicious "way of thinking about sexual activity, and of fearing it because of its many connections with disease and with evil."[38] No medical data about the relationship between sexual activity and bodily health without a preconceptual suspicion that there are mediating links to be discerned, signs to be interpreted, apparently discrete phenomena to be collected into a new system of understanding.

Foucault also asserts against Bonhöffer and Zahn that they do not analyze that shift whereby marriage emerged as a "universal form" with "mutual obligations that derive from it" (238), implicitly naturalizing the result of this more specific, even technical, process. Philosophy of the imperial period would also praise abstinence in a way that indicated both continuity and change. Abstinence, Foucault summarizes, becomes increasingly unhinged from Greek discussions of the ascetic practice as a mode of attaining to the "highest spiritual values" in the "forms of love." Rather, in the latter epoch, abstinence becomes increasingly linked to the idea of an inherent "imperfection" in sexual embrace. One sees a shift away from a projective ethics as a mode of reflection on the ec-static impulses of love and toward, as it were, a backward-looking morality in which the self is, as it were, being called *back* to itself (in repentence) or *back* to a preestablished or given normativity (in guilt).[39]

Foucault seems also at this point in his study of sexuality intent on pursuing a common background interest in some of his later work, the critique of a particular, and perhaps structuralist and psychoanalytic, model of negation or prohibition. He notes that those who are more rigorous in their refusals of sexual embrace, for example, are not measurable in terms of a stable distance of prohibition, whether the no of the father or the law of symbolic economy. Turning such generalized and representational models around, he considers how more austere forms of *askēsis* may be read as different and perhaps intensified forms of a positive *aisthēsis* of self-projection (238). In this respect, the difference between the classical Greek discourse and the Greco-Roman moralists is not constituted by an abandonment of the "uses of pleasure" for a prohibition in their stead. Rather, the latter moralizing mode is itself a different "ethics of pleasure." Expanding his phenomenologically inflected point, he notes that the more you attend to pleasure by way of a mode of self-mastery, the more dangerous it must necessarily tend to seem. In turn, the more dangerous pleasure becomes to the positive *aisthēsis* of self-mastery, the more this danger must be confined to marital contexts. As a final twist on this analytic scene, Foucault adds that one might discern that this greater confinement to marital relations is itself an indication of a highly *invested* incarceration of energies, an indication of their capacities to flow elsewhere. The point is similar to the one he makes in his 1973–74 lectures on psychiatric power, where claims that there is diagnosable a "great asylum tautology in that the asylum is that which must give a supplementary intensity to reality" in order to successfully secure its (projected) reality *as* real.[40] Or, in this case, it is the *investment* or surplus of intensity aimed at confining pleasure within marriage which supplements the very nature of this "natural" relation the latter moralists attempt to safeguard. Once so confined, it is as if there were a discursive need to invest marital sexuality with *more and more meaning* over time, this meaning operating as a kind of supplement necessary to bolster the value of a more narrowly circumscribed marital sexuality itself (239).

For our purposes, we must not miss an exceedingly significant detail of Foucault's conclusion. Note that at the end of his concluding remarks about the larger stakes and implications of his study he returns to the question of shared "code elements" between Greco-Roman moralism and the "moral systems" of Christianity. To repeat the same language of code elements in relation to the larger genealogical distinction between two forms of bodily ethics clearly, even surprisingly, indicates that the entire discussion of the conclusion—largely analyzing the breaks separating the classical Greek discussions of the fourth century and those occurring in Hellenistic and Roman periods—constitutes Foucault's effort "not to let the matter rest there" with the argument between Zahn and Bonhöffer. I do not think we can overestimate the significance of this repetition of language used to categorize Zahn and Bonhöffer, now in relation to these remarkably expansive figures within the Foucauldian genealogical tableau. Foucault certainly did *not* let the matter rest there, we might say, but he outdoes Zahn and Bonhöffer only with an equally striking traditionalism:

Epictetus becomes a stand-in for "Greco-Roman moralism" while Paul becomes the proxy for the "moral systems" of later Christian discussions. As he summarizes: "The code elements that concern the economy of pleasures, conjugal fidelity, and relations between men may well remain analogous, but they will derive from a profoundly altered ethics and from a different way of constituting oneself as the ethical subject of one's sexual behavior" (240). In other words, despite his efforts to subvert an older tale of Western culture in which Christianity and the Greeks play two distinct and (mutually supporting) antagonistic roles, here Foucault is trying to manage and maintain a genealogical *distinction* between a developed Christian moral theology and Greco-Roman moralism. That is not so surprising. What *is* surprising is that Foucault will attempt to situate that genealogical distinction in a profoundly traditional way, by staging the distinction in a tableau of Paul against the (Hellenistic) philosophers. Or, to return to the question of supplement investment in the maintenance of economies that could flow in very different directions, is it not here we see the invested distinctions that demand of Foucault his odd leaps in comparative and temporal contexts? As Halvor Moxnes writes, Foucault "compares the moral philosophers of the early Roman empire of the first two centuries with Christian writers from the fourth and fifth centuries, not with their contemporaries in earliest Christianity."[41] This aspect of Foucault's genealogy is even more apparent in the recently published lectures "on the government of the living." There, in a similarly striking leap, Foucault elucidates what he calls the crucial genealogical "hinge" whereby discourses about "conscience" undergo a fateful transformation.[42] There, too, Foucault finds himself comparing the moralizing writings of Seneca not with Paul (whom again he notes but does not explore in depth) but with the fourth-century writings of Cassian. The leap is, as it were, the supplemental "tautology" of an enactment which could very well operate in another mode.[43]

VICISSITUDES OF BEATIFICATION

To articulate the full irony of this situation, it is worth reflecting for a moment on the carefully organized and ploddingly elaborated Christian historiographical conservatism of Theodore Zahn, whose approach—strangely enough—ends up effectively being repeated by Foucault at the end of the published *History of Sexuality*. As a staunch German defender of a late nineteenth-century Christian orthodoxy against the inroads of "critical" modern scholarship on the New Testament, Zahn became the darling of an English biblical scholarship that often imagined itself called to use empirical research to defeat unbelieving and abstruse German theorizing about religion and culture. In a preface to the 1899 translation of Zahn's *Apostolic Creed*, for example, the English translators write:

> It is too often taken for granted that the trend of modern criticism is destructive of the ancient literal acceptation of the Creed which we revere as the faith of our fathers, and as the faith which we ourselves confess in our daily prayers. . . . At this critical moment it is a fact of great importance that loyal churchmen should be able to claim Professor Theodor Zahn as an ally in the great campaign. . . . The manly straightforwardness of the faith, expressed in the following pages, will commend itself to "all who love our Lord Jesus Christ in sincerity."[44]

A comparable but more famous English ally of Zahn in the battle against the influential Tübingen school of biblical interpretation was J. B. Lightfoot, perhaps the most influential English New Testament scholar of the nineteenth century. As in other ways, Lightfoot joined Zahn in attempting to defuse and defer a thinking of the (Christian) apostle that would emerge by a sustained search for similarities at work between Paul and the Stoics. On one occasion, for example, anxious about close verbal and thematic similarities between Seneca and Paul, Lightfoot wrote: "Did St Paul speak quite independently of the Stoic imagery, when the vision of a nobler polity rose before him, the revelation of a city not made with hands, eternal in the heavens? Is there not a strange coincidence in his language—a coincidence only more striking because it clothes an idea in many respects very different?"[45]

Lightfoot and Zahn will be united in the force and beauty of beatification, that aura of protective sheltering of their apostle from the consideration of the common which drives comparative thought. In Lightfoot the move toward sublimation, exceptionalism, or the general refusal of comparisons returns when, again struck by comparative similarities between Paul's letter to the Philippians and the writings of Seneca, Lightfoot finally rhapsodizes: "Here again, though the images are the same, the idea is transfigured and glorified. At length the bond of coherence, the missing principle of universal brotherhood, has been found. As in the former case, so here the magic words *en christō* have produced the change and realised the conception. A living soul has been breathed into the marble statue by Christianity; and thus from the 'much admired polity of Zeno' arises the Civitas Dei of St Augustine."[46] Paul as the guarantor of a Platonism for the masses indeed! Moreover, in light of my larger arguments about the rise and dissemination of Paul as an index of a pop Platonism, note how here, too, the link operates by twinning a Pauline exceptionalism with a Christian historical narrative which understands him to be its founder. Forget Zeno; it is Paul who paves the way to Augustine's philosophical system of beneficent governance. Further, *none* of the players in the nineteenth- and early twentieth-century debates over the disciplinary and comparative arrangements of texts and interpretive strategies were naive about the stakes of the game for the larger question of "Christendom" and its capacities as a stable apparatus of moral and social control. Like Zahn— and, strangely, Foucault after him—Lightfoot is extremely invested in precluding the idea that Paulinism should be read rather as a popularized Stoicism.

Zahn is usually even less cagy than Lightfoot about his reticence to compare biblical and philosophical texts. Dismissing nineteenth-century studies of the New Testament book of James in relation to philosophical discussions, on one occasion Zahn passes over comparisons of statements in James with those in the scriptural philosopher Philo, only to add: "Parallels from Greek philosophical literature, especially that of Stoicism, are even less pertinent. One might rather undertake to show that Epictetus had read James."[47] One might think the sarcastically preferred research project—of showing New Testament influence on Epictetus—to be a dismissive joke about the entire comparative enterprise until one reads Zahn's more developed encounter with those developing comparative studies of Paul and Epictetus (see below). Even without that story, on this occasion Zahn's refusal to think through modes of comparison is already noteworthy given some of the comparative categories Zahn had ready to hand. Earlier in his work on James, for example, Zahn compared the author of the New Testament text to the author of Proverbs only to write that "it would be going too far to say that there was any *particular mental affinity* between this author and James."[48] Or, following that extraordinary interpretive tradition whereby Jesus's brother James is imagined as the author of the biblical book by this name, Zahn intuits that the book of James does indeed express a mental affinity with the historical Jesus.[49] Ignoring a century of biblical scholarship on the problem of the historical Jesus in order to deploy a reconstructed personality read rather directly from the face of New Testament Gospels, Zahn comments: "There is not a single word of Jesus' quoted [in James], much less anything from the Gospels. And yet, although none of the sayings of Jesus are reproduced in exactly the form in which they have come down to us, it is possible to fill the margin of the Epistle with parallels of Jesus' discourses which resemble James more closely in thought than the parallels from Jewish literature, some of which are closer verbally."[50] Notice the rather stunning beatifications or subtractions of Jesus and James from their environments, with even Jesus only entering into a relationship with "Jewish" literature as a kind of second-order comparative moment. Foucault warned readers against being misled by the "misleading analogies," but Zahn certainly would not be duped! In fact, Zahn always polices a stark difference of category despite sometimes obvious threads of similarity meandering across his field of vision. Always, however, there will be for this reader a Christian specificity being intuited despite the otherwise misleading analogies, shrewdly perceiving beneath the comparative surface distinct "mentalities" that always—always already perhaps—leave Christianity unscathed, sheltered, safe as a self-same identity which should not be confused with that of the analogical interlopers from among pagans or Jews. At the same time, Zahn will find real analogical substance—screeds of parallels to scrawl into the margins of your New Testament, in fact—at work between "Christian" writings, even when the parallels to, as he puts it, "Jewish literature" are actually much closer.

These asides are important inasmuch as they begin to suggest something of the fundamental tendencies of Zahn when he approaches the question of the New Testament in relation to its Greco-Roman environment. The full irony of Foucault's failure to intervene in the nineteenth-century discussion, however, only emerges when we consider the speech Zahn gave about Paul and Epictetus when the New Testament scholar became rector of the Friedrich-Alexanders University in Erlangen (1894). In that speech Zahn nails his colors to the mast concerning the question of comparing the New Testament to Hellenistic philosophy.

BEATIFICATION; OR, PLATONISM FOR THE MASSES AGAINST STOIC IMMANENCE

The rectoral address of Zahn is a remarkable document by which to come to grips with the cultural and political locations of his larger oeuvre and, by implication, of Foucault's at the end of the published *History of Sexuality*. Zahn's speech begins with a rhetorical sheepishness about the academic loneliness of the modern theologian, a figure he imagines to embody an institutional search for the "historical appearance and abiding truth" of Christianity.[51] The loneliness of the figure emerges, we are told, inasmuch as this academic orientation has long since ceased to be the "common faith of a learned public," already a distinction echoed in that drawn above (by the English translators of Zahn's work) between a true (or, as the nineteenth-century Englishmen put it, a "manly") Christianity over against a merely modern version of the same (3). In Zahn's speech, as we will see, this distinction also functioned to distinguish in turn a metaphysical or representational morality from the thought of singularity and finitude.

Zahn's rhetorical sheepishness about being a lonely believer quickly turns into something of a different order, however, when the biblical scholar proceeds to deny that "theology" belongs to a "common science of religion," even while adding that both human finitude and the limitations of the other disciplinary formations make all (individuals and academic disciplines presumably) reliant on, precisely, *theological explication* of that massive historical weight of Christendom, disciplinary (or individual) specificity notwithstanding (4). Theology will be, therefore, the supplement, inflated into an imagined guarantee, of the very finitude of other academic disciplines. Playing out the modern academic tableau as a story of Christian origins or the story of the Bible's relationship to Western culture, this state of affairs is the case (he tells us) because of the way Christianity emerged from an "Old Testament pre-history" in order to explode as an expansive presence so forcefully that it indelibly marked world history, in any case all those individuals and academic institutions represented by his audience. Needless to say, Zahn seems to have overcome his initial rhetorical shyness! He proceeds to suggest that it is therefore impossible for the (otherwise) lonely theologian to be irrelevant, the disciplinary field he represents (remember, this is his rectoral address) appearing in unexpected but ubiquitous ways around the otherwise diversified search for understanding. Theology, as an identity of a historical tradition directly embodied in a believing academic curator, becomes in this way the guardian of finitude precisely because it exists vampirically on the same as the "one who knows" how to address it.

When Zahn moves toward the comparative question of Paul and the Stoics, his narrative story is a standard nineteenth-century tale. On the one hand, "Christianity" (with Paul imagined to be an original exponent) emerges as a universal value over against the localist limitations of Judaism. On the other hand—taking as a historical event Acts' imagination of Paul condescendingly and antagonistically arguing with the Athenian philosophers on the Areopagus—Zahn presents Paulinist "Christianity" as a critique of pagan polytheism. Thus working with three discrete characters—Judaism, Christianity, and paganism—Zahn presents something like a comparative *Bildungsroman* of increasing awareness of the larger, even global, contexts of life. A localist and insular Judaism, Zahn narrates, enters into the complex culture of the Greco-Roman world only to find itself amazed that pagan cultures were something more than simply reprehensible idolatries (presumably what "Judaism" had imagined prior to this encounter). As encounters do in a *Bildungsroman*, this one leads to an expansion of horizons and concomitant coping mechanisms. One of Zahn's (apparently astonished) Jews, Aristobulus, begins to promulgate the idea that Greek poets and philosophers had cribbed most of their work from Jewish writers. As Zahn narrates knowingly, such intercultural nonsense (*Unfug*: an extraordinarily interesting phrase given what he is about to say concerning Paul and Epictetus) is lamentably transmitted from Judaism to Christianity. Among the Christians, for example, one discovers similar ideological mechanisms and their productions in the early Christian fabrication of letters between Paul and Seneca. Zahn roundly condemns such apologetic maneuvers, though what strikes me as most interesting about his gesture is the way it interprets this fantasized and fabricated intercultural interaction or sharing as a result of cultural shock and envy (4). Zahn, as we will see, will rather play the "Christian" who definitely does *not* envy outsiders.

Similarly, the new rector claims only to "smile" at the foolishness of the *phantastische Erklärung* within which Alexandrian Jews—and later church fathers—believed themselves to be mutually explicating Greek philosophy and Jewish scriptures (5). Remarkably, the comparative problem of the *phantastische Erklärung* remains a problematic possibility for a modern period of thought as well, he argues, the crux issue being (for both periods, presumably) how one understands *apparent similarities* without falling into merely "external" forms of comparison, cultural mixtures that, presumably, are not acceptably or authentically enlightening. Oh, well, enlightenments have always been a little nationalistic. . . . Offering in this context a thumbnail history of comparative interpretation, Zahn suggests that while earlier church traditions tended to read analogies as a product of Christian influence on pagan culture, modern interpretation has tended to interpret the same as influence from the opposite direction (5). In any case, Zahn confides, *the question of priority, influence, and identity* (those great pillars of nineteenth-century discussion he will never question) is difficult to determine if we are simply discussing textual monuments and textual similarities. The problem is much more difficult if we are thinking about more diffuse "background" (echoes of the "mental affinity" question) of thinkers and traditions of thought, and Zahn sees in such a comparative enterprise potential indeterminacies and intermixtures that feel like "slippery footing" for his otherwise straightforward three-character play.

Longing, as it were, for a more secure foundation, Zahn makes several suggestions about how to proceed in the game of comparisons. Throughout, however, the theologian, questing for both the historical and timeless truth of Christianity—will never stray from the fundamental assumption that cultural value is expressed as influence, or that influence may be read as a kind of proprietary or property right of the dominant figure in the game of cultural "comparison." In this precise sense, of course, there is no comparative game at work here, only the game of influence, ownership, and hierarchy.

Inasmuch as there remains at least a formal (if perhaps rigged) mode of comparison, what is most remarkable to me about Zahn's intervention is the frequency with which he distinguishes Paulinism from the Stoicism of Epictetus by way of an orienting desire to maintain an image of a *kosmos* assuredly ruled by a figure of benevolent transcendence or a figure of justified governmental authority. Paulinism, Zahn would have us believe, saves us from that which might otherwise mark a philosophy of immanence, namely, from the immanent exceptionalism—or exceptionalism without stable justification—that would otherwise need to answer for the emergence and maintenance of structures of power.[52] Over against this crisis of justification for power, which Zahn associates both with Stoic and modern post-Christian philosophies, Paulinism for Zahn stands in for the security imagined to be afforded by submission to a benevolently transcendent rule. Without the panacea of Zahn's pop Platonism, we are left with a radical passivity that constitutes the risky or dangerous unfolding of a processual ontology of the event, a topic of immanence against which Zahn always reacts by evoking a specter of political danger. Without the benevolent paternalism of Zahn's imagined Paulinist God, Zahn consistently argues, is a world without divine "pity," a world in which minorities especially are in danger (20). As Zahn puts it, political philosophy needs an "Other" built in to its system or, perhaps better, an Other standing over this system, guaranteeing its goodness and making sure promises of safety to those who remain faithfully subservient to it (19). To find in Paulinism indications of other modes—immanent modes—of the resistance, turning, or folding in of a life-not-dying did not seem possible for the new rector or for his mode of relating his academic discipline, or his Europe, to the question of power and its justifications. And within this vexed constellation of solidarities and their justifications, Zahn would do his best to preserve an imagined Paulinism from (ancient and modern) philosophies of immanence.

But then, in his way, so did Foucault.

ON STUBBORN DISCURSIVE FORMATIONS

That there is such a peculiar intensity with which Foucault asserts the need to remain faithful to these same genealogical distinctions at just this point in his historico-philosophical diagnosis of "the West" is intriguing, and we need not simply confess ignorance of the master author's intentions on this score, given that the projected fourth volume of the history of sexuality—about the confessional "flesh" of Christianity—was not published. Much more worthwhile is to allow Foucault's inconclusive conclusion to work itself back into Foucault's larger oeuvre such that it becomes oriented by the pressure of these final references to the history of biblical research, and this in order to articulate further the genealogical stakes of the distinction between Paul, the philosophers, and the developed "moral systems" and institutions that would be Christianity in a later age. Indeed, *as Foucault states without much ado*, some of the late nineteenth-century biblical scholars he mentions were hoping to find, in their own engagement with "Paul and the philosophers," a way of unearthing (again, in good genealogical fashion) a Paulinist "basis of the moral imperative" in such comparisons with philosophy so as to see "whether it was possible to detach Christianity from a certain type of ethics that had long been associated with it."[53] They were relying on Paul, in other words, to serve as that ready-made stumbling block within the identity of modern Christianity, a genealogical fulcrum by which to invert the value of institutional mechanisms and the ethics they demanded. Might we even say they were

searching for a vibrantly obstructive kernel within the hegemonic operation of the Platonism for the masses?

At one level, it is the *seriality* of such a gamble on the early Christian figure that is most surprising, a surprising seriality that evokes the
"quasi-transcendental" machinations of the signature we discussed in the
introduction. Jacques Derrida, for example, is just right when he reads
the repetition of modern Europe's reliance on an ambiguously historico-
philosophical vision of "originary Christianity" as serially repetitive
enough to constitute a "little machine" whose automaticity is one of its
most striking characteristics.[54] The little machine works inasmuch as
this "originary Christianity"—in this case Paulinism—is looked to for a
source of critical resistance against modern European Christianity itself,
a form of immanent, genealogical critique if ever there is one.[55] For his
part, Foucault's own genealogy of immanent critique of culture named—
precisely—modern *biblical studies* as the agonistic territory from which
may be learned more general lessons about how to critique a system from
within.[56]

The significance of an agonistic reference to Paul as a mode of "outbidding," however, extends far beyond the obvious ecclesiastical orientation that Foucault diagnoses in the nineteenth-century biblical scholars.
Indeed, should we not broaden those earlier interests beyond recognition
(as it were) so that they include all those commonplaces in Foucault's
own genealogical interventions into the forms of power constituting what
even he sometimes periodized as "modern Western culture," up to and
including his multiple efforts to unearth a "political spirituality" against
what he imagined to be a failure of secular European political thought?[57]
It is not simply that one must consider here the discursive relationship
in Foucault's work between his observation of the Iranian revolution and
"Christian ritual," as suggested in the illuminating collection of Afary and
Anderson. It is certainly a matter of considering modes of subjective constitution through bodily practices.[58] But apart from ready-made projections of where a "political spirituality"—or perhaps a politico-theology or
materialist theology—must lead, in this case what is at stake is a matter of
patiently exploring the political and subjective territories that might yet
be unleashed or invented with a strategic reworking of the philosophico-
Paulinist archive. In precisely this respect is it not the case, at levels both
historical and philosophical, that we (literally) do not yet know (to borrow
from what Nietzsche said of the body) what a *Paulinist* can do?

By the time he wrote *The History of Sexuality,* of course, Foucault had already articulated psychological practices in Weberian terms as a more invasive and technically effective form of normalizing control over populations than were earlier confessional practices of "Christian society." It is worth pointing out such things as, at times, one might think the frequent self-descriptions of Foucault as *not* doing this type of hermeneutical labor might militate against this level of (reflective, comparative) functioning within Foucault's texts. But the same person to express anxiety about Paul, the Hellenistic philosophers, and later Christian institutions was also the one to claim that Enlightenment critique was a subversive form of reading inherited from medieval biblical interpretation, that the psychoanalyst's couch was an "updated" monastic confessional, and that ongoing critical practice should distinguish genealogically between "prophetic" and philosophical modes of *parrhēsia* or bold critical speech, in order to rightly judge "what we could call the 'critical' tradition in the West."[59] This latter example is particularly pressing in relation to Foucault's interest in the placement of Paul and early Christianity within his larger genealogy of sexuality. After all, the parrhesiast is to later scientific truth telling what the Greek lover is to later abstracted and formalized or generalized sexuality. In fact, Foucault's definition of bold speaking could be cut and pasted from his discussions of classical discourses of sexuality: "the commitment involved in *parrhēsia* is linked to a certain social situation, to a difference of status between the speaker and his audience, to the fact that the *parrhēsiastēs* says something which is dangerous to himself and thus involves a risk, and so on."[60] Bold speaking, like the potentially dangerous or excessive eroticism of the classical period, always occurred in relation to an outside, within a sphere of encounter that destabilized and opened up this encounter as at least a minimally indeterminate, incalculable, and therefore risky sphere. The alterity of such a sexual encounter, like the indeterminate effect of bold speech, was not susceptible to the roman à clef that was constituted by those techniques of introspection which later operated in the name of an implicit normalization or general theory of sexuality. And is this not an important genealogical link between "classical" models of sexual encounter, *parrhēsia,* and the placement of Paulinism in the archive of the "West"? To echo the question of Breton, how is it that a kind of "outside" of power may be maintained in each case? In the name of what would one resist the way techniques of introspection, from the confessor's booth to the psychoanalyst's couch, do not in the end serve only the grim task of normalization and routinization under an untouchable law? How is it, to echo Foucault's favorite philosopher, Heidegger, that sex and speech resist being forms of "standing reserve," that normalized, placed, and efficiently *available* form of energy which Foucault designated a "docile body"?[61] Is there, to repeat a fascination of Clayton Crockett, a constitutive *entropy* within these various ecological systems?[62]

Here, too, we see how Foucault's own incapacity to "let the matter [of Paul and the philosophers] remain there" testifies to the way the topic of Paulinism could—as if a node within a network or an accidental knot within a skein of yarn—organize or subvert words and things of another epoch entirely.[63] In such a context should we not say that, with the question about early Christianity's relation to a more general cultural shift in modes of bodily existence, Foucault's work also played out haunting questions about a projective "sketch" of the future that extend themselves, finally, into that epoch of marked immanence in political control that Foucault described with the term *biopower?* What *is* the place of Paul within Foucault's expansive genealogies of modernity that are replete with intriguing references to premodern Christian institutions, whether Foucault is describing Kant's critique of religion as a form of critique inherited from earlier exegetical debates or the drive to talk oneself to a cure on the psychoanalytic couch as a variation of earlier pastoral practices of the confessional? Particularly here, how would Paul, as a comparative node within this genealogy, figure into the discursive analysis of those modern *dispositifs* whereby individuals are called not only to "confess to acts contravening the law" but also pressured "to transform desire . . . into discourse"?[64] Whatever Foucault's intentions in including his brief engagement with Paul and Epictetus, or whatever Foucault had or would continue to plan in relation to "Christianity" and its flesh within his larger project on truth telling and sexuality, as a loose end the figure of Paul obtrudes here at the conclusion of the study on sexuality. Could we, for example, construe the Paulinist role in Foucault's genealogy as that site whereby power itself learns that it can be liberated to live "without law," strangely outside its economy, and thereby all the more invasively producing those interior spaces of the modern biopolitical form and the rationalized, docile bodies its demands might make transparent? This will be the issue for my reading of Pasolini's Paul. Or, as Foucault would put it earlier in *The History of Sexuality*: "We are informed that if repression has indeed been the fundamental link between power, knowledge, and sexuality since the classical age, it stands to reason that we will not be able to free ourselves from it except at a considerable cost: nothing less than the transgression of laws, a lifting of prohibitions, an irruption of speech, a reinstating of pleasure within reality, and a whole new economy in the mechanisms of power will be required."[65] And if that economy and its modes of incarnating itself in the self-diagnoses of the individual would be more totalitarian than the earlier, "repressive" mode of legal power, then has, as Jacques Lacan always insinuated (with different language) the era of biopower appeared only after finally discovering the Pauline proclamations about the "liberation" of spirit beyond the legal limits of law?

Paulinism, and perhaps an ambivalence about the immanence of power, dangles here at the end of Foucault's history, a loose and only partially assimilated appendix to Foucault's story. Moreover, given the history of discussion about Paul, it is not a surprise that Foucault would express a wonder here about, precisely, Paul and the (Hellenistic) philosophers. Whatever the role of Paul in Foucault's history, would such a role be isolable from the role of philosophy itself, particularly a philosophy struggling to liberate difference, singularity, and becoming from a metaphysics of presence, a metaphysics best glossed as a "Platonism" become ubiquitous cultural background? The apostolic, the religious, the visionary, and the apocalyptic will not have had a role detachable from the question of philosophy. But this is still to frame the question as one of retrospective representation. What is needed—increasingly—is a different mode of creative grasping of that *kairos* which Foucault himself seemed to miss. To that we begin to turn.

4

SINGULARITY; OR, SPIRITUAL EXERCISE (PAUL AND THE PHILOSOPHICAL IMMANENCE OF FOUCAULT AND DELEUZE)

Would you say [it] also expresses a crisis?

Absolutely, yes . . . I think he must have come up against the question of whether there was anything "beyond" power—whether he was getting trapped in a sort of impasse within power relations. . . . The first volume [of *The History of Sexuality*] did of course identify points of resistance to power; it's just that their character, their origin, their production were still vague. And that's just what he's telling himself in the very fine piece on infamous men: "Always the same inability to cross the line, to get to the other side . . . always the same choice, on the side of power, of what it says or has people say . . . "

What is this "line," or this relation that's no longer a power relation?

It's difficult to talk about. It's a line that's not abstract, though it has no particular shape. It's no more in thought than in things, but it's everywhere thought confronts some thing like madness, and life something like death . . .

This line, if it's so "fearsome," how can we make it endurable? Is this what the fold is all about: the need to fold the line?

Yes. . . . We need both to cross the line, and make it endurable, workable, thinkable. To find in it as far as possible, and as long as possible, an art of living.

—Claire Parnet and Gilles Deleuze

My parrhesiastic practice focuses on the execution of our sovereign,
Jesus the messiah, through whom the world has been crucified to me . . .
and I to the world. After all, in our collective becoming-messiah we
ground ourselves in neither circumcision nor uncircumcision, but only
in the forcing of a new creation.

—Paul to the Galatians (cf. 6:14f.)

IN DELEUZE'S MOVING CONVERSATION WITH CLAIRE PARNET ABOUT
the life and death of Foucault, I am struck by the way Deleuze's typical fascination with Foucault under the name of the fold and the double emerges
as a space within which to imagine the pressure of a crisis within Foucault's thinking.[1] How does thought, or life, escape power relations once
these are imagined, precisely, as ubiquitous? Could one cross a limit of
knowledge and power in order to experiment, and to experiment with
new communal forms? If so, has one crossed over a threshold of escape
from power, or would such a (spatializing, temporalizing) metaphor necessarily prove unhelpful? Moreover, and with a Hellenistic philosophical
inflection, in what way would such experimentation *answer to* a haunting
sense of trauma, of disappointment, and the threat of death, such that a
style of life affords an experimental therapy for the soul, for its fears and
its accompanying enslavements? And would this question not remain all
the more important even if these experimental quests for a freedom that
is also a shelter must be, by definition, hesitating, risky, and short-lived?

In keeping with the previous chapter, in other words, I want to claim
that Paul returns as an important figure with which to wrestle at a very
specific philosophical moment, a moment in an unfolding ontology Foucault himself does not resist calling an opening of and toward a (very circumscribed, thoughtful, even hopeful) "nihilism." If the strange messianism that is an aftermath of fidelity to the "crucified" returns at this point in
intellectual history with some forcefulness, then its arrival (to echo Walter Benjamin) peers at us through a very particular sort of philosophical
or theoretical aperture. In this section I want to take a measure of some
of the dimensions of this aperture as it operates within important parts
of Foucault's work. In doing so, I want to say more clearly than I believe
anyone has been saying up to this point why several fundamental problems within continental philosophy find such a nice articulation in Paul,
but also how a comparative or genealogical reading of Pauline texts might
unearth more important experimental insight still.

SINGULAR UNIVERSAL

Recall the classic moment when Foucault writes in *Discipline and Punish*: "The body of the king, with its strange material and physical presence, with the force that he himself deploys or transmits to some few others, is at the opposite extreme of the new physics of power represented by panopticism."[2] Above all, the spatial location of power has shifted in what Foucault at this point tends to articulate as a move from one economy of power relations to another, a shift in economy that effects a shift in the spectacular self-presentation of power to an image in which power "has its maximum intensity not in the person of the king, but in the bodies that can be individualized by these relations."[3] As each of our chapters argues in different ways, the spatial shift of aura or spectacular buzz (or, to echo Hent de Vries's important work, the "special effect") is the essential issue here. Without the locus of the sovereign's effervescent body, for example, how is it possible to represent diffuse mechanisms of individualizing, normalizing power if power is itself dispersed into a multitude of bodies, decentralized and as it were unlocatable, both everywhere and nowhere? One of Foucault's authorial modes throughout his career was about attending to such a formal and phenomenological problem. In this passage he declares brilliantly in a kind of Deleuzean vein that—without the ready-made *locus* of sovereign decision—the presentation and explanation of power relations becomes all the more "singular," indeed, all the more audacious than a mere king making decisions over life and death.[4] The audacity of the new spectacular economy emerges, ironically, inasmuch as it presents itself as a kind of normalcy, a routinized and efficient setup that best contributes to the proliferation of "life."

This is an important issue to drag from Foucault's prose here, as it points to the way an emergence of a logic of singularity was for him the essential distinguishing mark between his nineteenth-century "modernity," with its emergent biopower, and a "prehistory" as the nonmodern. The frequency and significance of such a move in Foucault should not be missed for Foucault's occasional stated hatred of the way "monumental" histories obfuscated a genealogical approach to the multiplicities of reality. In *The Order of Things*, for example, he summarized "the West" as having "known only two ethical forms":

> The old one (in the form of Stoicism or Epicureanism) was articulated upon the order of the world, and by discovering the law of that order it could

deduce from it the principle of a code of wisdom or a conception of the city; even the political thought of the eighteenth century still belongs to this general form. The modern one, on the other hand, formulates no morality, since any imperative is lodged within thought and its movement towards the apprehension of the unthought; it is reflection, the act of consciousness, the elucidation of what is silent, language restored to what is mute, the illumination of the element of darkness that cuts man off from himself, the reanimation of the inert—it is all this and this alone that constituted the content and form of the ethical. Modern thought has never, in fact, been able to propose a morality.[5]

"Our modernity," as he called it, cannot formulate a "law" or a "morality" or a representable "code" of conduct because, Foucault explains further, for modernity "thought . . . is itself an action—a perilous act."[6] Foucault sees in modernity something like a Heideggerian displacement of the economy of representation (where words are charted onto things) onto a more opaquely self-grounding economy of language, production, and life in which there is no *model* to re-present in thinking.[7] Instead, we might say (echoing Foucault's discussion of Deleuze), there are only *singular* exemplars which—for this reason—all the more opaquely or violently constitute the ground of their own operations. Outside a nomological economy whereby some "law" could function as the map by which to "deduce" good or useful action, the "imperative" of thought becomes all the more immanently, opaquely present a problem, indeed an essential Paulinist problem, as we have already explored in earlier chapters. In different language, in this latter *episteme*, as Foucault says, *thought is itself an act*. When Foucault concludes the section by saying that, therefore, "modern thought is advancing towards that region where man's Other must become the Same as himself," he is not suggesting the usual handwringing about an appropriation of the other by the same.[8] Rather, the point is that the existence of the same, as a singularity, would bear its own burden of alterity, would carry around with it its *own* shadow, and this shadow as a kind of opaquely disconcerting *imperative* of its own being. Thought or existence within this setup would always bear the cut of finitude, forever indicating the absence of stable models by always ever and only conjuring the singular other, my "ownmost" other, as Heidegger could have put it. The thought of self-grounding regions like life, production, or language result in a situation in which man is not contemporaneous with what makes him be—or with that upon the basis of which he is; but that he is within a power that disperses him, draws him far from his origin, but promises it to him in an imminence that will perhaps be forever snatched from him; *now, this power is not foreign to him; it does not reside outside him in the serenity of eternal and ceaselessly recommenced origins, for then the origin would be effectively posited; this power is that of his own being.*[9]

In addition to our construction of a genealogical echo chamber of Paulinism, the insight has astonishing implications for many of the standard construals of the ethical dimensions of Foucault's analyses of discourses, institutions, and power. The crucial issue is not at all that, say, the rationality of the clinic is bad or must be resisted because reason constructs its own other in the categories of madness, that prisons are bad or must be resisted because society founds itself on the designation and organization of the criminal, and so on. The astonishing insight is rather, much more simply but also as a profound paradox: these are the modes in which *existence* appears as such in the modern period. This realization in turn helps us to understand why the *generalization* of power relations, the dispersal from the centralized site of the sovereign—even their generalization in carceral and clinical institutions—does not, in Foucault's modernity, in *any* way imply that they become *less singular* than they were under the transcendent individual sovereign, a paradox that undoes not only the usual way of distinguishing the general from the particular but also a variety of Marxist dialectics that Foucault resists. Foucault's thought of a *generalized* epoch of power is here a perfect counterpart to Heidegger's thought of Being. In both cases what is intriguing (and paradoxical or aporetic) about power or being is that they are *not* (as Heidegger famously refuses in Kant and, indeed, in all "traditional" ontologies) "the most general categories."[10] Rather, liberated from the (imagined) totality in which generality or category traffick, the general itself becomes an instance or exemplar of existence in which the difference that constitutes it becomes, as it were, unplaceable. The existence, without representable model or a law to which it could remain obedient, becomes singular and singularly bearing the alterity which it itself is.

As I wanted to indicate with my initial quotation of Deleuze, I read Foucault and Deleuze as here exploring similar problems of a philosophy of *difference*, problems that ring throughout with the kinds of Paulinist echoes evoked in previous chapters. Moreover, it is in this respect, it seems to me, that some of the recent criticisms of the Deleuzeanism of Michael Hardt and Antonio Negri participate in a reading of Deleuze/Foucault (at this point) which is naive to this Heideggerian element in Foucault's archival work on institutions. For example, of course Deleuze was often interested politically in the way proliferations of dispersed (and singular) rhizomes overload and escape the centralized (and representational) root structures of "arborescent" systems. On this score it is often pointed out that various oppressive contemporary economies or structures operate in the same way as the singularly rhizomatic: capitalist consumerism and the U.S. military, for example.[11] At times these criticisms assume that the point of a Foucauldian/Deleuzean thought of the singular was to unearth a guarantor of an emancipatory outside of the "modern" economy of power both of them saw emerging around them, but this of course is precisely what seems *not* to fit the paradoxical link between the *generalization* of power relations and their essential *singularity* within this epoch. As Valérie Nicolet Anderson describes nicely, Foucault offers an immanent social ontology in which one "tunes in" to new modes of existence rather than "uncovering" an emancipatory *terra firma*.[12] No wonder Nicolet Anderson has become obsessed with Foucault in relation to Paul's conjuration of refuge for an experimental collective at the borders of political catastrophe (and what else could a crucified messiah be?).[13] And here our reading of Paul will rather closely mirror our reading of Deleuze: no concrete shoes, no originary foundation, just tuned in turnings and folding for the temporary crystallization of the new, the alternative, the resistant. Or, in an echo of the initial quotational bricolage of this chapter, neither the revolutionary nor the nonrevolutionary mean anything; what matters is new creation.[14]

IMMANENCE; OR, ("MODERN") PHILOSOPHIES OF SINGULARITY AND THE IMPOSSIBILITY OF ("CLASSICAL") EMANCIPATION

Similarly, we might wonder about the way the "modern" episteme to some degree—and paradoxically—recuperates the classical distinction between the immanent and the transcendent within an antinomy immanent to singular finitude itself. Is there in Foucault a similar dynamic as one finds in Heidegger, particularly that dynamic which led the young Heidegger back to Pauline texts as perhaps *the* indication of a logic of thrownness and the paradoxical facticity of being in a world without objective guarantee?[15] As we have just seen, in Foucault there is a sense in which the singularization of thought leads to an inversion of a *general* mapping of being. In the classical regime, despite the proliferation of different objects on the table of classification, everything could be "spread out to form a permanent table of stable differences and limited [i.e., delimitable] identities; it was a matter of genesis of Difference starting from the secretly varied monotony of the Like."[16] In the modern regime, by contrast, the "analytic of finitude has an exactly inverse role: in showing that man is determined, it is concerned with showing that the foundation of those determinations is man's very being in its radical limitations."[17] In a beautiful articulation of (specifically) Heidegger's "analytic of finitude" and its descriptions of thrown-ness—the same logic as that of the generalized singular of modern power relations—Foucault's "modern" sees, paradoxically, that the "contents of experience are already their own conditions."[18] Indeed, the effort *to match* constituted and constituting experience by the designation of "humanity" as essentially or radically finite effects a paradox that "shows how that [determining] origin of which man is never contemporary is at the same time withdrawn and given as an imminence; in short, it is always concerned with showing how the Other, the Distant, is also the Near and the Same."[19] Here again, the usual shibboleths about sameness and difference only lead us astray, as Foucault's point is to assert that, *despite appearances*, the hurly-burly of detail characteristic of the classical tables of classification only masked the sameness underwriting them, while the universalization of the analytic of finitude springs loose, under the name of the recuperated Same, an unprecedented potential for irrecuperable, irrecoverable difference. In lines that could have been written by Deleuze on the "minimal difference" or the "swerve" of *clinamen*, Foucault summarizes that the Same in the postclassical setup becomes "identity separated from itself by a distance," a repetition always of a *self-differing* Same.[20] In this mode, the Same as self-differing distance creates "a vacuum within the Same" in a way the proliferation of details and objects could not within the representational economy of the classical period.[21] It is sameness eternally recurring under the name of the "hiatus" that is difference.[22]

Or, to oscillate back and forth in our classical-to-modern theoretical problem, if the spectacular presentation of power relations becomes all the more singular, somehow all the more audaciously or spectacularly self-grounding, once released from its incarnation in the body of a sovereign monarch, then *opposition* to power in the latter epoch likewise becomes all the more difficult to conceptualize. One can ignore, contradict, and resist the dictates of the transcendent sovereign, the symbolic law of language, and so on, of course with sometimes violent repercussions or reprisals against the rebellious. But it demands a different order of thought to imagine ignoring, resisting, or contradicting the postsovereign *diffusion* of power that is nevertheless activated by scientific (which is often in Foucault to say generalizable) knowledge. As Foucault wrote, there is therefore a "slow, continuous, imperceptible gradation that made it possible to pass naturally from disorder to offence and back from a transgression of the law to a slight departure from a rule, an average, a demand, a norm."[23] With these lines which we must not forget when we seek to understand the forceful return of a philosophical Paulinism in our own time, we pass from an economy of power symptomatized or indicated by "the crime, the order of sin" to new apparatuses of measurement for the general population, new forms of capture that are now so diffuse within the population that the exceptional status and exceptional declarations of the sovereign no longer serve as the exemplary index of law and limit. No longer the Hobbesian or Schmittian decision of the sovereign distinguishing friends from enemies of the state, "the social enemy was transformed into a deviant," a transformation which demands a reworking of the idea of power and resistance alike.[24] As I discuss more in the following chapter, this formal issue determines the way that Paul's "return" in recent theory has been mediated by Pauline statements in Romans 7 wherein precisely the secession of economic distinction between law and exception is what comes to the fore.

How, after all, does one resist when mechanisms of power are imagined not to come from a repressive outside but to emerge by way of new and populace-wide apparatuses of measurement, all those mechanisms by which the new economy of power attempts to more effectively proliferate "life"? Much more pointedly, and to summarize a great deal of recent discussion of the viability of Foucault for ongoing critical theory, the real question for resistance in the new economy of power is this: how does one resist when power is that which is imagined to be making the mode or way life is the way life is? This duplication or radically immanent self-grounding of power is the traumatic issue in moments of Foucault, who tries increasingly and in different modes later in his career to imagine an unrestricted economy of power relations or a "network" in which "there is no outside."[25]

As mentioned, the logic of Foucault's story implies a new economy of power relations which are not *less* "singular" because now "generalized."

This is the essential issue for my current purposes, as the new economy is all the more grounded in specific, even (strangely) decisionistic, techniques of distinction-making, but without this distinction-making being localizable within the spectacular image of the sovereign. Here I agree completely with Jeffrey T. Nealon's discussion of power and resistance in Foucault's writings, particularly as he summarizes the relevant formal issues in an invocation of Kafka's parable of the gatekeeper in "Before the Law." As Nealon writes:

> Read through the lens of power and its genealogical intensification, Kafka's text functions as a kind of instruction manual for demonstrating the *costs* of misdiagnosing various forms of power: the man from the country performs his relation to power on a sovereign law model, which is to say he sees power as centralized, housed in a specific place or person. Hence he wants an audience with power, finally to confront the hidden law, which "he thinks should surely be accessible at all times to everyone; but as he now takes a closer look at the doorkeeper in his fur coat, with his big sharp nose and long, thin, tartar beard, he decides that it is better to wait until he gets permission to enter." The parable, however, shows us that biopower is wholly immanent to the socius rather than organizing it from above.[26]

Indeed, I think we could point out more forcefully than Nealon the significance of the parabolic statement of the gatekeeper to the seeker ("the gate was made only for you"), as it indicates nicely the structural link between the generalizing *diffusion* of power (precisely that which makes this economy of law different from an expression of the will of a sovereign) and the paradoxical *singularization* of the splitting of sovereignty and abjection. To make the parable speak the logics of Foucault's economy of power, *this gatekeeper*, situated at the limit of law, is a singular invention of an occlusion or blockage of *this* life from the authorization of it.

Consider the way Foucault himself is forced by his effort to articulate new logics of power into a number of profoundly labyrinthine statements due to the fact that he is trying to articulate how biopower is another way to describe the self-feeding *investment of its effects back into itself* without readily apparent outside or exit. He writes, for example, that a diffused panoptic "mechanism is not simply a hinge, a point of exchange between a mechanism of power and a function."[27] Rather, "it is a way of making power relations function in a function, and of making a function function through power relations."[28] Those who understand Foucault as too dark, too pessimistic, leaving no place for "agency," and so on, seem to me to miss the way the paradoxes, double binds, and aporiae of a text like this one emerge not from Foucault's effort to describe "more" of a particular way of construing power but from his effort to think (closely with Deleuze) a different mode or *ontology* of power relations altogether, one that is decentered and disseminated always only into its enactments or performances. In the next chapter we will read Pier Paolo Pasolini's Paul along the lines of the shift in power relations indicated when capitalism posits its own presuppositions, an indication that Lacan—even before the brilliant explorations of Slavoj Žižek on the issue—radicalized into the very nature of subjectivity itself, something we discuss further on in this chapter.[29]

To play on the language we have seen in Foucault, now a singularized, immanent power must bear the burden of its own *spectacular* "self"-assertion, its own semblance, or (as Giorgio Agamben has put it, nicely twisting the genealogical issues) its own "glory." Note, for example, how it is this intensely immanent construal of power which governs Foucault's description of the shift in the role of power from a repressive to a productive function. When power is not imagined as existing exterior to the life of the populace, he writes, when it is "not localized" even in "the general form of the law or government," then "there is neither analogy nor homology [to guide our thinking about power], but *a specificity of mechanism and modality*."[30] As described in chapter 1, we are not very far here from the turn in Althusser toward a phenomenological approach to the "modes" of production which, as we saw, became indistinguishable from the *performance of the call* of interpellation.[31] All power, we might say, has here become Pauline in the sense we discussed in relation to Breton, existing only in and as a kind of kerygmatic power which is "weak" in the sense that it exists only *in* its being believed. When power becomes immanent to life and those tactics believed to measure it, in other words, cultural critics are stuck with an "exorbitant singularity" that "masks" its sovereign impositions all the more by becoming indistinguishable from the measurable "way" of life itself.[32] This exorbitancy, this excess which "makes" the given by acting as its effect constitutes a kind of swerve, a kind of faith which minimally displaces this given from a state of resting in itself. Thus it is not "more" of a particular construal of power that renders inoperable the step outside it, but an epochal, paradigmatic shift in *the thinking of power* which governs Foucault's radical reworking of the inside/outside of power: "We must cease once for all to describe the effects of power in negative terms: it 'excludes,' it 'represses,' it 'censors,' it 'abstracts,' it 'masks,' it 'conceals.' In fact, power produces; it produces reality."[33]

This line within Foucault's work seems to me the really difficult and productive problem accompanying an inventively comparative "return" of Paul for contemporary theory and its political formations. It is the problem, in fact, that necessarily (and despite the epochalism of some of Foucault's statements) led him to an exploration of singular *styles* of life, even if Foucault tended to leave Paulinism as a figure of representation and sacrifice to the original rather than to inflect him along the lines of the technologies of selfhood he saw in Paul's philosophical contemporaries. These *styles* are those *differences* without totalizing rule capable of justifying judgments about them, and to think about them is to think about lives and living that are singularly relational, comprehensible not under the nomination of a category or norm (which Foucault on important occasions happily terms *law*), but rather as a unique sphere of relationality. As Paul might have put the matter to his hesitant colleagues in Galatia, the only way to judge whether you have received the spirit or become part of the (creatively processual) "strange federation" is simply to taste the savor of the very experience in question, a statement we might explicate with the gloss: "My stupid colleagues, who has drugged you? Only one thing do I want to know from you: did you experience the liberation of spirit while living like Jews in Jerusalem or when you simply affirmed our conversations while living as you do in Galatia? Having started the movement in this style, will you now displace its convincing vibrancy by demanding that you now live like someone else?" (cf. Galatians 3:2f., 5:1). Here Heidegger's appropriation of Paulinism was right on the mark, in the sense that it understood Paul as an exemplar, ultimately, of life which could *only* be judged from out of a singular *style of care*, of *concern,* which is itself the animating force of judgment rather than knowledge. Foucault, as we have already seen, tends to read "Christianity" as on the modern/epistemological side of what he describes as the eventual "inversion between the hierarchy of the two principles of antiquity," namely, the principles to *know oneself* and to *care for oneself.* In keeping with a potential modern break with knowledge as justified judgment in the form of application of an external rule, Foucault casts a genealogical eye back to "Greco-Roman philosophy in the first two centuries" in order to think with them the issue of thought as a singular *style* of life (philosophy as *bios*), and in so doing allies himself very closely to Heidegger. Unlike Heidegger, however, Foucault did not seem to press the very legacy of early "Christianity" for indications of alternative paths not taken, other modes of creating solidarities between oneself and others besides rule-based docility or (which amounts to the same thing) the experience of truth through self-renunciation. But we should distinguish here between what Foucault himself *did* and the framework of the driving problematic that drove Foucault to the archival projects he did pursue. By the same token, it should be clear by now that the basic story Foucault sketches also determines his late-career interest in *risky* political speech, that singular style of creatively countercultural solidarities expressed in the media of Greco-Roman experiments with *parrhēsia*. It was the (Deleuzean) interest in the *style* of philosophical *bios* which attracted the late Foucault to the formulations of Hadot, a thinker with whom he is otherwise separated by a profound intellectual and political gulf.

Likewise, for the moment, it is worth mentioning that this issue of style or singularity seems a problem many interpreters of the philosopher misunderstand. Recalling some standard clichés, we should point out that it is not simply that Foucault "goes too far" in his "pessimistic" views about the effectivity of specific disciplinary tactics, that panoply of specific, modern "micropowers" as so many measurable gestures, activities, habits of mind and affect. The difficulty here for the cultural critic occurs instead at the level of Foucault's *model* whereby "life" and even "being" merge seamlessly into a thinking of "power."[34] In that respect, we must hear echoes not only of the specific historical or genealogical stories Foucault tells (of the prison, of psychoanalysis, of population statistics, and so on) but also of the consistent, if often unmarked and unfootnoted, references to Nietzsche and Heidegger, the latter being that philosopher Foucault once claimed to think about the most but write about the least, the former being the philosopher who—as it were—interpreted Heidegger to Foucault.[35] Power becomes another name for "thrown" life, invested life, potential life—in a word, power names, simply, "factical" life. The comparison is useful inasmuch as it seems to me the case that most of the interpretations of Foucault's descriptions of diffuse, dispersed power relations are premised on the idea that there must be some stable or self-same *terra firma* (in Aristotelian terms of which Heidegger was fond, a *hūpokeimenon*) that could exist *without* those energetics Foucault designates *power*. But it was the Heideggerian (also Deleuzean) effort to think contingencies (perhaps "history") as *constitutive* of the various strata of reality rather than as epiphenomenal, detachable "ornaments" on a stable structure (like a *hūpokeimenon*) that, essentially, inverts the common understanding of power (as that which is, possibly or contingently, imposed from without) so that power may be read less locally, less detachably, as simply what "produces reality."

I confess that I find Lacan's oddly paradoxical formulations about power-as-solicitation to be more useful, ultimately, than some of Foucault's. But what is interesting about the thematics of power in Foucault's writings is not whether he has become too pessimistic (and so on), but rather the ways we can in his writings observe the striking paradoxes (again, comparable to the thematics of Heidegger's facticity and *Dasein*) as demands for a reworking of our usual ways of thinking. Most importantly, Foucault transforms how one would understand "resistance" to power. Here we should remind ourselves that it was a similar problematic which inspired Lacan to reverse the anxiety of "old father Karamazov" about the death of God, inasmuch as (the old father believed) the death of the divine sovereign would mean that "everything is permitted."[36] If the sovereign (divine) monarch, the paternal law which functions as the system's fulcrum, leverage point, or external ground is removed—Lacan countered—then the problem is rather that *nothing is permitted.* In a question that takes us to the heart of similar paradoxes about freedom from law, the play with rhetorics of slavery, and the idea of freedom to belong "to another," in Paul, we are invited to wonder how—without the external measure of repressive prohibition—one would even distinguish between muling subservience and bold transgression.

To stay with the Karamazov story and its Lacanian inversion for a moment (we will discuss Paul and Lacan in the following chapter), the collapse of an "outside" position from which power is exerted (but also in terms of which power is sheltered, preserved, saved) cuts loose an explosion of indeterminacy and ambiguity about power and its contestation. Or, to make the line fit with what is to follow in and outside of Pasolini's Paul, with this collapse of an external sovereign power emerges Foucault's occasional despair about the possibility of "liberation"—as well as all those moments of exhilaration in which those interpreters of Foucault, Michael Hardt and Antonio Negri, proclaim that, finally, "biopolitical" immanence has liberated the significance of *productive bodies.* And just here, between the utter loss of a site of emancipation and a paradoxical explosion of new life, will be situated the return of Paulinism in these writers.

INSIDE THE OUTSIDE OF THE LAW OF BEING: IMMANENCE IS BIOPOWER

One must interact with Foucault, therefore, on the question of immanent "biopower"—power made immanent to (aporetically) measured life itself—with attention to the background philosophical model rather than by way of simple empirical questioning about whether Foucault's analyses of specific modern tactics of measurement and control "go too far" in their sense that there is no substratum, no *subiectum* or subject, on which an external "power" could inscribe itself. After all, by what measure would we measure the relation, or separate the distance, between "subject" and "power"? As is often the case, this problem of thing, measure, mediation, and epistemic recognition here echoes very closely those delicious paradoxes of media-philosophy and philosophy's technologies in relation to which Hegel challenged Kantian critical reason from the ground up. Recall the beautiful section from the beginning of the *Phenomenology of Spirit*, a section worth quoting at length:

> For, if cognition is the instrument for getting hold of absolute being, it is obvious that the use of an instrument on a thing certainly does not let it be what it is for itself, but rather sets out to reshape and alter it. If, on the other hand, cognition is not an instrument of our activity but a more or less passive medium through which the light of truth reaches us, then again we do not receive the truth as it is in itself, but only as it exists through and in this medium. . . . It would seem, to be sure, that this evil could be remedied through an acquaintance with the way in which the *instrument* works; for this would enable us to eliminate from the representation of the Absolute which we have gained through it whatever is due to the instrument, and thus get to the truth in its purity. But this "improvement" would in fact only bring us back to where we were before. If we remove from a reshaped thing what the instrument has done to it, then the thing—here the Absolute—becomes for us exactly what it was before this [accordingly] superfluous effort. On the other hand, if the Absolute is supposed merely to be brought nearer to us through this instrument, without anything in it being altered, like a bird caught in a lime-twig, it would surely laugh our little ruse to scorn, if it were not with us, in and for itself, all along, and of its own volition. For a ruse is just what cognition would be in such a case, since it would, with its manifold exertions, be giving itself the air of doing something quite different from creating a merely immediate and therefore effortless relationship.[37]

As Michael Hardt and Antonio Negri argue in their book *Commonwealth*, the turn from stable, transcendental structures of cognition (here: Kant) toward an immanent phenomenology (Hegel) is a move that necessarily questions the proper limits—or property rights and divisions of labor—of common being itself.[38] As such, Hardt and Negri point out, the move toward an immanent phenomenology is a move that bears a strong family resemblance to the Foucauldian gesture of handing over without reserve "the subject" to an immanent realm of power relations constituting a "biopolitical" sphere. This sphere, of course, is one in which—as in Hegel's post-Kantian phenomenology—all dreams of stable structuring roles on the "outside" of such immanent divisions of labor appear as a "ruse," an obfuscating and even comical moment of thought, the humor of which is generated by the way—we should note—that in this passage divisions of labor and represented proprietary structures do not and cannot coincide. Indeed, in this transformation from Kant to Hegel (or, in fact, the early materialism of Marx) to the late Foucault, Hardt and Negri find a clue for the unleashing of productive bodies into a sphere in which no structures may circumscribe themselves as safe and unquestionable realms of the transcendent. This move, Hardt and Negri claim, will constitute liberation in a biopolitical space of the "phenomenology of bodies." But it is also the move which constitutes, with some caveats, the fascination with Paulinism in the work of Giorgio Agamben, Roberto Esposito, and Eric Santner, to name several important touchstones.

Hardt and Negri are perhaps the most *hopeful* of interpreters of Foucault when they see in the death and dissemination of sovereignty a profound opening for political subjectivity. For Foucault, they argue, the death and dissemination of central authority is not simply the death of the sovereign monarch but the death of all self-protectively abstract and stable sovereignties that might be articulated in terms of transcendental argumentation, whether Kantian categories or even categories of nameable and self-same material substrata, as in the "subject" of the early Marx. What is beyond these epochs of "transcendental" power is, therefore, an epoch in which there is no fulcrum found in any "outside" of the immanent space of bodies and their productions. Unlike many of Foucault's interpreters, however—who tend to see this transfer from one economy of power into another as the end or annihilation of all spaces of resistance, Hardt and Negri focus on the way it is likewise the end or annihilation of all spaces within which active power could be safely cordoned off from the effects of bodies and their productive capacities. Freed from a deferral to transcendent structures of thought, Foucault, and we in his wake, are able to traffic in a "phenomenology of bodies" that is indistinguishable from "biopolitics": "Its first axiom is that bodies are the constitutive components of the biopolitical fabric of being."[39] Echoing Hegel's demonstration of the "ruse" of Kantian schemata, they write: "Labor, freed from private property, simultaneously engages all our senses and capacities, in short, all our '*human* relations to the world—seeing, hearing, smelling, tasting, feeling, thinking, contemplating, sensing, wanting, acting, loving.' When labor and production are conceived in this expanded form, crossing all domains of life, bodies can never be eclipsed and subordinated to any transcendent measure or power."[40] Or, as Giorgio Agamben might put it, the transcendence of any transcendent measure would necessarily exist only so long as its self-performance as a kind of aura or "glory" would. Life as fad and intensity, a constitutive concern for a while (to echo Heidegger). Or, in keeping with the way these dynamics often play out today, organizing, juridical measures only exist so long as the managers making a living off them—so to speak—can convince everyone of the grandiosity of the particular *mode* of management implied in their apparatuses of measurement and organisation. Note, incidentally, that it is precisely the perennial possibility of the splitting off and co-optation of immanent, phenomenological life by a would-be manager and his metrics that causes others like Roberto Esposito to resist the immanent politics of phenomenological bodies. Speaking of Hardt and Negri through Foucault, Esposito writes of the latter:

> It is as if Foucault himself wasn't completely satisfied by his own historical-conceptual reconstruction or that he believed it to be only partial and incapable of exhausting the problem; indeed, it is bound to leave unanswered a decisive question: if life is stronger than the power that besieges it, if its resistance doesn't allow it to bow to the pressure of power, then how do we account for the outcome obtained in modernity of the mass production of death? How do we explain that the culmination of a politics of life generated a lethal power that contradicts the productive impulse?[41]

One might even say, comically, that this is the contemporary quest to understand the original sin which seems to stick to modern immanence, a catastrophe at the heart of immanence which is all the more difficult to grasp now that stably transcendent political structures (i.e., transcendent power relations) seem to have lost their capacity to afford us any sense of their legitimacy. Indeed, the driving question of Esposito's efforts to articulate the odd sticking to life of a dangerously supplementary realm of threat and sacrifice is framed by Esposito as a Pauline question about how law, ironically, *produces its own transgression*, how juridical norms lead to death. It is therefore with an avowed Pauline inflection that he continues his reflections on Foucauldian immanence: "This is the paradox, the impassable stumbling block that not only twentieth-century totalitarianism, but also nuclear power asks philosophy with regard to a resolutely affirmative declension of biopolitcs. How is it possible that a power of life is exercised against life itself?"[42] Esposito is clearly correct that the strictures—and even sacrifices—inherent in the productive management of, always, some specific version of life are not simply "two parallel processes or two simultaneous processes."[43] The insight is crucial not only for his criticisms of Hardt and Negri, but also for his conjuration of Paulinism. Elsewhere, for example, Esposito reads the Pauline "problem of law" in terms of the old *katechon* myths, concluding that it is with this aporetic problem of law which is significant to note:

> Whence its constitutive antinomy, binding it to that which it opposes, and opposing that to which it binds. The *katechon*, one might say, more than simply deferring *anomie*, is what keeps enchained its two possible expressions: one that translates the meaning of law into work, and the other that frees it from the compulsion to work. . . . Superimposing satanic *anomia* onto messianic *anomia*, making the one the exact double of the other, the *katechon* subjects the community to the power of a law that simultaneously reproduces and enslaves it.[44]

The political problematic of agency and liberation within Foucauldian immanence return full blown as a rumination on Paulinist paradoxes, perverse inversions of value, and the hollowing out of power for the sake of rogue agencies. Such is our moment.

PAUL WITH BAUDRILLARD AND JOB

The problem of the horror of life turning against itself in order to secure itself is, of course, not missed by Hardt and Negri. Nor do they miss the odd significance of ancient Paulinism as a comparative touchstone in relation to which to process these issues. One should not miss, for example, the way Negri's own ontological explorations of the biblical book of Job (*The Labour of Job*), begun in an Italian prison, were borne of a "question of how to develop an adequate understanding of repression so as to resist

it and to find a way to interpret political defeat as a critique of Power."[45]
The reading is integrally related to Negri's understanding of the age of
biopower, as Job presents us (Negri argues) with a negotiation of unjust
power relations precisely *after* all hope of any justificatory ground *outside*
this oppressive, invasive relation—any stable "measure"—begins to seem
impossible. Negri reads Job's situation as does the divine voice (or the narrator) at the end of the biblical book, both claiming that the efforts of Job's
counselors to justify the patriarch's suffering in terms of some calculation of cause and effect were for nothing.[46] Job's refusal of the calculable
justice of the would-be counselors, in fact, coincides with Negri's own
break with Marxism, a theoretical and practical project grounded in "a
culture of measure."[47] Without external leverage or measure by which to
distinguish oppressive power from space of resistance (or, incidentally, by
which to discern measured ground by which to *justify* resistance), it is no
wonder that Negri claims it was Job who "led [him] to a close friendship
with Foucault."[48]

Nor should we miss the way the aporiae and deadlocks of power/resis-
tance arrived at here repeat very closely a problem that had been haunting Marxist analysis for some time: the problem in the study of religion
of the explanation of myth.[49] In a way which repeats the basic structures
of Hegel's move beyond Kant that we described previously, the young
Hegelians forced the collapse of standard earlier explanations of religion
as useful ideology manufactured by ruling classes in order to dupe the
masses.[50] Just as in representational cognition, so with belief: stable representational and proprietary economies are displaced into productive
events, acts of organization, the open-ended agonism and performative
indeterminacy of which is unavoidable.

In this respect, the criticisms of Foucauldian notions of power by Jean
Baudrillard seem to press on an open door in the sense that they repeat,
rather than contravene, Foucault's work. Playing on the same young Hegelian move toward immanence without stable transcendental coordinates,
Baudrillard writes—with a dismissiveness that seems to me more self-
serving than illuminating—that Foucault "substitutes a negative, reactive,
and transcendental conception of power which is founded on interdiction
and law for a positive, active, and immanent conception, and that is in fact
essential."[51] In this immanence, Baudrillard continues, there comes to exist
a profound ambiguity, therefore, between "desire" and "power."[52] Exactly.
And while Baudrillard urges us to "forget Foucault," his criticisms seem
rather an important supplement to a (Foucauldian) genealogy of power

which Baudrillard assumes as well but tends to articulate in slightly different modes. Baudrillard's supplement concerns the question of resistance to an ontology of cultural process in which nothing can escape relational emergence, therefore calling into question the significance, or possibility, of resistance or the constitution of an outside of power. Significantly in relation to our articulation of Paul, Baudrillard opposes an economy of "seduction" to those ontologies of production and force that he senses are finding a peculiar apotheosis in the work of both Deleuze and Foucault. Against these ontologies, seduction "withdraws something from the visible order and so runs counter to production, whose project is to set everything up in clear view, whether it be an object, a number, or a concept."[53]

Baudrillard's thinking about seduction has not yet been brought into discussions of Pauline notions of kenosis (cf. Breton) or the twinned emptying of divine and imperial power, not to mention the way Paul, Bartleby-like, suggests that believers prefer to live "as if" worldly structures were "not" (cf. Phil 2, 1 Corinthians 7, 15). But the link needs to be processed. Just for a start, for example, and in a way that aligns Baudrillard with Stanislas Breton's meditations on the cross and the nonpower of the neuter, the kenotic exodus from being, and the void at the heart of determinate existence, Baudrillard's criticism of Foucault remains obsessed with a strangely *auratic* or spectacular forcefulness of, precisely, a *withdrawal* from the space of organized contestation, a withdrawal from that position within a contest which would constitute force, power, or the political in the first place. Foucault—and indeed a long history of materialist political critique—have not yet thought radically enough about how to escape (rather than to reformulate) the problem of power, thinks Baudrillard:

All forms of power have endeavoured to camoflauge this fundamental challenge in the form of force relations such as dominator/dominated and exploiter/exploited, thereby channelling all resistance into a frontal relation (even reduced to microstrategies, this conception still dominates in Foucault: the puzzle of guerrilla warfare has simply been substituted for the chessboard of classical battle). For in terms of force relations, power always wins, even if it changes hands as revolutions come and go.[54]

In his repetition of traditional oppositions even at the moment of their radical reformulation, Baudrillard finds missing (in the very positivity of Foucauldian power) a lack that solicits a more profound "*exorcism*" (his terminology) of power than is possible in the old master-slave language of power and resistance.[55] As we will see shortly, Deleuze's reflections on the potential subversion inherent in radical passivity explores the same philosophico-political terrain. And in the next chapter we see Lacan and Pasolini unearthing the same nonpower within power relations constituting the (merely) auratic or spectacular power of a consumerist economy. For the moment we note that Baudrillard's criticisms echo Walter Benjamin's formulations of a *pure* or sacred revolutionary violence (as opposed to calculated or instrumental violence) that, in turn, is comparable to the reading of Paulinism by Giorgio Agamben. Baudrillard writes, for example: "But the turnaround Foucault manages from power's repressive centrality to its shifting positivity is only a peripateia. We stay effectively within political discourse—"we never get out of it," says Foucault— although we need precisely to grasp the radical lack of definition in the notion of the political, its lack of existence, its simulation, and what from that point on sends the mirror of the void back to power. In effect, *we need a symbolic violence more powerful than any political violence*" (my emphasis).[56] "Consider yourselves dead . . . but alive" as Paul would have said to the partisans of a messiah already effectively repressed by Roman authority. Or, in an echo perhaps even more striking: "You have died (with the failed messiah). Why then do you submit any longer?" Indeed, alongside Breton we should read Paul and Baudrillard as alike deploying perverse (almost non-) strategies for a reflecting back to power, as in a mirror, a void. This interest in a kind of opening onto a new economy afforded by *inoperativity* or a void *within* effective economic relations seems, on my reading, to be a useful point of comparison inasmuch as *all* of these thinkers share with the ancient Stoics a fascination with a peripatetic "turn" *within* a plane of immanence, a turning around which itself threatens the very hinge along which domination and submission remain operable. In this respect, Paul is not only comparable to Baudrillard but also to Gilles Deleuze. Deleuze tended always to imagine Paul in a clichéd Nietzschean mode, but what he says of the inversion of power in Sacher-Masoch is perfectly apropos of the Pauline statements we have noted:[57] "In Lacan's words, the law is the same as repressed desire. The law cannot specify its object without self-contradiction, nor can it define itself with reference to a content without removing the repression on which it rests. The object of law and the object of desire are one and the same, and remain equally concealed."[58] We should pause over the words, taking a moment to think them through, indeed, with a new genealogical constellation.

IMMANENCE; OR, PAUL AMONG STOICS
AND OTHER PERVERTS

Then comes the end, when he hands over the kingdom to God the
father, after he has *destroyed every ruler and every authority and power.*
For he must reign until he has put all his enemies under his feet. The
last enemy to be destroyed is death. . . . When all things are subjected to
him, then the Son himself will also be subjected to the one who put all
things in subjection under him, so that God *may be all in all.*

—Paul against the Platonic dualists of Corinth
(cf. 1 Corinthians 15:24–28)[59]

Stoic: Your understanding of the matter is correct. You see, I do not
accept payment on my own account, but for the sake of the giv-
er himself: for since there are two classes of men, the disbursive
and the receptive, I train myself to be receptive and my pupil to be
disbursive!

Buyer: On the contrary, the young man ought to be receptive and you,
who "alone are rich," disbursive!

Stoic: You are joking, man! Look out that I don't shoot you with my inde-
monstrable syllogism!

—Lucian, *Philosophies for Sale*

While there is a great deal of talk these days about the surprising, even
"messianic," relevance of some Pauline texts for a thinking of power within late capitalist culture, it needs to be added that it is precisely a kind
of Stoic element within Paul tha tends to generate his contemporane-
ity for us. Above all, it was a fascination with philosophical immanence
which, for the Stoics, provided the subversive hinge for all of their value-
inverting games of paradox, a subversion whose comedic and deflationary
aspects the brilliant Lucian never seems to miss. Note, for example, the
way that, in *Coldness and Cruelty*, Gilles Deleuze engages in philosophical
reflection on sadism and masochism as two different modes of subverting
effective power or what he calls, significantly (and as did Foucault), law.
There Deleuze writes about the way a transition from one form of law to
another, or from one form of political constitution to another, seems premised on a "divine interval" which is itself extralegal. As he suggests, this

"vanishing instant" testifies to its "fundamental difference from all forms of law."[60] What is remarkable about Deleuze's engagement is that he reads *both* sadism and masochism as *modes of unhinging* law, modes of discerning within it a vanished moment of nonlaw within law or a moment of unpower (as he described it elsewhere) within power.[61] This discernment, moreover, operates only as a kind of inspiriting *participation* in this secret non-force within force, an odd "bubble" (to evoke Peter Sloterdijk once more) which subtracts itself from the very economy within which it first emerged.

Again, for my purposes, it is important to say that Deleuze's reflection on Sade and Masoch is premised on a thinking of immanence, and it is precisely the *immanence* of the aporetic life of law which opens law to its own subversion. In Deleuze's interest in the simultaneous or egalitarian emergence of *both* proscription *and* proscribed, we encounter a dynamic comparable to Heidegger's refusal of a transcendent metaphysical Frame, which leads Heidegger, significantly, to a thinking of being in which forgetfulness and veiling become *constitutive* of being itself. A comparison between Deleuze and Heidegger is here important to note in relation to the fact that often notions of the critique of totalized systems from "postmodern" philosophies of difference tend to focus on what is *lacking* from the whole. In both these philosophical instances, however, we could just as well say that the *lack* (of framing, justifying, or stabilizing totality) emerges as if directly from an *excess* of information, an excess of information that unhinges the earlier workings of the system itself (whether Heidegger's metaphysics or Deleuze's economy of law). Consider that in the case of Deleuze it is as if *law* can no longer bear the too-present actors who constitute the drama on its stage of legal operations. The pervert, so to speak, whether sadist or masochist, finds rather *too much* on hand, a kind of excess in relation to the workable economy of law or norm. She finds, as it were, that her place on the stage of normativity is operable only because of a larger machinery of staging (of movements, of sets, of words and gestures) which exceeds her but with which she could identify with a gesture which dramatically transforms the drama in question. Note Deleuze's specific and very Pauline example here: feeling the whip intended to suppress his unlawful or inappropriate sexual desire, the masochist finds that the very thing intended to prohibit desire has given him an erection.[62] The erect member of the smitten masochist is, therefore, an indication of what Deleuze refers to, in another intriguing echo of the Pauline tale, as the "ways of twisting the law by excess of zeal."[63] In an isomorphism we need to understand more and more, the "pervert" has gone mad with a properly Pauline madness, as if knowing that the prohibition is really an invitation to enjoy the very thing proscribed. The slap, the rebuke, even the whip are absorbed into the extraordinarily zealous knowledge of the masochist: that the punishment is itself the means, rather than the obstruction, to the promised land of no-longer-forbidden delight. And with the salvation of the pervert is discovered something of singular importance.

Consider here that we are reading Deleuze, perhaps one of the greatest Stoic physicists in the history of Western philosophy. One does not learn so much of a tactic by which to circumvent or short-circuit law so much as one catches a revelatory, emancipatory glimpse of the *nomos* of an immanent universe. Deleuze is clear: the pervert does not *try* to "overthrow the law" (89). She realizes instead that she is herself a crystallization of that "divine interval" constitutive of, reducible to, law. It is a radical Stoic immanence which throws into comedically, erotically charged clarity the lie of the Aristotelian mean and its measure of masters and slaves. As Deleuze writes, "In every case, law is a mystification; it is not a delegated but a usurped power that depends on the infamous *complicity* of slaves and masters" (86, my emphasis). And to see the staged, performed, enacted complicity of these actors is already to see emerging (to evoke Romans 7 once more) another law at work in our members. It is to realize that one is playing one's part in a larger drama, and all the more so as we do not play these directly or straightforwardly. This, I am suggesting, is the Deleuzean *prokopē*, or progression in thought, those displacingly ascending or expansive modes of identification by which we are led out of our individual bit parts in order to identify, precisely, with the hegemonic totality in which we find our roles. No wonder that, in order to explain the subversive revelation of this Stoic immanence, Deleuze would resort to that trademark topos of Stoic counterculture, the *paradox*: "A close examination of masochistic fantasies or rites reveals that while they bring into play the very strictest application of law, the result in every case is the opposite of what might be expected (thus whipping, far from punishing or preventing an erection, provokes and ensures it). It is a demonstration of the law's absurdity."[64] And with the inversion through immanence of the cause and effect of law or prohibition we return to Heideggerian immanence as well. I am particularly interested in the way Heidegger points out that the collapse of stable metaphysical frames completely ruins mechanized readings of cause and effect, a topic we will explore in our reading of Pasolini and Lacan. In place of this primal scene of linear cause and effect we have the event, the *Ereignis*, in which not just the specifics of cause and effect, but causality as a structure, becomes arrested under the sign of a radical contingency, read as a singularized "repetition" or performative enactment outside of which there is nothing, whether ground or original. Or, once our apostles and perverts have given us a *demonstratio* of "the law's absurdity," we have glimpsed a universe constituted by the joke, a singularly comedic act none of us will escape except, as Deleuze has suggested, by "mystification" or "usurped power."[65]

It is in this precise sense that one might *accept wholeheartedly the critique* of Foucault as a Spinozist "quietist," precisely the charge laid against him by Edward Said and—often without the specific reference to Spinoza—many others. As Said put it in *The World, the Text, and the Critic*:

> Foucault's theory of power is a Spinozist conception, which has captivated not only Foucault himself but many of his readers who wish to go beyond Left optimism and Right pessimism so as to justify political quietism with sophisticated intellectualism, at the same time wishing to appear realistic, in touch with the world of power and reality, as well as historical antiformalistic in their bias. The trouble is that Foucault's theory has drawn a circle around itself, constituting a unique territory in which Foucault has imprisoned himself and others with him.[66]

How interesting that Spinoza claimed that no one philosophized so like himself as the apostle Paul![67] What Said's criticism of Foucault fails to think are the paradoxical and often bizarre ways in which *inversion is internal* to the force of cultural expression as such.

Nor should we miss the way it is precisely a kind of intensified Stoic immanence which becomes the premise for the Deleuzean politics of inversion, not by the "step outside" of immanence (nor still some vitalistic essentialism of "life") but rather by way of surprising "foldings" of it and within it. And once we move beyond Nietzsche's effort to see Paul as always believing in or peddling the big Other of a metaphysical or ultimately conciliatory frame, we can immediately recognize important moves of a kind of Paulinist baroque radicalism. Against Said, the answer to the "problem" of political contestation tends to be read in Deleuze as the "demand" to invert the inside into the outside, to create ways to show "emergence" or to show how a new "exterior" space can unexpectedly become a temporary and processual subject-ground. Thus not at all far in important respects from the "aleatory materialism" of Althusser, such processes become the Deleuzean "event" whereby a new political subject emerges from the flux for a period of life indistinguishable from its affirmation of a kairotic chance.[68] In short, what is being explored by Foucault and Paul alike is what is being said by Deleuze: "resistance" must free itself from dialectical oppositions that work out into repetitions of the same types of scenario, the same hierarchies of power. For all these thinkers, forget oppositional politics: we must have—to repeat this chapter's initial gloss on a Pauline text—a politics of new creation. Or, differently, there is no real freedom in "opposition," but only in new creation, a politics (if we should still call it that) of a "self" (if we should still refer to this term) emerging at once as both a radical passivity and a surprising involution of the effective powers through which it emerged in the first place. As we might say, "Consider yourselves dead . . . but alive."

This, incidentally, is a Paulinism beyond Nietzsche, indeed a materialism for the masses. At one level, such maneuvers, conjurations, or proclamations will afford only a series of minor transformations of life under empire, life in its immanent technological manufacture, but these minor transformations can in turn constitute an assemblage of minimal differences in which we may yet sense the emergence of a remarkable difference, even a difference that makes all the difference. Immanence does not yield stuckness, except on a superficial level. Rather, it yields the capacity for remarkable "turns" which do not so much overturn power relations as undo them, reconfigure them, and in ways essential for recent cultural theory. At the end of Baudrillard's effort to outbid a Foucauldian biopolitics, for example, it is no wonder that we get a hopeful invocation of a Kafkaesque zombie-Christ, Baudrillard's dead being raised not to hot-blooded life (which would be to repeat the triumphalism of presence and positivity Baudrillard himself diagnoses at the heart of ontologies of production) so much as to a realm of simulation, seduction, and the generation of ungrounded, rogue, or noninstrumental "desire-effects."[69] You have died, Paul might have put it, so why do you submit any longer? In this way Baudrillard's "forgetting" of Foucault—ironically, by pressing Foucault to his (fully acknowledged) paradoxical limits—is extremely close to Breton's reflection on a kenotic, Pauline *logos staurou* or "word" of the cross. It is in this respect that one begins to sense some of the ways in which Baudrillard's critique of the alleged traditionalism of Foucault's articulation of power and resistance are themselves reinforcements of things Foucault had himself said clearly at that point. More importantly, however, in exploring the parrhesiastic and counterintuitive or paradoxical topoi of Stoic immanence, both Baudrillard and Foucault veer much closer to a materialist Paulinism than they ever recognized. In his paean to the Heideggerianism of Blanchot, for example, Foucault plainly stated some of the assertions Baudrillard pretends to use against Foucauldian biopolitics. There the analyst of the micropolitical writes, for example, that one must not think of a dialectical "contradiction" (which would totalize and stifle the play of difference in the oppositional poles) but rather of a "contestation that effaces" the very coordinates of the field in which it emerges.[70] You have died. Why do you submit? Beyond submission, beyond mastery, Paul comes close to Sacher-Masoch and the paradoxical inversions of power in a game of immanence we have yet to process fully.

FROM FOUCAULDIAN RESISTANCE TO PAULINE REVOLUTION: VICISSITUDES OF ANTIMYTHOLOGICAL VIOLENCE

The question of fairness to Foucault aside, we should note here that the reflections of Baudrillard on the zombie-Christ and Negri's reading of Job as a Pauline creation submitted to *mataioti* or "futility" (cf. Romans 8:20, a clear echo of the "futility" of the Septuagintal translation of Ecclesiastes) are very close to Slavoj Žižek's articulation of Paul's "communism."[71] In each case, all are attempting much more than a simple *ethical* reflection about how to think power "otherwise" than as strength and knowledge. Indeed, they are close to Breton's lifelong corpus (up to and including his thinking in *Saint Paul*), which may be read as a metaphysical or (perhaps more accurately, postmetaphysical) *ontological* musing about *how such a revolutionary project might be possible.*[72] To put the question in Baudrillard's terms: what does it look like to think beyond the political, oppositional model of Foucauldian biopolitics and resistance? How would one navigate a space of a postpolitical or even, to echo Benjamin, a properly *sacred* violence?

In this sense, and Baudrillard's caveats about formulation notwithstanding, explorations of Paulinism by Breton and Žižek are never very far from Baudrillard's efforts to think around oppositional, productivist, politics of metaphysical realisms. Nor are they ever very far from reflections of Antonio Negri, who suggests, in his own ontological explorations of the book of Job (*The Labour of Job*), that Paul had in mind *the catastrophe of Job* when Paul wrote that "since, in the wisdom of God, the world did not know God through wisdom, God decided through the stupidity (*mōria*) of our proclamation, to save those who believe" (1 Corinthians 1:21).[73] One can see why Negri would find in Job's reflection on injustice and inexplicable catastrophe a profound link with Paul's message of a failed messianism or a crucified messiah, not to mention why, as a political prisoner himself (and this, importantly, regardless of exactly how one understands his incarceration), Negri was struck by this particular constellation of texts.[74]

How can failed political ventures—or inchoate carceral sufferings—ground a critique of power? More aggressively, how is it that organized power cannot resist, cannot close itself off from, the excluded realm of a failed coup—or from that cost in suffering demanded for the maintenance of power's coherent identity? For Breton, Baudrillard, and Negri alike, the Paulinist question is not merely ethical but also ontological: can one *think* an executed messiah, and this as a peculiar form of cultural critique? Or, do executed messiahs themselves afford the space and time of cultural transformation? The problem is not only a Pauline problem, as if buried away in the past, or as if not a question we may yet be compelled to repeat.

Generalizing or formalizing the particular catastrophe at the core of Paul's intervention, Žižek compares this aspect of the crucified within Paulinism to the "necessity of a dead bird" in Christopher Nolan's film *The Prestige*. The scandal of the crucified in Paul finds itself in conversation with the ineluctable material remainder or stupidly obtrusive passion that Žižek finds also as a constitutive element in materialist philosophies, where all the self-enclosed idealisms and autotelic grounds of the philosophical reflection find themselves thrown off the rails by way of "material" obstructions. Traumatic, uncanny, and disruptive, this "zero level" of identification Žižek universalizes until it becomes genuinely common or even communistic.

In other words, in an intriguing repetition of the Pauline moment, here the *dispossession* named in the executed messiah thus becomes communal property and a new source of political critique or, perhaps said better via Baudrillard, a transformation of the regnant political *seduction*. In presenting, even identifying with, the necessary "dead bird" (Žižek) of power's self-performance as a mode of political "glory" (Agamben), one tells the secret of power precisely by performing it so profoundly that the specific elements of theatricality and (necessary) performance appear directly. The masochistic submission of Paul to power implied by his intention "to know only Christ, and this [Christ] *as crucified*" (cf. 1 Corinthians 1:2), gives rise not just to one zombie-Christ (as in Baudrillard) so much as multiple communities of the undead "body of Christ," each of them experimenting, in their communal organization, their concepts of power, and the sexual/familial practices, with singularly inventive new modes of having "died with Christ" so that a new mode of "life" could slip through the cracks in the very split between the colonial Roman and colonized Jewish communities. Where there was once a squaring off of power and resistance, now there was what Larry Welborn describes as a Pauline "theater of fools" in which an army of singular zombie-Christs are walking around, as if not capable of judging properly whether they are either dead or alive.[75] Cicero (as we have seen) would have blanched.

Such dynamics may be usefully compared to what Michael Taussig explores in a different context as the enactment of "defacement" as a "labor of the negative" within which there emerges, precisely, "an orgy of disproportion" which may yet reconfigure the everyday appearance of things.[76] Paul—himself fetishizing, wearing as a mask, or otherwise memorializing and enacting what otherwise would have been simply another Roman execution of a would-be messianic leader—is not far from Taussig's explorations of the moment when (as Paul would have put it) *ta mē onta*, things that "are not" appear in order to "destroy" the "things that are" (1 Corinthians 1:28). Perhaps just there is the link between Paulinism, ontology, and the political, linked in the image of an implicit threat, even if always "weak" and "stupid" (cf. *to mōron, to asthenēs* at 1:26), that the so-called Christ-ians—now identifying as "crucified" with Christ and thus "dead" to ready-made or worldly interpellations (cf. Galatians 2:20)—may perform or masquerade an excess for which the summary putting away of Jesus could not have taken account.[77] Perhaps this larger drama itself is what Paul was talking about when he wrote that "if the *archai* [rulers] had known what they were doing [in excluding or rendering inoperable the theologico-political hopes appended to Jesus], they would not have killed him"! (cf. 1 Corinthians 2:8). In any case, one of the tasks presented by these philosophico-Paulinist constellations is to uncover the way radical dispossession irrupts in the contestation of existing, world-constituting logics, allowing for the emergence of a different political masquerade oriented around the formerly uncountable, zero-level status of the excluded.[78] And whether we are describing a contemporary biopolitical immanence or an ancient resurrection movement, what we are talking about is the performance of masks, personae, and "glories" with no ground outside their theatrical enactment. As remarked in an earlier chapter, we could thus render Paul's famous statement to the Corinthians in this way: "We testify to messiah executed, which is only scandal and stupidity except for those interpellated by this testimony. Those so interpellated should look at their emergence as things which do not exist now assembling together for the destruction of what is."[79]

PERFORMING, FOLDING THE EMPTYING OF POWER

Or, as Judith Butler writes, Foucault's subject of power is a body "for which materialization [as a substratum, as a body] and investiture [by power] are coextensive."[80] Such is Butler's mode of framing the way that, in Foucault, we are trying to think an economy of relations in which there is no neutral "outside" onto which "power" would inscribe itself, if "power" begins to function as the level of ontology itself. The question, then, is straightforward, and Butler's *Psychic Life of Power* grapples with it consistently: "Where does resistance to or in disciplinary formation take place?"[81] Or, in a more dialectical mode, if the interiority of the modern subject is intimately related, indeed an effect, of an exterior realm of techniques, tactics, and disciplinary apparatuses, "how are we to understand 'interiority' in Foucault?"[82]

As it must, given Foucault's story, Butler's reading becomes oriented around questions of the "self-subversion" of power and sites of "resistance" that *are not* themselves power, moments of power's "failure" to interpellate subjects into its machinations.[83] Or, to spin the questions as an echo of Paulinism, Butler's reading becomes (necessarily) oriented around questions of tragic self-subversion or self-emptying, the (im)potential for weakness to affect or become a sort of power, and the capacity for such moments of inversion or short-circuit to hollow out within power relations a self-enclosed or invaginated space of communal subjectivity.

It is on these points, we might add, that Butler's reading of Foucault and subjectivating techniques becomes very similar to philosophical receptions of Paul by Giorgio Agamben or (for that matter) Stanislas Breton. In both philosophers, Paul's writings are of acute interest precisely because of the way they stage a community-founding identification with an event of crucifixion (and therefore effective suppression) of a messianic figure *as* something that subverts power. It is useful to play on language of "event" here, as Badiou's Paul stands in stark contrast at just this point. For Badiou, the event is, rather, resurrection, a difference in interpretive focus that is mirrored, for example, in the way Badiou sometimes chides Simon Critchley's story about *negativity* as a source or ground of new forms of political subjectivity. As Critchley introduces his political intervention, "Philosophy does not begin in an experience of wonder, as ancient tradition contends, but rather, I think, with the indeterminate but palpable sense that something desired has not been fulfilled, that a fantastic effort has failed."[84] Indeed, Critchley explores the impetus for philosophy against the backdrop of a nihilating force that threatens to annihilate the highest values, thus gutting our motivations for community action. It is precisely at this point—the emptied (or "kenotic") and ultimately gutted deity of, say, Philippians 2—that Paulinism returns as a significant interlocutor for Critchley's project, precisely inasmuch as this return does *not* seem simply to repeat, say, the oppositions between meaning/non-sense, God/death-of-God, motivation/passive nihilism that tend to be assumed when Critchley names his project as a "secular" one. Indeed, if Paul now returns as this uncanniest of guests, a figure of a new materialism, he does so because he found himself scheming community formation and resistance at the moment of messianic failure, and this with no real guarantee of persuasive or social success. No wonder Paul made a great deal out of "proclamation" and the centrality of "trust"—obviously he had no other leg to stand on than such ephemera, if something like "life" and "freedom" (as he liked to say) were to be ripped out of a messianic corpse or if the brutal reduction of a messianic movement to the "slave's death" of Philippians 2 was, impossibly, to be resisted. No wonder Paul seems to feel, at the moment of finding in this community's identification with the "slave's death" a glimmer of a threat against the crucifying *archai* or rulers, simultaneously a sense that the entire movement is a kind of cosmic joke, all the more laughable for its weakness and exposure to extinction (cf. 1 Corinthians 1, 4:8–13). Here Critchley's sense of the tragicomic is perhaps a useful way back into the Pauline tableau. The Paulinists' disavowal of death's power, their allowing Jesus's death to be "for" them (thus acting as if they were beyond death's "dominion") nevertheless *remains* a merely virtual community of people identifying with that death and the undeadness they discover in it without a real sublation or overcoming of the originary trauma. The movement generally remains, in Paul (though not much longer), a "scandal" and a spectacular joke, as Paul sometimes acknowledged (cf. 1 Corinthians 1:23, 4:9f.).

In each instance, Paul's writings are worth thinking about inasmuch as they imagine this moment as one in which "nothings and non-beings" (cf. *ta mē onta,*) miraculously emerge to "annihilate" the categories and self-understanding of the ready-made world in what we might call (in one of those beautiful Britishisms) a peculiar kind of piss-take (1 Corinthians 1:28). We discussed earlier the way Breton follows Rudolf Bultmann in important respects to find in Paul an example of "heroic meontology" (or heroic theory of nonbeing), a project that fits well with Butler's interest in a mute, weak resistance (and therefore a *form* of power) that nonetheless *is not* in itself a power capable of "dismantling the [interpellative] injunction or changing the terms of subject constitution."[85] Butler wants to think, with Foucault, not the liberation of a "hidden or repressed" subject existing "outside" the "law" of power, but rather the capacity (of what? from where?) for "a refusal" of subject formations that cannot contest the dominant forms of social discipline that they only seem *not* to mirror.[86] How to think, as Timothy Mitchell describes in a different but significantly related field, the emergence of a "virtue of recalcitrance"?[87]

The point should be clear by now, and Butler's slippage in vocabulary between "power" and "law" (of subjectivation) may mark the occasion to push our conversation more decidedly in a Pauline direction, if only to prepare the way for that revelation of a Paulinist "scandal," the significance of which means a great deal for the projects both of Foucault and Pasolini. *How are we able to think, to be, transgression, sin, crime, once power becomes identified with normalizing bios, with life itself?* How are we able to think, or to act, as a transgressive force once power becomes another name for being itself? How are we able to articulate an effect of transgression *on* law that originates not from outside law but rather from law itself? How does "law" (of life, of being)—to repeat Paul's intriguing statements in Romans 7 or Galatians—*produce its own transgression*? (Or, in an ontological mode: how do we think prohibiting law and transgressive desire *as the same thing*?). As we will see in the next chapter, Pasolini's Paul provides a useful "machine with which to think" (as Deleuze used to say of the great books of philosophical history) in relation to these pressing Foucauldian problems.

Finally, it is worth mentioning that, in another encounter of Paul and the philosophers, Jean-Luc Marion also allowed Paul to function as the "intervention of an instance" in a larger genealogical "outwitting" of Western ontology. Without exploring details, Marion notes correctly that one may discern the "lexicon of the Greek philosophers" in Pauline statements about *ta (mē) onta*, particularly in relation to the question of the one becoming the other (e.g., Romans 4:17; 1 Corinthians 1:28).[88] Like Breton of the "underground current" of a new materialism, Marion suggests that, unlike the discourse of the science of being, here the transition (say, for *ta mē onta* to become *ta onta*, or vice versa) "befalls them from the outside" by way of a call that is a "wholly extrinsic establishment."[89] Despite the fact that his book is an exploration of this divinely interpellating exteriority as "without being," Marion generally seems very anxious to resist a Žižekian, Badiouean, Baudrillardean materialism, though what seems to have been the anxiety on Marion's mind at the time was rather a Derridean form of atheism. As I am saying, however, some of the interpretive moves being performed by Marion are otherwise isomorphic with these stances.[90]

As I have said from the beginning, I am not really interested in aged or prefabricated territorial disputes between theology and philosophy, God and materialism, or the community of the crucified and philosophical accounts of political agency, but rather in the question of contemporary biopolitical spaces. In that sense, how *does* the discourse of the partisan of the crucified cut across a discourse of being? How, in that light, would one understand Jon Sobrino's echoes of 1 Corinthians 1:28 in his articulation of the various ways in which the poor of Latin America "are not"? This constellation of identities leads Sobrino to consider what might happen if the poor name this non-being as the communal space of "the crucified." With such a performative identification, Sobrino believes, the group will emerge into its place within a larger "copro-historical" genealogy that, he hopes, may yet transform the consumerist commitments of the first world and, importantly, "de-ideologize human rights" talk, once these commitments, and this ideology, likewise realize that nothing has become something, *the* indication of an epochal transformative moment.[91] Despite initial appearances, then, a formulation like Sobrino's is close to Baudrillard's reflection on those history-defining moments in which factions took up a place of what Paul called *ta mē onta* or what Baudrillard calls the place of the nothing. As Baudrillard writes:

> Let us consider now the *real* history of class struggle whose only moments were those when the dominated class fought on the basis of its self-denial "as such," on the basis of the sole fact that it amounted to nothing. . . . When the class itself, or a fraction of it, prefers to act as a radical non-class, or as the lack of existence of a class, i.e., to act out its own death right away within the explosive structure of capital, when it chooses to implode suddenly instead of seeking political expansion and class hegemony, then the result is June '48, the Commune, or May '68. The secret of the void lies here, in the incalculable force of the implosion (contrary to our imaginary

concept of revolutionary explosion)—think of the Latin Quarter on the afternoon of May 3.[92]

LATIN QUARTER '68, JEWISH QUARTER 44: DISPLACED NETWORKS OF ANTIMYTHICAL VIOLENCE[93]

Indeed, think, too, of the Jewish quarter in the Roman colony of Corinth in 44 when a wandering vagabond of a crucified messiah organized a cell of little "crucifieds," parodically taking the sting out of the effective imperial forcefulness that counted Jesus as one of the serial repressions constitutive of the maintenance of empire. The violence of this gesture Paul registered at the level of variations of the same identitarian predilection to extrapolate signs of cosmic or divine beneficence in the effective history of the world: "to the Jews, foolishness, to the Greeks, stupidity." But the violence of an identification with a serially repressed messianic figure was also registered at the level of a faint hope that this *form* of identification with the crucified might be part of a heterotopian "rule" in which "all authority" might itself be emptied (cf. 1 Corinthians 15:24–5). Among other things, to remember the Jewish quarter of 44 alongside the Latin quarter of '68 is to recognize that Baudrillard, too, places his hope in the zombie-Christ, brought back from the dead in ungrounded desire-effects that do not try to found a new form of power so much as to find precisely in power's ungrounding and emptying a paradoxical form of emancipation.

I want to add one final figure to this little *testimonia* collection of isomorphic immanence and Paulinism. Here one needs to mention the way John Riches, in his excellent commentary, *Galatians Through the Centuries*, points out that the philosophical master of the Kyoto school, Keiji Nishitani, discovered in Galatians 2:20 ("it is no longer I who live, but Christ lives in me") potentially a significant indication of the West's misrecognition of itself and its alleged philosophical commitment to the concrete individual self. Against the usual either/or of these cross-cultural encounters (all tricked out with an allegedly Western self versus Buddhist nonself), Nishitani began to ask Christian philosophers and theologians: "Who speaks these words, actually? Paul? Or another?"[94] The Paulinist koan, as it were, invites an experience of the self that is deferred, mirrored, and decidedly nonpresent, an indication of what Nishida described as "immanent transcendence" and, indeed, an indication of an "I" that is itself "'a creative event out of nothingness.'"[95] As Ueda Shizuturu describes, the effort to think the "I am" as a form of groundlessness, and this ground-lessness as the origin of life *ex nihilo*, constituted an important moment in Nishitani's efforts to overcome (Western) nihilism by way of a kind of intensification or radicalizing of nihilism to the point that it negates itself (in Shizuturu's words, "to overcome nihilism through nihilism"). It is *as a figure of such an enterprise* that Paul emerges here as a significant link in an aggressively globalizing "Western" constellation that Nishitani want-ed to analyze (as both poison and cure) by way of the juxtaposition (and assertion of profound identity) between Nishitani's two Christian think-ers, Meister Eckhart and Friedrich Nietzsche. Interestingly in light of Albert Schweitzer's suggestion, mentioned already, that Nietzsche "could have been Paul," here the identifying link between Eckhart's passive affir-mation of life "without a why" and Nietzsche's active nihilation of modern, Christian values is precisely the Paulinist identification with the crucified, through whom "I" have become crucified to the world and it to me (cf. Galatians 2:20). Indeed, Shizuturu explains how Nishitani's exploration of a Paulinist link between Eckhart and Nietzsche fits his articulation of an ontology in which there is *neither the divine nor the human*. In Nishitani's making a koan out of a Pauline theologoumena, we discover a project not unlike Eric Santner's discoveries in Paul of a figure of the "undead," that life which is neither merely creaturely nor merely divine, but some point of indistinction between the two.[96] By the same token, Nishitani's Paul is here very close to Giorgio Agamben's notions of both Paul and politics, namely, that they circulate around the "empty throne" of power, the center of power as, precisely, a void in quest of a spectacular proxy.

5

SEIZURES OF CHANCE

Paulinist Agencies in Neocapitalist Contexts

Tell me, those wanting to be submitted to law [*hoi hūpo nomon thelontes einai*], do you not listen to the law?

—Galatians 4:21

In Lacan's words, the law is the same as repressed desire. The law cannot specify its object without self-contradiction, nor can it define itself with reference to a content without removing the repression on which it rests. The object of law and the object of desire are one and the same, and remain equally concealed.

The fact that anarchy can only exist in the interval between two regimes based on laws, abolishing the old to give birth to the new, does not prevent this divine interval, this vanishing instant, from testifying to its fundamental difference from all forms of the law.

—Gilles Deleuze and Leopold von Sacher-Masoch, *Masochism*

IN MANY WAYS AND NECESSARILY TO MULTIPLE ENDS, IT IS THE moment to seize upon an opportunity to (re)stage a work that the great Pasolini, by chance, could not himself fund. If so, our own putting into place of imaginary mises-en-scènes for a screenplay Pasolini left behind would immediately set in motion a complex comparative machinery, whirring away to effect an operational wonder about the now-time within which chance occasions and imaginary props afford a chance to bring a screenplay, not to mention an apostle, to life again. In fact, Pasolini wrote in his notes for a screenplay (written in 1966 and again in '68) of a kind of *inevitability* of "transposition," continuously emerging "mutual implications," and a retroactive demand for a new "coherence" over these "series" produced by the very unleashing of "analogy." One senses the rhythm of a repetition already, perhaps, of that ancient literary movement whereby— from Daniel to the popular books of Enoch or the Testament of Abraham—the so-called apocalyptic text was always and necessarily imagined as having been mysteriously "sealed up" for a period of time during which the text (retroactively, to be sure) "waited" for those latter-day events and constellations that would conjure or effect its belated release, break its "seals" as the authors of Daniel or Revelation liked to say.[1]

Pasolini would write in his own *Tristram Shandy* of a novel, *Petrolio*, that the real question both of temporality and of causality is therefore: what codes eventually emerge into operativity making events narratable, temporalized? Among other things, *Petrolio* can be read as a repetition of the quest to approach the codes or *schēmata* of and in the very appearing of narrativity, a quest on which linear temporal flows and coherent narrations of cause and effect often enough flounder or are inverted. Exploring the codes and conducts in question, a sort of editorial narrator intrudes onto a scene wherein *Petrolio*'s Carlo finds himself perusing objects in a used bookstore in Rome, an offscreen narration (as it were) appearing, at the last, to add some additional notes as if for the improvement of a future edition of the account: "Note in pen on a page of the Argonautica (Greek-English): 'Pay no attention! Every great writer writes only to fill the blank page with marks' and in smaller letters: 'Every great writer loves centones [patchworks of authorial scraps] above all. The culture of every great writer is medieval.'"[2]

Such is the necessary scaffolding also for, as it were, our Greek-Italian-English encounter with Pasolini's apostle as well, whether angelic messengers for us unseal a temporality decidedly out of joint, authors and origins slipping into the void of a blank page on which are scribbled medieval centones, or whether we speak not of angels but latter-day technologies of modern literary pastiche and cinematic bricolage. In any case, the effects are the same, these assemblages of agencies, agencies as assemblages, leaving us stranded only ever to wonder about, so to speak, the software programs of culture operating behind our screens. However we situate the screenplay, the audience of Pasolini's plan for a film about Paul encounters a decidedly scrambled temporality and a proliferation of analogical potentials.

Naturally, just like all those apocalyptic authors in this new and old movement of thought, here we too will have necessarily played something like a willing pseudepigraphic role in the restaging of a piece that never really was, our own roles bearing more directly than is usually the case all those structures of an authorial, directorial fiction. We will have written, will have staged *as if*—above all *as if* there were no alternatives to the ironic trickeries and spatiotemporal displacements of identity and its causes which constitute the eventualities of our (inevitably Greek-Italian-English) project. With this evocation of an ancient and returned pseudepigraphic, apocalyptic staging in mind, let's play out the rules of the ancient genre by enacting a temporal collage which itself seems to summon so naturally a host of angelic or virtual testimonies, as if another angelic testimony were for us as well the primary staging device by which any illumination, the very light of *apokalypsis*, might arrive.

RECUPERATING ANGELS

These figures have become exemplary for you, as if written for your rumination, on whom time's ends have come.

—1 Corinthians 10:11

In a rhapsodic retrospective analysis of the rise of biopolitical immanence—which he glosses nicely as an emergence of an economy which calculates on "the soul at work"—Franco "Bifo" Berardi reflects on Italian critical theory in the 1960s and '70's, particularly a moment Berardi associates with 1968 and a realization that "social composition and the formation of revolutionary subjectivity can be explained neither by the idealist hypostasis of a human nature to be realized through historical action nor by the analysis of the implicit contradiction in the structure of productive relations. Neither the presupposition of a humanity needing to be redeemed, nor the analysis of capital are sufficient to understand what happens on the scene of 20th-century history, on the stage of working class struggles and of capital's restructuring."[3] The formulation is part of Berardi's compelling retrospective rumination on the emergence of economies which seemed, increasingly, already to have co-opted or to have functionally incorporated some of the collective identities or cultural logics which, prior to this point, had seemed to afford a relatively stable ground outside these economies or (which comes down to the same thing) a relatively fixed end toward which these economies tended.[4] In this respect, Berardi proclaims the slow fading into oblivion or communal obsolescence of two sites from which to imagine the launch of emancipatory cultural critique. When a "presupposition of a humanity needing to be redeemed" and, indeed, the struggle for recognition *within* a pan-logicism of market calculation begin to appear as beliefs or operations whose time has past, a belief in a new epoch of power relations announces its arrival, one that signals in turn the necessity for new exemplars of transformation, resistance, and solidarity. In ways at least comparable to the diverse work of Mario Tronti, Antonio Negri, Paolo Virno, Giorgio Agamben, Roberto Esposito, and Michael Hardt, here Berardi's retrospective also gambles on the possibility that the newly invasive or relatively more totalizing and immanent mode of economic calculations will yield new forms of significance for productive bodies imagined as singularities.[5] Herald of new forms of life, Berardi's analysis calls for a rethinking of soulish passion or singularity, a topos which comes to appear in this economy as neither a human factor to be imagined in an external relation to the power of capital nor as a self-enclosed identity in the name of which one could suspend the permanent revolution of capitalism for the sake of stable recognitions and proprietary limits therein.

Berardi's retrospective bidding adieu to earlier modes of critical theory is an important interpretive messenger, so to speak, for our figuration of Pasolini's screenplay about Paul, on which Pasolini worked between 1968 and 1974. After all, Pasolini's piece is, from start to finish and from draft to draft, plagued by the question of desiring production, particularly as it constitutes constellations of desire, freedom, and the frames or regulating institutions whereby desire intersects with forms of speech and recognition. In this respect, the *apokalypseis* or revelations of Pasolini's Paul are integrally tied to Pasolini's brilliantly anachronistic placement of the apostle between fascist power of the late 1930s and what Pasolini often described as an epoch of permissive power or repressive tolerance emerging in the late 1960s. Situating the apostle of a law-free evangel of liberty between epochs of fascism and consumerism itself demands further reflection on that political question which spurs important interventions throughout Pasolini's writings (e.g., *Lutheran Letters*, *Heretical Empiricism*) and his films (e.g., *Love Meetings*, *Salò*), namely, does the transition from a repressive oedipal economy to an economy of relations named by the consumerist incitement to desire and enjoyment actually accomplish, socially speaking, a political form of control that a repressive fascism itself could never accomplish?[6]

Echoing Berardi's analysis, for the Pasolini of the late sixties and early seventies, it was as if crucial sites of ostensibly transgressive desire had themselves been installed as integral mechanisms in a feedback loop constituting a much more invasive and effective economy of control and, as Pasolini liked to say, normalization. In a prescient wonder comparable to those which drove Michael Foucault's early work on the history of sexuality or Jean Baudrillard's early diagnoses of the consumerism of mass media's sexual imaginary, Pasolini famously noted his own anxieties in the shifting cinematic significance of the represented sexual body. Evoking a recurrent phallic terminology in his work ("Tetis"), he writes: "Even though, in *The Arabian Nights*, and also in the next film [*Salò*] which will have 'ideology' as its explicit theme, I will continue to represent *even* physical reality and its blazon, Tetis, I *regret* the liberalizing influence that my films have contributed, in practice, to a *false* liberalization, actually desired by the new reformist and permissive power, which is also the most fascist power in history."[7] Foreshadowing Berardi's anxieties about the incorporation of resistance and earlier struggles for recognition into the rhythms and algorithms of capitalism, Pasolini goes on to describe uncertainties about whether, with "the last years of the sixties" the political gamble on "the body" as "the only preserved reality" in relation to capitalist normalization or governmentality itself was not giving way to a suspicion that the erotic body was caught up in a machinery of normalization feeding directly into the ritual maintenance of new identities even better adapted to a "neocapitalist" or consumerist economy (246).

As if by some impishly perverse agency, even new thresholds to which Pasolini himself had brought Italian cinema seemed to him to have collapsed into a mere simulacrum of transgressive resistance to normalization. Pasolini here points repeatedly to his successful release of a cinematic image of a "sexual organ in detail and close-up," an evental cinematic threshold which constitutes, by any measure, a new limit of scandalizing representation or at any rate an "enormous cock on the screen" (246, 247). But this transgressive breakthrough in the struggle for the representation of the desiring body had begun to signify for Pasolini only the flame of a potlatch ceremony, precisely the *destruction* of a transformative excess, its *sacrifice* rather than its emancipatory conjuration into presence.

This image is an important one for our constellation of apocalyptic signs and apostolic narrations, one we should keep in mind when we recall Pasolini's Paul stranded, as it were, between '38 and '68. Pasolini is very clear on this point, claiming in his statements about sexual imagery in cinema that, both sexually and politically speaking, the rebels of the latter regime of power are anything but what they appear: "Today, the youth are nothing but monstrous and 'primitive' masks of a new sort of initiation (negative in pretence only) into the consumerist ritual" (246). Indeed, picking up on Pasolini's suggestion that this experience of his own work pushed him toward cinematic presentations of sex with "*'ideology' as its explicit theme*" (my emphasis), it is noteworthy that he foreshadows *Salò* in such a light, namely, as a fascism which is indistinguishable from a brutal command to enjoy. As Andrea Righi remarks on the film as part of his genealogy of biopolitics: "Pasolini's use of sexuality in *Salò* is crucial to understanding the consequences of this false idea of freedom. In consumer society individuals are at the same time victims and victimizers; they take advantage and are simultaneously exploited by a system that is based on an endless cycle of production and consumption."[8] Such certainly seems to have been Pasolini's apocalyptic diagnosis, and it is here, situated by a demand to understand a relatively more seamless economy of production and consumption, that the filmmaker and critical cultural theorist sets to work the conjuration of a return of the Pauline legacy.

In the late sixties and early seventies, these and similar diagnoses of a harrowing transformation of the ontologies of power and resistance began to circulate throughout Europe as if a climate change were beginning to be registered. The sensitive were charting similar alterations in temperature within Paris, for example, and in ways that constitute an intriguing further context within which to articulate the emergence of Pasolini's Paul. It was in his seminar of 1969–70 that Jacques Lacan began with a rather astonishing statement, one clearly directed against popular understandings of May '68 and its aftermath: "What analysis shows, if it shows anything at all . . . is very precisely the fact that we don't ever transgress. Sneaking around is not transgressing. Seeing a door half-open is not the same as going through it. We shall have the occasion to come back to what I am introducing now—there is no transgression here, but rather an irruption, a falling into a field, of something not unlike *jouissance*—a surplus."[9] This evocation of a discursive world without transgression marks a subtle shift in Lacan's thinking about power, even as it opens a new lecture series which developed some of Lacan's most compelling insights about the castration, lack, or nonexistence of the big Other as the final frame or guarantee for judgements about power relations.

Reconfiguring earlier diagnostics in light of what he often describes as a kind of "experience" of newly emerging cultural logics, it is here on the "other side of psychoanalysis" that Lacan diagnosed an oddly *ambivalent* supplementation of the lost Other, that lost cause in relation to which we might "desire to be submitted" (as Paul says in the initial citation above: 'Tell me, those wanting to be submitted to law, do you not listen to the law?'). Whether or not we would hope to be so submitted in order to ground antagonism and rebellion or obedient compliance would make little difference. In either case, the big Other's nonexistence itself abandons both would-be transgressors and rebellious revolutionaries alike to a difficult necessity of rethinking the very nature of desire in relation to cultural or symbolic authority. The transgressively desiring body, to recall Pasolini, is here in Lacan's analysis no more a "preserved reality" outside the structures of power than it was in the later writings of the filmmaker. In Lacan's discussion of a freedom now difficult to conceptualize or place, we are forced to manage an excessive weight of the immanence of desire in its relation to a merely virtual big Other. We are forced to manage the weight of this relation precisely because we do so without the shelter or justification of a belief that the law, the father, or the repressive regimes of money or power exist, precisely, apart from this ritualized investment in them. In such a scenario it is structurally impossible to distinguish transgressive desire from Pasolini's "'primitive' masks" donned for a ritual through which we would have conjured the presence of the Other in question. Without eliding genuine antagonisms between the different theorists, the same *problem of desire* (which is to say a very similar "problem of the law"), as an awareness of the structural or economic ambiguity of transgression, marks other watershed contributions that emerged at the same moment in the work of Gilles Deleuze and Félix Guattari (*Anti-Oedipus*, 1972), Jean-Francois Lyotard (*Libidinal Economy*, 1974), Jacques Derrida (*Dissemination*, 1972), and Jean Baudrillard (*The Consumer Society*, 1970).[10]

THE ANCIENT PAUL IN AN OPEN ECONOMY
OF SURPLUS VALUES

It is worth reflecting in this respect on the way that the Paulinism of Jacques Lacan, so to speak, has often been associated with his interest, during the earlier 1959–60 seminar, with Paul's text of Romans 7, a form of thinking that has shifted in slight but important ways by the time of his lectures on "the other side of psychoanalysis" ten years later. Recall that in the ancient text of Paul the apostle imagines an economy whereby a perverse mode of power operates behind the back of an otherwise docile or submissive imaginary self, this hidden operation functioning to effect the self's problematic splitting or doubling. While it is not the place fully to explore the implications of this fact, recall as well that it is possible that Paul played out this splitting of the subject in Romans 7 as a repetition of a theatrical tableau of Medea, whose desire to act violently against other impulses within her became a favored touchstone for Hellenistic philosophical diagnoses of the "problem of passion."[11] It is in this mode that Paul writes: "So I find it to be a law that when I want to do what is good, evil lies close at hand. For I delight in the law of God in my inmost self, but I see in my members another law at war with the law of my mind, making me captive to the law of sin that dwells in my members. Abject person that I am! Who will rescue me from this body of death?" (Romans 7:21–24).

A long history of Christian readings of a peculiar passage in Paul's letter to the Romans about law and the production of transgression have oriented themselves by a supersessionist narrative that unhelpfully imagined what were in actuality Paul's partisan Jewish interventions *within* a vibrantly diverse first-century Judaism to constitute (instead) the "Christian" *break* with Judaism. As Paul never called himself a Christian and would have refused the supersessionist implications of such a terminological distinction, neither the terminology nor the teleologies underlying this traditional narrative prove illuminating for contemporary encounters with Paul. Nevertheless, this traditional orientation has often functioned very effectively to exclude all other modes of thinking about ancient or (by analogy) contemporary identity in relation to prohibition, or about the plurality and limits of different legal codes, none of which topics were either far from ancient discourses on *nomos* or irrelevant for latter-day reflections on power.[12]

For our purposes it is useful to allow Romans 7 to operate as a machine with which to think the problem Righi articulates, the idea of an economy of a consumer society whereby the producer/consumer is *simultaneously* victim and victimizer, and this because of a capacity—as the ancient Paul put it—"to seize a chance opportunity" (7:8, cf. *aphormēn de labousa*) to create a surplus desire or excess of relation within the otherwise fixed poles of the juridical scene. As we will see, this comparative constellation articulates an impish mode whereby an open economy of power relations can be formulated as the possibility for any of its moments to be subtracted from the dominant form of structured power, a potential which ends up meaning that the form of power itself *only* emerges retroactively, therefore, in relation to this (open) operation of exceptionality or surplus. Put differently, Paul's quirky articulation of what is often traditionally named the theologico-political "problem of the law" in Romans 7 emerges hand in hand with an epoch in which capitalist power as production of surplus operates at once expansionistically but also eventually as an emergent production of surplus relationalities that deforms earlier models of cause and effect.

In the text of Romans, notice the way in which the dialectical standstill or suspension of agency within the juridical economy does not simply operate in the splitting or doubling of the inner man/wretched man of this scene, fissuring his agency into antagonistic strategists (cf. 7:21–24). Much more striking than this Platonic splitting of agencies, I think, is the way there is here clearly a matching split or duplication of *nomos* as well, as if the agency of *nomos* itself appears as *both* prohibition *and* transgression of the same. In this passage there is apparently hit upon a "law" of law itself, as if having "discovered" a law within law or a code inside of code, a little shadow of law producing its opposite, resistance to it, active rebellion and criminality rather than docile acquiescence to appropriate limitations. "So I find this law: when I want to do the good, evil lies ready to hand. . . . [That is] I see in my members another law (*heteron nomon*) at war with the law of my mind (*nous*)" (cf. 7:21f.). Here the very impasse or obstruction within the otherwise smooth functioning of power in a system of juridical compliance itself comes to name *another nomos*, namely, the *nomos* of the way the arrival of the commandment is always a repetition of the "springing to life again of sin" (cf. 7:9), a return of the repressed which displaces the "I" from itself, effectively "killing" it (cf. 7:10). And this displacement and splitting of the I, we should not miss, emerges from a "chance" that is susceptible of being grasped as a "production" (cf. *kateirgasato* 7:8) of a surplus capable of inverting the value of the intentions of the actor in question. The "problem of law" as the "problem of passion" in Romans 7 returns forcefully at a moment when new types of production of surplus value seem, precisely, susceptible to a value-inverting seizure in an economy that grows by transgressing its own limits.

It is this little shadow of law, this excessive surplus within law, which, in this intriguing passage, effects a doubling and self-suspension of juridical authority as an imagined form of emancipation.[13] Elsewhere in his writings, Paul, playing the role of overheated partisan, seems much more comfortable than he does in Romans 7 with presenting the juridical economy of *nomos* solely as an agency of enslavement or as an apparatus for the production of transgressors. One could certainly wonder on reading his letter to the Galatians whether Paul imagined the juridical economy to found itself *only* by way of the manufacture of criminality as the exception to juridical norms (see, e.g., Galatians 3:10–13, 19, 22f., 4:3, 9). In the later letter to the Romans, however, Paul seems more intent on supplementing the otherwise short-circuited, suspended, or exhausted polarities of agency into which the juridical economy seems to have fallen. Indeed, note just how in the Romans text "sin" is relied upon as a crucial supplementary agent, this "third" agency being imagined as the localizing *cause* of the displacements of activity and passivity within the otherwise short-circuited functioning of juridical economy. In what many commentators over the centuries have even imagined as a kind of response to possible views of Paulinism emerging from the more trenchant earlier letter to the Galatians, Paul presents a virtual conversation with an interlocutor who asks: "So what are we saying, that the law is sin?" to which he responds: No! Rather, it is *sin* which "seizes an opportunity" within *nomos*, this extralegal act of partisanal warfare itself yielding the perversely split (and perhaps Medean) scenario described in the seventh chapter of Romans.

However, despite Paul's efforts to stabilize the otherwise destabilized juridical economy by way of the naming of "sin" as a supplemental agency, the nameable *cause* of disturbance, note that the *function* of the agency of sin within this Pauline tableau is simply the function of the power of exception making through a potentially productive surplus and its appropriation which displaces the status of otherwise-perceived laboring roles. We might read, therefore, "sin" as the retroactive appendage of the "chance opportunity" itself, that agent always already the effect of a more primordial zone from which arises the potential for partisan co-optations, rogue attacks, and potentially revolutionary emancipations alike. Consider that it is no accident that Paul appropriates in this passage the favored lingo of "seizing a chance" from a panoply of Greek texts on military history. Random occurrences, chance encounters, enable the polemically inclined to "seize" or "take" the opportunity afforded by chance, transforming the nature of sovereignty in a kairological moment of opportunity that effects new orders of power. The seizure of chance in these texts constitutes a kind of Schmittian act of appropriation, though one not at all merely at the disposal of regnant powers. On the contrary, regnant power maintains itself by immunizing itself against the arrival of these unformed moments of chance. As the first-century Jewish historian puts it, much more effective than defeating one's political enemies is to immure the current situation of power against the "chance" (*aphormē*) of viable contest in the first place.[14] Paul's exposition of works and the weaponization of surplus against would-be workers here fits such descriptions exactly. Note, for example, that Paul's scene here emerges against the backdrop of a lack of power in law—he names its status as *adunaton*—opening the way to understanding the productive economy of commandment as one constituted through an originary "weakness" or inoperativity within the (active, sovereign) law—(passive, docile) flesh pairing (cf. 8.3, *to gar adunaton tou nomou en hō ēsthenei dia tēs sarkos*).

It is only at first glance, therefore, that Paul's tale seems like it sides with traditional sovereignty, as if bemoaning the weakness of effective order and longing for a moment when the role of *nomos* in a representational economy of commandment could be stabilized. Many commentators, docile sorts themselves perhaps, assume that Paul *merely* laments the deformation of the sovereign command of *nomos* at the hands of the radical partisanship and interventionism of "sin." But this is to miss the implications of the way Paul has here made sin a partisan properly speaking, postrepresentational and insurrectionist, what Paul himself calls (in a line of great interest to Jacques Lacan and George Bataille) sin's manifestation through the (inoperativity or surplus activity of the) commandment to be "sin beyond measure" (*hina genētai kath' huperbolēn hamartōlos hē hamartia dia tēs diathēkēs*).[15] Here, too, we should pay attention to the specific modes in which Paul maps his discussions of sin's partisanship onto the seizure of the chance motif, a motif that was never in the ancient Mediterranean contexts *simply* about the anxiety of the powerful to immunize their situation against it. Seizing the *aphormēn* or chance was also, we should never forget, about the capacity for transformative insurrections, a discourse of partisans without acceptable political representation, none of which was far from the advocate of a brutally murdered messianic figure.

Jacob Taubes earlier intervened in the political history of Pauline reception to develop a genealogical subversion of the dictatorial exceptionalism of Carl Schmitt, Taubes looking to Paulinism for a mode of attending to transformative contingency or the (as if *ex nihilo*) *surprise* and openness of transformative sovereignty, just as Schmitt did. But Paulinism, Taubes argued, enables a way of attending to the same rogue potentials, except that one could think them, he stated famously, "from below" rather than from the position of Schmittian institutions or dicators. In this project

Taubes never picked up on some of the things we are describing here, including the rather astonishingly inverted Schmittianism we might find in Paul's use here of Schmitt's beloved theological term of the *katechon* or "suppressive" capacity of power.[16] At Romans 7:6, for example, it is through the community's adamant identification with the criminalized and effectively suppressed messianic figure that they "have died" to the effective grasp of *nomos* generally. The Paulinist insurgency is described as excepting itself from the juridical economy, the crucified having thus subtracted themselves from the effective force that, he writes, "suppressed them" (*nuni de katērgēthēmen apo tou nomou apothanontes en hō kateichometha*). Far from the suppressive power of rule against chaos, here it is the Paulinists who have, precisely, subtracted themselves from the suppressive power of the legal order.

Far from being a "Christian" break from Judaism, here Paul's rhetoric is in keeping with a rich and diverse tradition of early Jewish partisanship and contestation of inherited norms of all sorts. Note, for example, that the first-century commentator and philosopher Philo of Alexandria could also imagine that a divine law installs within itself the *aphormē*, as if Philo, too, were reflecting on the possibility of a divinely sanctioned chance (chance as divine sanction) for the deformation of identity, causality, and the economy of commandment. Thus, Philo writes, in legal traditions of scripture, strangers are given a "chance" or opportunity to appropriate legally those goods and rights which were not officially or originally afforded them because of their identity as outsiders (cf. *Special Laws* 2.118.2). Philo also narrates key moments in the surprising scriptural deformation or revolutionary transformation of the identity of the people by way of the terminology of chance, as when a non-Israelite prostitute becomes the crucial bearer of the people's legacy, indeed the very "origin" of their justly constituted *polis* (cf. *On Virtues* 222.6). Similarly, identifying with the partisan against repressive power structures, Josephus, too, understands that what was the eventual *destiny* of Moses (to be the cause of both the downfall of the Egyptians and an emancipatory exodus of the Israelites) nevertheless had to occur in a moment of chance openness to transformation (namely, the invasion of Egypt by the Ethiopians). Josephus's Moses, just like Paul's sin, effects the transformation of agencies, territories, and sovereignties by "seizing the opportunity," both writers appropriating the same Greek terminology of sovereignty and partisanship (cf. *Antiquities of the Jews* 2.239.1).

In other words, the seizure of chance is itself the unformed, deforming moment in the economy of identity, sovereignty, and commandment whereby radical transformation may be effected. Or, as I have already intimated, one might even say the drama of divinity in these ancient texts is *nothing but an attentiveness to this open space of transformation*, almost a monotheistic variation of the question of causality and openness that the polytheistic traditions deified as *tuchē* (or chance). After all, the potential seizure of chance is at once imagined as both the origin and possible revolution of modes of life, the singular aura or surplus value of which has always been the stuff of religion. To add one further genealogical twist, we might even say that, in keeping with another of the ancient meanings of seizable *aphormē*, in Paul's confounding of the efficacy of *nomos* by way of the chance opportunity of this economy's inversion we have a witness to that *"capital" which funded* both the promise and the debts of ancient religiosity, the surplus value or excessive forcefulness of its stability *and* its openness to radical transformation.[17]

In light of this ancient discourse, it is worth remembering Pasolini's sense of a catastrophe at work in the inversion of an image of cinematic rebellion into a form of normalizing participation within a more diffuse and consumerist political economy. It is worth thinking, in other words, that whether one intends to fulfill the law or to transgress it, there is "another law" in excess of law capable of subverting both intentions. Both moments of relating to the juridical or representational capacities of a "code" are traversed by a monstrous opening whereby a kairological chance apparently could be "seized" at any moment, and it would make little difference whether this seizure renders the obedient as transgressors or the transgressive the new obedient. This is the Paul of the underground current of a new materialism, and perhaps someday we will understand that Paulinism has always been part of that archive of contingencies, partisanships, and their always contingently discovered "laws." What else is that partisan Paul's own seizing upon what could otherwise no doubt *only* be read as the effective operation of imperial juridical power, namely, a Roman crucifixion of yet another serial messianic figure within first-century Jewish culture? As discussed above, Paul latched onto the suppressed aspect of his messianic figure in a way that can only be described as doggedly obsessive: "I intended to know nothing among you except Jesus Christ, and this one *as crucified* (*kai touton estaurōmenon*; 1 Corinthians 2:2). Or, in that inimitable style of the Paulinist partisan: "You stupid Galatians! Who has cast a spell on you, before whose eyes Jesus Christ was clearly performed *as crucified!*"(Galatians 3:1).

Remember that we should hesitate before we retroject later Jewish and Christian rationalizations of Paul's seizure of *this* (to say the least, not so promising) chance opportunity. Paul's appropriations of a messianic figure who was both humiliated and executed by occupying forces was much more interventionist, fragmentary, and surprisingly open-ended than these later justifications (and, often enough, co-opations) recognize. In so hesitating to allow latter-day ideologues to rewrite the risky, tentative performance of the earlier moment, we are more likely to attend to the modes in which Paul and his cohort struggled, essentially, to fold the effective operation of imperial power back onto itself, as if to hollow out a bubble of unsurveilled powerlessness within effective power itself. "No way will I ever boast except in the cross of our lord, Jesus Christ, through which the world has been crucified to me, and me to the world" (Galatians 6:14); "But if we have died with Christ, we believe that we will also live with him. . . . Consider yourselves dead . . . but alive" (Romans 6:8, 11). In dying to law by their dogged identification with the crucified, Paul claimed that the believers had been subtracted from the suppressive or katechontic power of the juridical order.

To put the matter differently, was not the secret of Paulinism already that his own *kairos* or now-time of a surprising event (cf. Romans 5:6, 9:9, 13:11), the moment which for him constituted the transformative power of a new age, was precisely in keeping with (or formally the same as) *the operation* of sin's "seizing an opportunity"? This is the case despite the way that Paul *likewise* attributes to the aleatory or supplemental forcefulness of a chance perversion of efficacy within "the commandment" a structure of agency or causality by invoking the name "sin." Put more dramatically, we should not be misled by the ostensibly gut-wrenching, soul-searching rhetoric of a split subject: "Who will rescue me from my split subjectivity?" (cf. 7:14–25). After all, it was only because Paul's catastrophically criminalized Christ was taken by the apostle as the messiah's having "been made sin for us" that Paul was to have anything creatively emancipatory to say about his Christ at all (cf. 2 Corinthians 5:16–19, 21). It was this suppressed messiah which was for him the exemplary clue that the merely believing may "become" outside the economy of the manufacture of representative transgressors. It was, in other words, not only sin which seemed to have learned the affinity between partisanship, transformation, and seizing on a subversive chance. If the *nomos* of the current order makes transgressors of you, you might consider how transgression itself speaks doubly as the end of transgression, even as a kind of redemption to be seized upon.

My assertion is that it is the very topic of a free-floating *surplus* of production within the economy of power relations which hovers above *both* the ancient Paul *and* his return in late capitalism. This is a genealogical puzzle whose effects remain to be worked through. Nevertheless, playing the good neo-Paulinist, Lacan was inviting his would-be revolutionary students to a similar mode of thought as Paul's, certainly no less perverse, rethinking the role of desire within machinations of power and resistance with implications we should not miss. For example, Gil Anidjar has given a very nice Schmittian reading of Paul, focused on Paul's politely diminutive little question: "In telling you the truth, have I become your enemy?" (Galatians 4:16).[18] As Jacob Taubes tried to do earlier, Anidjar here forges an important link between Paulinism and different types of Schmittian exceptionalism that have yet to be worked through in depth. Above all, we should note the many *modes* in which the *kairos*-obsessed partisan conjures an apostolic *polemos* from within inherited forms of habituated activity or from representative figures of the larger established communities. As Philo of Alexandria explores interestingly, the taking of inference or interpretive tack within a tradition is a result of a seizing upon the *aphormē* of a chance (cf. *Who is the Heir of Divine Things?* 300.3ff.).[19] This is the same tale that the early Derrida, as we have seen, would name the swerve of *clinamen* and the very "materialism" of his early theory of "writing." In keeping with Philo's standardly Jewish hermeneutic tradition, it is this partisan tack whose inferences split, divide, and solicit the new and surprising (or, perhaps, the monstrous) which we see everywhere in Paul. Thus being circumcised in moments of Paul's polemic becomes, somehow, a "cutting oneself off" from messianic benefit (cf. *katērgēthēte apo christou*); the beneficent father Abraham mutates into an anarchic "father" of an impossibly generated people, genealogy replaced by an aggressively virtual form of lineage constituted, as it were, only "before" the representations and stabilities law (cf. Galatians 5:4, 3:16–18, 29, 4:31). The Paulinist orgy of disproportion also raises its head when Paul asserts that the shining aura of Moses down from Sinai was veiled, yes, but veiled only *because of an embarrassment about the fact that this shining "glory" was already fading away* (cf. 2 Corinthians 3:13).[20]

Like Lacan's Joyce, Paul the partisan repeats tradition while deforming it, deforms it while repeating it, following the singular declinations and inflections of the seizure of chance (and, as we have pointed out, in keeping with his Jewish hermeneutical contemporaries).[21] For the Paulinist, the messianic age as much as "sin" was capable of "seizing an opportunity," and this to turn agency and agencies against themselves, splitting their operations into conflictual multiplicities of identity and radically altering their capacity to maintain themselves as hegemonic forms of power in the process. Playing the role of a kind of "sin without measure" in relation to the effective economies of "commandment" constituting Roman imperial domination over the intractably rebellious Jews, for example, Paul declares that the Roman transformation of a would-be messiah into a form of stupidity and failure should itself be grasped as a moment of divine wisdom and triumph of the undying divinity of the partisan (cf. 1 Corinthians 1), indeed a divinity that has given rise to a new "city-council" (*ekklēsia*) of the undead, a council consisting of those who act as if *already* dead so that they might live beyond the "suppressive" or katechontic economy of *nomos*. Carried away by the unending, undying life of this very gesture, Paul even boasts that if the "rulers" knew what they were doing when they put down this messianic figure they wouldn't have done it (1 Corinthians 2:8). His point here is not simply that the rulers were "mistaken" in their crucifixion of the rebel from Palestine. Much more in keeping with his argument the issue is rather that, in their very enactment of imperial control and legal condemnation of a messianic figure from a dissident state, the "rulers" became susceptible to the doubling, splitting, undying power of the divinity of emancipatory partisanship. Roman imperial power, too, knows not what it does, living as it does off of a surplus or excess that is only imagined to be owned.

The analogies between Paulinism and the "problem of power" in the late sixties are perhaps most vibrant when imagined as part of a pastiche of the multiplicity of modes in which seizures of chance afford new modes of *undoing the power of power, rendering ineffective the coding of codes or reversing the value of effective history*. In a word, it is in the generalization of the role of the partisan with the unregulatable development of "neocapitalist" economies that solicits a "return" of Paul and all those topoi of life inhering in death, a decree of salvation attaching to the imperial condemnation of a criminal, and so forth. As a figure of thought and analogical provocation, Paul returns as a peculiarly forceful touchstone within an economy whereby we are all subjects of, and subject to, the capacity to seize on a chance opportunity in order to destabilize the very force of normativity.

SEIZURES OF CHANCE; OR, THE CAPITALIZATION OF MASTERY

As one last angelic/analogical testimony, one last witness for the illumination of Pasolini's Paul, note how Lacan's 1969–70 lecture course mentioned before signals a subtle rewiring of Lacan's previous statements about the authority of law in relation to transgression, say, in his seminar on the ethics of psychoanalysis (1959–60). In the earlier lectures Lacan's attention was not so much on the economies whereby transgressive *jouissance* feeds back into structures of authority and control, though the implication is already there, but rather on the modes whereby *jouissance only* appears as such in relation to its prohibitive opposite:

> We are, in fact, led to the point where we accept the formula that without a transgression there is no access to *jouissance*, and, to return to Saint Paul, that that is precisely the function of the Law. Transgression in the direction of *jouissance* only takes place if it is supported by the oppositional principle, by the forms of the Law. If the paths to *jouissance* have something in them that dies out, that tends to make them impassable, prohibition, if I may say so, becomes its all-terrain vehicle, its half-track truck, that gets it out of the circuitous routes that lead man back in a roundabout way toward the rut of a short and well-trodden satisfaction.[22]

By the time we get to the post-'68 discussion of the Other in psychoanalysis the specific Lacanian inflection of the "problem of law" has shifted in an important way, indeed in keeping with the same shift in logics that marks Pasolini's anxiety about 1968 as a more effectively fascistic power than 1938. Lacan's intervention from "the other side of psychoanalysis" ends, rather, with a repetition of the initial suggestion that "analysis shows" us power structures marked not by *transgressions* but by *detours* of power.[23] This shift in focus is perhaps flagged best by the invocation, at the beginning of the latter seminar, of a world *without transgression*. The concepts are not entirely new, but inflected differently. Indeed, Lacan refers to "an experience" that his theoretical modelings repeat in a different mode (164). This experience is, in turn, in keeping with a sense that what he calls "the master's discourse" effectively co-opts opposition because it has "needed to go beyond certain limits" in order to maintain the aura, the authority, the effectivity of its "name" (167f). This transformation beyond "limits" which themselves constituted the recognizability of the master-slave dialectic Lacan calls a "capital mutation . . . which gives the master's discourse its capitalist style" (168). Put differently: "In the master's discourse, for instance, it is effectively impossible that there be a master who makes the entire world function. Getting people to work is even more tiring, if one really has to do it, than working oneself. The master never does it. He gives a sign, the master signifier, and everybody jumps. That's where you have to start, which is, in effect, completely impossible. It's tangible every day" (174).

Consistently within the later writings of Lacan, the more pressing issue is that—with the disappearance of the sovereignty of the lawgiver or the big Other—paradoxically there is a *proliferation of the modes of control whereby a virtual Other might anchor itself*. As she puts it in her excellent discussion of the radical immanence of a desiring economy—which she glosses, through Spinoza and Lacan alike, as "secular causality"—A. Kiarina Kordela writes, "To say that the subject is the cause of itself amounts to the assertion that *everything* can be the cause of the subject, under the precondition that the subject 'agrees' that this is its cause."[24]

Differently put, it seems *at just this point* that the problematic appears which inspired Lacan to reverse the anxiety of "old father Karamazov" about the death of God, inasmuch as (the old father believed) the death of the divine sovereign would mean that "everything is permitted."[25] If the sovereign (divine) monarch, the paternal law that functions as the system's fulcrum, leverage point, or external ground is removed—Lacan countered—then the problem is rather that *nothing is permitted*. Without the external measure of repressive prohibition, how would one even distinguish between muling subservience and bold transgression, and in relation to what structure of power? Rather than the link to Romans 7, perhaps here the intriguingly retroactive textual connection to make would be to point out that it is Paul who opposes grace/faith and work/law in order to demonize the law in Galatians (as enslaving, as a curse, as given by questionable angels rather than by God, as mere calculation, and so on), only to turn around in Romans to declare: "Do we overthrow the law by faith? No way. Rather, we uphold the law" (Romans 3:31). The constellation of Pauline contradictions is intriguing in the sense that Lacan's problem here is the way the *withdrawal* of a localizable, representable prohibition only makes it possible for a massive influx of other forms of coercion and mastery, all of which can appear (retroactively) to have played the role of cause. As Lacan puts it, such is the "capitalization" of the (earlier) role of the "master."

As the Karamazov story and its Lacanian inversion imply, the collapse of an "outside" position from which power is exerted (but also in terms of which power is sheltered, preserved, saved) cuts loose an explosion of indeterminacy and ambiguity about power and its contestation. And just here, between the utter loss of a site of resistance and a paradoxical explosion of new life, appears Pasolini's Paul. At any rate, Lacan believed that the new economies of power precluded anything like a Christian or post-Christian "good news" of the *overcoming* of the order of law, particularly as an anarchic freedom, as it were, beyond the law. As he quips, "It is certainly not as an attempt to explain what sleeping with the mother means that the murder of the father is introduced into Freudian doctrine" (120). Put differently, the promise of analysis is certainly *not* that "in some way psychoanalysis frees us from the law" (119). Indeed, it is difficult not to hear echoes of a comparison between Paul and Oedipus when Lacan describes Oedipus as having transgressed the limits of power or *nomos* only to discover that, without these limits he has no buffer between himself and the *lack of power* which constitutes power as such. In Oedipus's conversion, so to speak, to a life beyond law, "what happens to him is not that the scales fall from his eyes, but that his eyes fall from him like scales. . . . In other words . . . the essence of the master's position is to be castrated" (121).

Stranded between '38 and '68, forced to reconceptualize power and emancipation in a world without the legitimation of founding origins or assured ends, Paul returns as a participant indication of a world in which power increasingly resides in the surplus or excess over the representational. Pasolini's Paul returns, in this context, as both the herald of radical openings, ecstasies of new ages always about to appear, but just as much as the foreclosure of the open. No wonder Pasolini sometimes imagines the author of Acts, that first soporific institutional co-optation of a singular Pauline partisanship, to be a satanic figure. This is perhaps power's secret, as if its own weakness were the most effective form of conjuring ritual supplementation and an investment of credit or faith from ritual adherents (whether transgressive or subservient would make no difference). After all, there is participation in the ritual maintenance of the powerless master or else a more direct facing the powerlessness itself, the master's or ours.

CONCLUSION

New Beginnings

The text, however, as we find it today tells us enough about its own
history [*seine eigenen Schicksale*]. Two distinct forces, diametrically
opposed to each other, have left their traces [*ihre Spuren*] on it. On
the one hand, certain transformations got to work on it, falsifying the
text in accord with secret tendencies [*geheimen Absichten*], maintaining
and extending it until it was turned into its opposite. On the other
hand, an indulgent piety reigned over it [*eine schonungsvolle Pietät
über ihm gewaltet*], anxious to keep everything as it stood, indifferent
to whether the details fitted together or nullified one another.
Thus almost everywhere there can be found striking omissions
[*auffällige Lücken*], disturbing repetitions [*störende Wiederholungen*],
palpable contradictions [*greifbare Widersprüche*], signs of things the
communication of which was never intended [*Anzeichen, die uns
Dinge verraten, deren Mitteilung nicht beabsichtigt war*]. The distortion
[*der Entstellung*] of a text is not unlike a murder. The difficulty lies
not in the execution of the deed but in the doing away with the traces
[*ihre Spuren*].
—Sigmund Freud, *Moses and Monotheism* (trans. Katherine Jones)

It is confirmed likewise by Caius, a member of the church, who arose
under Zephyrinus, bishop of Rome. He, in a published disputation
with Proclus, the leader of the Phrygian heresy, speaks as follows
concerning the places where the sacred corpses (τὰ ἱερὰ σκηνώματα)
of the aforesaid apostles are laid: But I can show you the trophies of the
apostles (τὰ τρόπαια τῶν ἀποστόλων). For if you will go to the Vatican

or to the Ostian Way, you will find the trophies of those who laid
the foundations of this church (εὑρήσεις τὰ τρόπαια τῶν ταύτην
ἱδρυσαμένων τὴν ἐκκλησίαν).

—Eusebius, *Ecclesiastical Histories* (2.26.6, 7)

READ SIMILARLY TO NIETZSCHE, FREUD FOR ME WAS CORRECT
inasmuch as he understood Paulinism as a kind of counterpoint to the
"religion" of the people of Moses. But Freud was still not sleuthing hard
enough, not doing enough dreamwork on the force and forms of cultural
memory, when he considered Paul himself as actually having instituted
the operative break between Judaism and Christianity. For all his shrewd
reflections on revolution, institutionalization, and its repressions, Freud
still read Paul like Martin Luther, participating in an aged panoply of a
triumphalistically anti-Jewish and implicitly pro-imperial tradition inasmuch as he finds in Paul a founder of a new religion, Christianity, which
was in essential (read ideal) respects, *not* Jewish. Of course, Pauline Christianity was imagined by Freud as internally or dialectically related to Judaism in the sense that he imagined Paul as operationalizing repressed Jewish guilt for the murder of its patriarch. Or Freud's Paul promised a holism
of identity as salvation, a promise Freud interpreted as an infantile fantasy
for security that only operates against the backdrop of the very "Judaism"
this fantasy would disavow as its insecure, unsaved alter ego. Fair enough,
shrewd enough, but once again, that the very split between these "religions" and these stable economies of redemption would *itself* need to be
excavated for its own mode of splitting repressed and represented authority was not an issue tackled in *Moses and Monotheism*. Like Nietzsche,
that the *archē* of Christianity, its "greatest son" or its "original," was so
split seems not to have been on the table. The result is that Freud's perennially provocative intervention into the theologico-political memory of
the West, appearing at nightfall of an unprecedented anti-Jewish violence,
insinuates a dispossessingly foreign element into the founder of Judaism
even as it leaves Paul, as a genealogical counterpoint, relatively unscathed.
"To deny a people the man whom it praises as the greatest of its sons is
not a deed to be undertaken lightheartedly—especially by one belonging
to that people [*Einem Volkstum den Mann abzusprechen, den es als den
größten unter seinen Söhnen rühmt, ist nichts, was man gern oder leichthin
unternehmen wird, zumal wenn man selbst diesem Volke angehört*]."

Indeed.

What I have explored in the course of this book, however, are some of the ways that, on the other side of the sublimating narrative of "Christian origins" there appears an apostle as a Jewish partisan or sectarian whose singular project alternately failed and passed away before its being simultaneously buried and beatified by a great machinery of Christendom and its pop Platonic narration of "Christian origins." Subtracted from these types of Eusebian foundations, it is my assertion that Paul becomes a crucial figure in a very different archive, one we hit upon following a path nominated as an "underground current" of a new "materialism." Along this path we found in Pauline texts indications of new figures of a kind of materialist spirituality or an immanent religiosity that—by definition—remains a profound affront to a Western tradition which has so loved to imagine Paul, rather (and for all kinds of reasons), as a proclaimer of a transcendent frame, metaphysical guarantee, or teleological baptism of the brutalities of effective history.

For us, Nietzsche's critique of this eventual constellation organized in and under the name of Paul in this tradition was apt: Paulinism really has become, and not just recently, a "Platonism for the masses." But there are—and continue to be—occlusions, elisions, repressions, and murders in the co-optation of Paul into this metaphysical framework which threaten, always threaten, to burst loose. And (does anyone need proof of it today?), when the mechanisms break down or shake loose in the machinery of a dominant form of enculturated Christendom, then the breakdown of this labyrinthine apparatus allows all manner of economies, all manner of governances of self and others to spin in different orbits. Such things are more important and wide reaching than most of us have yet begun to realize.

At a fundamental level then my genealogical gamble here is simple. It is indeed possible to shove beyond the imagined Paulinism of Nietzsche and Freud alike, a gesture which has in important respects not yet been accomplished by some extraordinarily important recent philosophers and cultural critics in recent decades. In doing so, I argue, we challenge an essential story of what a good Constantinian like Eusebius would call "Christian origins," with the result that one of the stable narrative touchstones or justifications of a popularized Western metaphysics begin to open onto new territories as well. Nietzsche rightly diagnosed both Western ontotheology and Western ontotheology's obsession with Paul as its founding figure, its most effective purveyor of a Platonism for the masses.

As Nietzsche himself once wrote, however: "The most enlightened get only as far as liberating themselves from metaphysics and looking back on it from above: whereas here too, as in the hippodrome, at the end of the track it is necessary to turn the corner."[1] Nietzsche's apothegmatic image has always haunted me in relation to his own excoriation of Paul. Fine, excoriate Paul as the founding disseminator of a Western metaphysics in which a belief in transcendent guarantee effects a "higher swindle" on everyday life, a life which in turn becomes fleeced of its own gravity, its own significance. But, in order really to "turn the corner" in the immanent structures of recurrence constituting this life, why is it that we would at all be interested in reading Paul—even antagonistically—as the "one who knows" or even as the one who thinks he knows, about the economic transactions of transcendent guarantee or stable Platonic idealities? Do we really assume that Paul was nothing like Freud's Moses, that Egyptian, as if (to play on the Egyptians of Hegel and Lacan as well) Paul were no mystery to himself? One of the uncomfortable questions of this book, which I posed to Nietzsche, to Freud, to Althusser, to Derrida, to Foucault, and to Deleuze is just this: why are *we* reading Paul in such a docile, traditional way? What are *we* preserving or protecting in *not* exposing Paul, as it were, to the unjustified, unsaved—or, simply, immanent—forms of always singular life in which we claim to believe? In each instance, I argue, this way of reading a biblical text (perhaps above all a biblical text!) is to set oneself up as *wanting* to escape metaphysics, all the while preserving oneself as the one able to look down on this moribund condition, or over at it, as if it were an object, a given entity, or an alter ego. And so these thinkers have continued to read Paul protectively, continued to cover him up in the glass of a museum casing, and this in order to guarantee an important distinction between their postmetaphysical present and a pop Platonic religiosity they rightly disavow.

A more radical stance must be taken, however, and we take it when we read in order to turn the corner *with* Paul, steering him, his texts, and his little chariot of Western foundationalism around the corner in an arena of immanence from which none of us will escape, but in which we may yet find surprises and which we may yet transform. One should be brutal about the issue. Does not the difference in these two interpretive approaches not itself constitute the difference between, on the one hand, a mere *idealistic declaration* of a "step outside" the Paulinist narrativities and Platonist metaphysics of the West and, on the other, an actual transformation of the very framework of this metaphysics itself? Convinced that this is the case, I was also persuaded that Nietzsche, Freud, Derrida, Foucault, and Deleuze have done us no favors in their failing to confront the issue head on. We must now more patiently engage in a shrewd genealogical *Verwindung* of a hegemonic Pauline narrative which in important respects continues to plague recent "radical" readers of Paul, from Stanislas Breton and Alain Badiou to Daniel Boyarin. Forget Nietzsche's mere disavowals of Paul and the foundationalist metaphysics of the West: we must rework the cultural function of the apostle, as if to allow another gospel to ring out from him, as if to witness to another type of collectivity or other solidarities confronting other political catastrophes, all these forming alongside a repetition of this name now *within* the path of an "underground current" of a new materialism. In an axiom I have tried to clarify in the different sections of this book, what we need is a rethought political or social canon of Western "origins," one in which we find in Paul a "materialism for the masses," an origin itself split into a multiplicity, constituted by difference, and therefore the farthest thing from a foundational idealism.

Like Freud's project to intervene in always singularly interwoven threads of politics, history, and religion around the names of Moses and the West, this book takes seriously the idea that, for an essential founding patriarch of Christianity as well, the beatified imago of the original founder is already an effect of a violent imposition that consolidates profound cultural power—and indeed an implicit model of political identity—by being repeated unremarked. Alongside Freud's dreamwork and textual excavation on Western cultural memory, therefore, here I have presented readers with tales of a very recent discovery of Paul's concrete shoes. The revelation is disconcerting, awful even—an apostolic body turning up now with concrete shoes—and all the stranger as this surprising turn of events is only made possible by a series of technical developments within apparently disconnected forensic and archaeological spheres, above all recent work in continental philosophy and biblical studies.[2] Nonetheless, what has been unearthed is as solid and real as can be, and there he is, not just any old cat in some squishy bag all putrescent down by the river's edge. No, we have here a founding apostle—some will call him the inventor of Christianity—and there he is (it's as clear as day), a sacred corpse all fitted up with concrete slippers. My work simply brings to light what has been obvious all along about this apostle, almost from the beginning no more than just bones and quick drying cement. If you don't believe it, just call Eusebius.

As we see in Paul's last extant writing, at the end of Romans (15:30–32)—as it were the final words of Paul—he seemed to recognize that he was destined to wear shoes of the cement variety, and he begged others to help him prolong his life amidst their looming threat. To be subtracted from your own legacy, hidden inside its veneer in fact, is no joke. Freud was not wrong to have suspicions that it is hero worship itself—all those paens to the founding father—in which we see the contortions of a cover-up. In this respect the figure of Paul—whom even Freud continued to read as the purveyor of promises of a Platonistically styled econonomic transaction guaranteeing salvation (those "foundation stones of a new religion founded by Paul")—is even clearer than Moses. Even more, in a peculiar turn of events in keeping with Freud's sense of repetition of drama in multiple spheres, as many alleged corpses of Paul as can now be unearthed all turn up as if carefully fitted with the same *type* of concrete shoe. Nietzsche named both the mass-produced similarity of these simulacra, and their similar types of concrete shoes, a phenomenon of a pop metaphysic whereby the real issue of worldly life was imagined to be siphoned off and securely guarded in another sphere altogether. This "massive phenomenon" of life as an organized savings plan was Nietzsche's higher swindle, a popularized metaphysic that spreads around when we let bankers become the preachers of a world they'd like to run. Linking the story backward to Plato and forward to the internally regulated self-effacements of modern Europe, Nietzsche of course named the entire complex a Platonism for the masses, imagining Paul as its great evangelist. Remaining within the orbit of Nietzsche's analysis, Freud diagnoses the psychic economy of this cultural mode as a form of idealist misidentification—in short, a volatile narcissism constituted by imagined participationist holisms.

At which point perhaps we sleuths really need to call in other agencies, as the scope of the crime scene we have stumbled upon starts to balloon into a conspiracy on the grandest of scales. Good detectives, we should note for the record that *when* these varieties of a Pauline corpse must have been exhumed so as thus to be retrofitted with the same *type* of concrete accoutrement can only occasionally be determined. What we *can* say is that the corpses in question seem to have been exhumed and laid back to rest—heavier each time—with some regularity. All we can say is that it is as if someone had a lot invested in making sure *this* particular type of body would never come floating to the surface. As one says, all hardboiled by the edge of a river, this body is not just any old cat in any old bag. But who would go to this trouble, why, and how, this mad quest to exhume and retrofit Paul and those who look like him with the proverbial concrete shoes? Who indeed would be so hell-bent on making sure that this type of corpse remains, back there, at the beginning, sunken down to where all good founders should stay, buried away with the foundations? Why, at any rate, would *we* participate in this crime, this madness?

AKHENATON, MEET MR. APOSTLE

Like Freud, I gamble everything on a quirkily political potential of the new subjective or psychic economy as it comes to grips with the possibility that its beatified or sublimated imago was always a corpse hidden in plain sight. To say it like a psychoanalytic *kerygma*, here we are invited to join an unruly alliance of those who believe that to tinker with Paul, as it was to tinker with Moses, is to monkey with a profoundly and perennially invested lever of identity. As always, this *kerygma* necessitates a genealogical intervention, and it is time for us today to consider more seriously the modes in which a reworking of the figure of Paul implicate both ourselves and our forbears in an Adam/New Adam story for our own moment. At the very least, we must realize that to reconfigure Paul in the cultural memory of this tradition will always have implied a shifting within four terms that are simply too intimately oriented by or implicated in the cultural memory of Paul for it to be otherwise. These names, the West, Europe, Christianity, and Judaism, are all alike too intimately, awkwardly related to the history of this figure, and none will remain indifferent to its cultural repositioning.

Now as much as ever, there is a remarkable array of political and intellectual issues being organized in and through the name of Paul, sometimes, in good Pauline fashion, by the force of surprising talk, awkward promises, and temporary cohabitations of a life-changing sort. The array of issues in play in these movements are all too important to ignore. Consider Freud's lines reproduced earlier. Perhaps it is the New Testament, that always already operationalized covenant or charter of a religion that often stands in as "the West"—both in this West's religiosity and in its secularity—which has always had altogether too many junior sleuths and all too few Detective Dupins of the sort Freud seems to describe. The psychoanalytic interpreter of found and founding contracts is clear enough. The excess of sleuths and paucity of detectives appear in and as a community of interpreters who tacitly agree not to attend to communications of that which was never intended. They are a collective of subjects anxious about what must not be seen and therefore a community haunted by sign-objects which squirm rather precariously at the edges of the community of meaning as that which must be refused entry as so many illegitimate emissaries from an unthinkably unintended communication. No wonder Freud links unintended communications to suspicions of a corpse ineffectively disposed of.

If Freud dreams in *Moses and Monotheism* (*Der Mann Moses und die monotheistische Religion*) of a coming biblical interpreter, the psychoanalyst imagines this tracker of unintended communications as all kitted out in the tricks of the detective trade, above all with an attentiveness to the *void* of omission or gap, coupled with an odd interest in "disturbing repetitions," inexpressive singularities or *atoms*, like a nervous twitch that points somewhere only ever by repeating itself. In this sense, Freud's Bible in the cultural memory of the West will always have been tied to a hesitatingly ambivalent *anxiety,* which defines the self-maintenance of a singularity that could always be otherwise, communities of readers constitutively exposed to the possibility of haunting communiqués that were never intended to be sent. When the maintenance of canonical boundaries starts to involve unintended refrains from agents unknown, then definitionally we must wonder whether there is a body buried somewhere.

Freud's revisionist narration of Moses as the sublimated Jewish imago of a murdered Egyptian was therefore structurally familiar to the analyst. Familiar with the scene, he knew that voids and repetitions are echoes—so many miniature or minimal afterlives—of the stilled heartbeat from the corpse immured in the wall, perhaps of the dismembered body stuffed underneath the floorboards, all the more a "trophy" (as Eusebius acknowledges) because so blazingly silent, secret, hidden in relation to what it *could* indicate to those catching a glimpse of it. Whether such corpses were dismembered and stuffed here and there or dropped wholesale down into the foundation materials themselves, we can never be sure. For Freud, piety will have been an interpretive epoch constituted by *not* attending to mute signs, *not* wanting to learn too much, *not* wanting to acknowledge the swerve of unintended signs and the transformatively revelatory *pressure* of singular repetitions.

FOR A NEW MATERIALISM AGAINST RELIGION'S CULTURED DESPISERS

As the one stuck with this case, my promissory overview for my readers was simple: if you stay with me at the crime scene in order to photograph, to size up, and to chisel away at these concrete shoes, the resolution will be dramatic. I never forgot the traits of a recent film trailer. Once the shoes come off, once a body can float back to the surface, you will be returned, fully satisfied and a little wiser, to the title of the show. And is not the body floating to the surface the emergence of a new Paul indistinguishable from a new materialism? For my money, such a denouement would be worth the emergency lights, chilly air, and yellow tape at the crime scene of a significant textual murder, all those strong indications that the shoes on the corpse in front of us might herald striking inversions or shake-ups of reigning social hierarchies and the ready-made identities which take shelter therein to imagine themselves either inside or outside "religion."

Above all, I have tried to make clear how, in cases like these, it does not do us any favors these days to remain true to a demythologizing political and social critique of religion as ideology so long as this gesture obfuscates structural similarities between ourselves and the religionists. Nor is it useful to take up the mantle of the atheist who steps outside religion if that mantle is woven with the same threads or shares the same hues, cost, and function of precisely the "religion" it is said not to be. As I have argued, it is my contention that it is a new materialism, specifically, that must necessarily challenge the tried and true game of agonistic mimickry, competitive "outbidding," all variations of the old master-slave dialectic which—we should know by now—does not promise winners so much as a common exposure to death. Most importantly of all, however, a new materialism which remains indifferent to earlier tactics of Enlightenment does so as, precisely, an act of fidelity to what Gilles Deleuze called a plane of immanence or the peculiarly groundless ground of all efforts to think phenomenological immanence. In fact, we need to go a step further in order to be more precise than general talk of ignoring the distinction between the inside/outside of "religion" and in my case we can do so by saying that one exemplary figure in particular has returned with remarkable forcefulness, as if summoned back from the dead by, precisely, unflinching efforts to move forward with a philosophy oriented around both difference or multiplicity and immanence.

COMING INSURRECTIONS

Paul is significant in my philosophico-political genealogy of the accident and the encounter which spurs thought because he has become a discursive lynchpin in the self-description of "the West" which can now subtract itself in relation to this structure in two catastrophic ways. In both cases the catastrophe occurs by including and acknowledging that which I have been arguing has only been *included out*, actively forgotten, strategically included *as* something so as to suppress some other intolerable something. As the economic, military, colonial histories of the West continue to play themselves out, I find we can include Paul in this way as that type, that uncanniest of guests, who knows about us things we tend actively *not* to know about ourselves. On the one hand, I have argued that we can subtract the lynchpin, the origin, the founding father from a story of Western religion as Christianity by pointing out that Paulinism was ultimately shortlived, ephemeral, an explosion of impossible rhetoric about the transformation of embodied and engendered habituations for the creation of the new. Within a generation the rhetoric had worn thin, the habituations or lived embodiments of received power relations demanded that the church—to survive in this world—would actively sacrifice the apostle to received models of community (on the one hand) or adopt a suicidal refusal of the same (on the other). As a genealogical moment, therefore, Paulinism is peculiarly worth thinking about. Somewhere between a repetition of the same and a refusal of this same repetition by way of a suicidal gesture is Paulinism: ephemeral, strange, a moment of suspension and tensing that expressed itself in a language of time and hilarious, mad, and maddening inversions of value. To meditate on such moments is to expose ourselves to them.

I have tried to explore a few of these Paulinisms which are, precisely, *subtracted from* the architectonics of Christianity (where Paul becomes—suspiciously and in a self-congratulatory way—an "early" or "original" version of an imagined global triumph), but also subtracted from typical philosophemes in the sense that the apostle becomes a bearer of that "underground current" of a "materialism" in which accident and the encounter with (or folding of) an outside spur a thought of new kinds of solidarity. Without being underwritten by a triumphalistic grand narrative, without the guarantee of philosophies of representational mimicry or transparent consciousness, my Paul becomes in this context—in a more Deleuzean vein—an assemblage of affects without stable sensibility, unregistered and only misleadingly representable effects of forces that came and went, which were corralled into Roman families and gendered hierarchies (again, on the one hand) and a refusal of the sexual body (on the other). For us, Paul is not the founder of Christendom but a site in which are registered affects lost in time and disconnected from the body.

Throughout, I have argued that we should maintain a kind of Deleuzean disinterest in that great machine of judgment which is the distinction between religion and the secular. This great machine and the sacrificial judgment it always and already extricates, veils a multiplicity of sites of social invention and political creation that rather should remain available, free, unowned, virtual exemplars we might affirm, repeat, or name differently. I even added that this Deleuzean indifference toward the prefabricated difference of this particular apparatus of judgment might be read as a latter-day repetition of Paul's reckless appropriation of the Hellenistic philosopher's paradoxical boast (that the poor sage owns all things) for the common life of his communities: "all things belong to you" (1 Corinthians 3:21ff.).

In advocating a Deleuzean nominalism toward these massive entities (religion, the secular), I of course did not intend to make it any easier to place a biblical figure like the apostle Paul in relation to that equally massive (and intimately related) archive that is "the West." On the contrary, to refuse the rules of this fundamental game is to liberate rogue elements of thinking that should begin to plague this tradition in new ways. That is, I have been arguing, the case in thinking about the legacy of Foucault in relation to the figure of Paul. In this respect, note that Alberto Toscano, in his important book on the category of the fanatic, criticizes the theological genealogy of Western political economy to be found in Agamben's *Kingdom and the Glory.* Toscano claims that there is a profound problem with Agamben's substantializing narrative of two millennia of history in which a contemporary society of the spectacle, for example, becomes a latter-day indication of a spectacular (and disempowering) theology of humanity as God's image and the economy as the organized, managed, and organized machinations of the divine sovereign:

> Where Foucault had located, beginning in the mid-eighteenth century, the emergence of "governmental reason" in the early discourse of political economy and the concurrent practice of administering the health and productivity of populations, Agamben turns the clock back two millennia: to the writings of Aristotle and Xenophon on the economy, then to the fate of this notion within the theology of the Church fathers, beginning with Paul. In the process, he abandons Foucault's commitment to discontinuity, as well as his related nominalist disdain for the assumption that substances, essences or universals can be registered across different historical domains.[3]

In doing so, Toscano claims, Agamben "decodes a hidden theological machine behind the operations of the secular world" in a way that betrays Foucault's commitment to Nietzschean genealogy in which "'the secret is that things have no essence or that their essence was fabricated in a piecemeal fashion from alien forms.'"[4] But what if a nominalist interest in the primacy of the contingent organizing apparatuses of capture over their substantial self-same did not preclude comparative games of explication, as that engaged in by Agamben, but rather proliferated them beyond (all) measure? This, essentially, is my gamble, and no straightforward gesture to the stability of "the secular" could safely discredit it. It is within this game of an open-ended archive, a West without grounding coordinates in names like theology, religion, or the political, that I think a reading of Paul becomes all the more compelling, if all the more dangerous as well. As Clayton Crockett sometimes reminds us, it was Deleuze who said that it is a conceptual commitment to the death of God that yields a world in which *everything* can become a theologeme.[5]

NOTES

PLATONISM FOR THE MASSES

1. Eric Santner, *The Royal Remains: The People's Two Bodies and the Endgames of Sovereignty* (Chicago: University of Chicago Press, 2011), p. 138.
2. By the same token, while there is now an extraordinarily important cottage industry within historical studies about the Jewish Jesus or the Jewish Paul, it is almost never recognized within these studies that a historical tradition of narration (Paul as first Christian, origin of Christianity) and a tradition of metaphysics (identity as grounded or originated in the self-same) were profoundly intertwined. Nietzsche was right: Christian narrations of Christian origins were a popularization of Platonism. The reason the "Jewish Paul" stories have failed to be as important a cultural force as they might be is because historians wanted the one cog in the massive apparatus of this pop Platonism to be overcome (in the form of relinquishing its passé supersessionist Christian origins stories), even while they almost completely ignore the matching metaphysical mechanism, the very question of identity and groundedness. What I have here called a more thorough revolution of thinking will only be possible if we put a wrench simultaneously in both sets of interlocking gears, so to speak, and to do this we need to stop *leaning on identity politics*. As should be very clear already, the question of Judaism is essential to a transformation of this

cultural machinery, which is why we cannot efface the important issues by collapsing everything back into an ultimately quietistic identity politics. I say more about the theme and some of the important historians in this tradition in my introduction, "Paul and the Philosophers: Return to a New Archive," in Ward Blanton and Hent de Vries, eds., *Paul and the Philosophers* (New York: Fordham University Press, 2013).

3. With *problem* and *apparatus* I begin to flag an issue of a repetition which is itself a singularity, an issue of a philosophy of difference that will be central to the chapters to come. For the moment, for those interested, see, e.g., Gilles Deleuze, *Difference and Repetition* (London: Continuum, 1997), p. 198, *A Thousand Plateaus* (Minneapolis: University of Minnesota Press, 1987), p. 399; cf. *Foucault* (Minneapolis: University of Minnesota Press, 1986), p. 76ff. See also *"What Is an Apparatus?" and Other Essays* (Stanford: Stanford University Press, 2009).

4. Cf. Hans Ulrich Gumbrecht, *The Production of Presence: What Meaning Cannot Convey* (Stanford: Stanford University Press, 2004). Gumbrecht's anecdotal labor in "Materialities/The Nonhermeneutic/Presence" (pp. 1–20) always meant a lot to me, as some of my earlier work (e.g., *Displacing Christian Origins*) had emerged during a period when Gumbrecht's *Materialities of Communication* (Stanford: Stanford University Press, 1994) project were for me a very fresh approach to the humanities, not to mention my much appreciated introduction to the work of Niklas Luhmann and Friedrich Kittler. Note the respective concluding chapters in Caroline Walker Bynum, *Fragmentation and Redemption: Essays on Gender and the Human Body in Medieval Religion* (New York: Zone, 1992), and *Holy Feast and Holy Fast: the Religious Significance of Food to Medieval Women* (Berkeley: University of California Press, 1987); see also *Christian Materiality: An Essay on Religion in Late Medieval Europe* (Cambridge: MIT Press, 2011). I think one can say the same thing of her more recent work on blood, inasmuch as the auratic evocation of "living blood" is a mode of hierarchizing and liturgically enacting the issue of "lineage." In other words, the *materiality* of such an investigation is, as in Gumbrecht, not in any reduction of the conceptual drama of "religion" or symbolic structures but rather in its mode of linking auratic, excessive attachment to historical and empirical "bearers" of such events of signification. Cf. Caroline Walker Bynum, *Wonderful Blood: Theology and Practice in Late Medieval Northern Germany and Beyond* (Philadelphia: University of Pennsylvania Press, 2007); Jonathan Goldberg, *The Seeds of Things: Theorizing Sexuality and Materiality in Renaissance Representations* (New York: Fordham University Press, 2009).

5. While others could be mentioned as well, note the important appropriation of Deleuzeanism for a new materialist spirituality which becomes indistinguishable both from a "resurrected" Paulinism and a new political ecology in Clayton Crockett and Jeffrey W. Robbins, *Religion, Politics, and the Earth: The*

New Materialism (New York: Palgrave Macmillan, 2012); Clayton Crockett's essay on the Pauline/Deleuzean event in Blanton and de Vries, *Paul and the Philosophers*; Roberto Esposito, *Bios: Biopolitics and Philosophy* (Minneapolis: University of Minnesota Press, 2008), pp. 157–169, *Communitas: The Origin and Destiny of Community* (Stanford: Stanford University Press, 2009), and *Immunitas: The Protection and Negation of Life* (New York: Polity, 2011), pp. 59–80; Santner, *The Royal Remains*, pp. xxi, 129–141. Bradley carries through some of his remarkable work on originary technicity by way of the "theo-logico-political" in Arthur Bradley, *Unbearable Life: Essays on Biopolitical Theology* (London: Routledge, 2014).

6. Cf. Giorgio Agamben, *The Kingdom and the Glory: For a Theological Genealogy of Economy and Government* (Stanford: Stanford University Press, 2011); Eric Santner, *On the Psychotheology of Everyday Life: Reflections on Freud and Rosenzweig* (Chicago: University of Chicago Press, 2001), *The Royal Remains*; Esposito. *Bios.*

7. Jacques Derrida, *Archive Fever: A Freudian Impression* (Chicago: University of Chicago Press, 1996), p. 7.

8. Ibid., p. 1.

9. Agamben, *The Time That Remains* (Stanford: Stanford University Press, 2000), pp. 138–145.

10. Again, as was the case with regard to *apparatus* and *problēmata* in note 3, the "signature" indicates a kind of phenomenal event which itself precedes and constitutes our usual thinking about discretely separable subjects and objects or events separated in time. (In addition to note 3 in this chapter, see also the excellent work of Eric Alliez, *The Signature of the World: What Is Deleuze and Guattari's Philosophy?* (London: Continuum, 2005). "In *practice*, the question is that of a theory of thought capable of diagnosing in our becomings the ontological condition for the real experience of thought" (ibid., 2). Pushing the same genealogical method also back to a Foucault who remained in this respect very close to Deleuze, Agamben engages the issues in Giorgio Agamben, *Signature of All Things* (Boston: MIT Press, 2009).

11. There are many touchstones evoked here, from Hegel's kenotic creator to Heidegger's subversive craftsman tinkering away at his "jugs." More recently, Peter Sloterdijk brilliantly sets the old metaphysical traditions loose in search of a new form of therapy of the soul in *Spheres*, vol. 1: *Bubbles: Microspherology*, trans. Wieland Hoban (Los Angeles: Semiotext(e), 2011), cf. pp. 29ff.

12. It may be that at some point we would all diverge in our respective hopes in the question of identity and multiplicity or the promise of representational notions of democracy, but there is an important articulation of these types of "repetition problems" in a related critique of dominant forms of reading Paul in Denise Buell and Melanie-Johnson Debauffre, "Beyond the Heroic Paul: Toward a Feminist and Decolonizing Approach to the Letters of Paul,"

in Christopher Stanley, ed., *The Colonized Apostle: Paul Through Postcolonial Eyes* (Minneapolis: Augsburg Fortress, 2011), pp. 161–174.

13. See, for example, my chapter "Reason's Apocalypse: Albert Schweitzer's 'Fully Eschatological' Jesus and the Collapse of Metaphysics," in Ward Blanton, *Displacing Christian Origins: Philosophy, Secularity, and the New Testament* (Chicago: University of Chicago Press, 2007).

14. She will perhaps see herself in paragraphs like this one, chips which have fallen as we worked close by (with a tip of the hat to Max Müller) in the same Scottish woodshop. Thanks here to Yvonne Sherwood for many conversations on many planes to many conferences about Derrida, the self-described "last and the least" of the Jews.

15. Note the perfectly phrased opening gambit: "To deny a people the man whom it praises as the greatest of its sons is not a deed to be undertaken lightheartedly—especially by one belonging to that people." Sigmund Freud, *Moses and Monotheism* (New York: Random House, 1996), p. 3.

16. Cf. Niall Ferguson, *Civilization: The Six Killer Apps of Western Power* (New York: Penguin, 2012).

17. For an important recent effort to rewire Heidegger's reading of Nietzsche—by way of Paul—see Didier Franck, *Nietzsche and the Shadow of God*, trans. Bettina Bergo and Philippe Farah (Evanston, IL: Northwestern University Press, 2012). Franck would disagree here with my articulation of the *Romanitas* and technicity of Nietzsche's stance, but for the sake of his excellent and insightful book I could forgive him this oversight.

18. Goldberg, *The Seeds of Things*, p. 43. There is a great deal more to discuss in this excellent book, and I hope that my next book on Paul, spiritual exercises, and biopolitics will afford the space to do so.

19. Of course, the modes of this cohering of a new identity are already far afield from those surrounding the historical Paul. As Pervo summarizes nicely: "Paul is without doubt Luke's hero, but Luke does not present the leading feature's of Paul's theology, nor does he reveal some of the more salient features of his biography. For the author of Acts, the heritage of gentile Christianity was under attack, and Paul could only be defended through some major modifications." Richard Pervo, *The Making of Paul: Constructions of the Apostle in Early Christianity* (Minneapolis: Fortress, 2010), p. 156. See Pervo's book for a fuller discussion of some important distinctions between the Pauline letters and the Paul of Acts. For a similarly useful basic overview of generally accepted scholarly distinctions between Acts and the Pauline letters, see John Dominic Crossan and Jonathan L. Reed, *In Search of Paul: How Jesus' Apostle Opposed Rome's Empire with God's Kingdom* (San Francisco: Harper, 2004), pp. 27–41.

Likewise, of course, the moves being made in Acts to naturalize a distinction between "Christians" and "Jews" are only initial movements in that direction, certainly not yet those of an Augustine or a Eusebius. But these tendencies are in fact already present here, geological shifts that will eventually select for narratives of Christian origins as supersessionist apparatus of capture.

20. Before the quasi-transcendental *apparatus* and *signature* of Foucault, Deleuze, Derrida, and Agamben, there was a vibrant buzz operating between cliché and archetype wthin the writings of McLuhan, a great thinker we should not forget, e.g., Marshall McLuhan, *From Cliche to Archetype* (Toronto: Gingko, 2011).

21. Essential for the breadth of its survey and its critical perspectives is an article by Todd Penner, "Madness in the Method? The Acts of the Apostles in Current Research," *Currents in Biblical Research* 2, no. 2 (2004): 223–293. Among some excellent recent work on Acts, Penner's work here and elsewhere (cf. *In Praise of Christian Origins: Stephen and the Hellenists in Lukan Apologetic Historiography.* (London: T&T Clark, 2004)) makes clear the *many* ways in which the text and diverse legacies of Acts could be reworked and rethought along genealogical lines, modes which would overflow the specific tale being spun here between Freud, Nietzsche, and Paul. Or, similarly rich and important, note the related work of Willi Braun, Ron Cameron, and Merrill P. Miller in their respective efforts to unearth modes of thinking earliest Christianities without collapsing these into hegemonic rhetorical and political narrative structures of Acts (e.g., *Redescribing Christian Origins* (Atlanta: SBL Press, 2004); *It's Just Another Story: The Politics of Remembering the Earliest Christians* (London: Equinox, 2013)). In fact, a kind of classic which should be republished is Ron Cameron's "Alternate Beginnings—Different Ends: Eusebius, Thomas, and the Construction of Christian Origins," in Dieter Georgi, Lukas Bormann, Kelly del Tredici, and Angela Standhartinger, eds., *Religious Propaganda and Missionary Competition in the New Testament World* (Leiden: Brill, 1994), pp. 501–526. As I say, there is a great deal worth mentioning these days. I will point to some others further on, though it goes without saying that a full treatment of Acts in the constitution of Western cultural memory is another project in its own right. Here I am only sparking a few fires by situating Acts polemically between Roman suppression of first-century Jewish rebellion, Eusebius, and the hegemonic discourses of "Christian origins" which seem ubiquitous from the Evangelical churchman to the deconstructive cultural theorist.

22. And do we not here hit upon one further painful irony in the functioning of Christian origins stories? That is, it was only after a predominantly gentile Christianity began to press for a retroactive *naturalization or self-protection of its own identity* that there was invented the image of the monolithic, conservative, reactionary "Jew," the very one who could not yet see his way to the cosmopolitan realities of diversity.

23. The title of one of his lectures on Pauline texts.

24. It is on the subject of ambivalence, for example, that a more elaborate geneal-ogy of Acts within Western cultural memory should be taken up. One excel-lent starting point would be the work of Joseph B. Tyson, which (as historical reconstruction and also reception history) I admire a great deal. See Joseph B. Tyson, *Luke, Judaism, and the Scholars: Critical Approaches to Luke-Acts* (Columbia: University of South Carolina Press, 1999). Thanks to James Crossley for steering me toward Tyson's study.

25. Christopher Mount, *Pauline Christianity: Luke-Acts and the Legacy of Paul* (Boston: Brill, 2002). See his discussion of Irenaeus as an indication of second-century developments in the reception history of both Acts and Pauline texts, with shifts in the reception of Acts increasingly determining the future of the Pauline texts (cf. 11–44).

26. Ibid., p. 33.

27. You can see my interest in clichés becoming archetypes, in the sense that I am here *primarily* interested in the possible naturalization or retrojection of a Jewish/Christian distinction. This focus need neither ignore nor be obscured by the interest of Acts in both fetishizing the idea of a "true Israel" or of appending this appellation as a characteristic of that group whose other name will increasingly become Christian rather than Jew"

28. Indeed, the parallels between the Jerusalem elite of the Gospel of Luke and "the Jews" of Acts is an intriguing story in itself, part of the way the author of builds a system of echoes between the redemptive figures of Jesus and Paul. Both figures appear in four trial scenes, are exonerated by the Roman figures in the episode, and then punished because of the pressure of Jewish groups.

29. As Todd Klutz argues in an important reading of the exorcism stories in Luke-Acts, even the miracle tales were geared toward downplaying the tensions between Paul and his compatriot followers of Jesus in Jerusalem: "Due chiefly . . . to his need to highlight unity and harmony within the Jesus movement, Luke puts most of the blame for Paul's difficulties on the shoulders of the outsiders; and consonant with this tendency, two of the themes summarised above serve primarily to define and underscore the boundaries between those inside and those outside." Todd Klutz, *The Exorcism Stories in Luke-Acts; a Sociostylistic Reading* (Cambridge: Cambridge University Press, 2008), p. 242. Which is to say that the rhetorical and narratological management of an inside and outside remains, at every level of Luke-Acts, necessary.

30. Sanders's work seems to me as crucial as ever, all the more important when we shift our focus from authorial origins and intentions toward the "apparatuses" or paradigms of interpretability as these begin to exert themselves through the earlier texts (which is to say once we move away from the origin of Acts toward Ignatius, Eusebius, Nietzsche and Freud). Jack T. Sanders, *The Jews in Luke-Acts* (London: SCM, 1987), pp. 11–13.

31. See Christina Petterson, *Acts of Empire: The Acts of the Apostles and Imperial Ideology* (Taiwan: CCLM, 2012), especially ch. 4, p. 96f.

32. This aspect of Acts is all the more interesting when imagined against the backdrop of a radical critique of Roman imperial authority, as the ambivalence (about the discursive role or value of Rome) highlights the way that it is *in relation to Rome* that Acts wants to constitute a distinction of identities (and political entities) between "Christians" and "Jews." As I have suggested already, it is precisely *in* ambivalence that the essential collaborationist political moves are being made.

33. In this respect, for me C. Kavin Rowe's *World Upside Down: Reading Acts in the Graeco-Roman Age* (Oxford: Oxford University Press, 2009) misses aspects of its opportunity to participate in a promising reworking of inherited traditions of political theology by way of the text of Acts. On the one hand, as I have already mentioned, I agree that there are a number of open legacies to be reworked within Acts and its afterlives, and Rowe provides useful and creative readings of Acts' Christianity as a challenge to political habits outside this group. Still, for me the book collapses a potentially radical hermeneutical tradition into a remarkably conservative interest in "narrative" (a code for something he imagines as a "foundation" and a "totality" which also functions as a "norm," cf. 166). "Hermeneutics as politics" (to borrow from the work of Stanley Rosen) is thus transformed into a mere identity politics, replete with anxieties that a Christian commitment to truth is excluded by dominant forms of religious studies in North America. This overlooking of the radicality within the hermeneutical tradition is not unrelated to Rowe's imagination of Carl Schmitt (or Giorgio Agamben) as foundational metaphysicians of the sort he himself wants to be (cf. pp. 110f., 169). The same could be said of Rowe's reduction of the relevance of Jan Assmann for the study of Acts to Assmann's interest in the political legacies of monotheism over against polytheism.

In terms borrowed from Jacob Taubes, for me these characteristics function to make Rowe's study an exceptionalism "from above"—which is to say an exceptionalism on the side of "myth-preserving violence." This we see clearly at times, for example in Rowe's references to given Christian "narratives" which must not be questioned in their demands for new sacrificial victims (consider the concluding section and the role of a "normative conceptual base" in that text). In other words, despite its important readings of Acts and pagan politics (which I like), in other important respects the book is for me very much a contemporary "Platonism for the masses." Identity is imagined to be given and received from a stable past, indeed a form of "original Christianity" appearing as a quasi-transcendental "narrative" from Acts. Ineluctably this quasi-transcendental "narrative" constitutes a *type* of universal which can only maintain itself in the "negation" of competitors or the passive reification of the (imagined or unquestioned) legitimate limits of that passively received identity: "what will we not tolerate? what kind of diversity is unacceptable? Answering these questions invariably requires recourse to a more comprehensive [*sic*] pattern of thought" (166).

34. Cf. Friedrich Nietzsche, "What I owe to the Ancients" in *Twilight of the Idols*, trans. R. J. Hollingdale (New York: Penguin, 1990), p. 117.

35. For example, see discussions of *objet petit a* and transference through the notion of the *agalma* as this emerges in Lacan's striking engagement with Plato's *Symposium*. *The Seminar of Jacques Lacan*, book 8, *Transference* (unpublished translation by Cormac Gallagher from unedited French manuscripts).

36. See, for example, Jacob Taubes, *The Political Theology of Paul*, trans. Dana Hollander (Stanford: Stanford University Press, 2004), *From Cult to Culture: Fragments Toward a Critique of Historical Reason* (Stanford: Stanford University Press, 2009), *Occidental Eschatology* (Stanford: Stanford University Press, 2009). The discovery, editing, and interpretation of Taubes's fuller correspondence with Schmitt is a real breakthrough for understanding the larger stakes of Taubes's interventions. See Thorsten Palzhoff and Martin Treml, eds., *Jacob Taubes—Carl Schmitt: Briefwechsel* (Munich: Fink, 2011). The English translation appears as *To Carl Schmitt: Letters and Reflections* (New York: Columbia University Press, 2013). Note also the important collection of Randi Rashkover and Martin Kavka, eds., *Judaism, Liberalism, and Political Theology* (Bloomington: Indiana University Press, 2013). Finally, I confess I cannot quite understand the Paulinist interventions of Taubes without seeing how they are inflected as fragments, visions, and fantasies in the novel of Susan Taubes, *Divorcing* (New York: Random House, 1969). That story I will hold for another occasion.

37. Cf. Shmuel Trigano, "'The Jewish Question' in the Return to Paul," in Blanton and de Vries, *Paul and the Philosophers*. Trigano's work is important—essential even—though I think he and many others quite wrongly assume there is anything *representational* about "the universal" in recent work of Badiou and Žižek, something both philosophers are (both often and consistently) at pains to refuse as a debilitating form of traditional metaphysics and dangerous politics.

38. I pick on Professor Trigano's work here with admiration and in order to reflect myself on how his important criticisms and (theologico-)political concerns may function more forcefully in other contexts than his own. I hope to say more about his larger work in a different context. For now I note simply the updating and genealogical expansion of his earlier *L'E(xc)lu* in a reading of Romans as a paradigmatic moment in Western political economies in Shmuel Trigano, *Democratic Ideal and Shoah: The Unthought in Political Modernity*

(Albany: SUNY Press, 2009), pp. 85ff. What I cannot accept are Trigano's assertions—as if parroting a long history of Christian exceptionalism—that there is anything *original*, and therefore, *non-Jewish*, about Paul, the very assertions which ground Trigano's reading of Romans.

39. Comedy, as a philosophical topic with profound implications for questions of a genealogy of "religion," is a topic I will pursue more rigorously in the next book. Initial indications of these directions can be found in Ward Blanton and Yvonne Sherwood, "Shallow Graves: Toward a Philosophical Comedy of Tears Over the Serial Dying of Gods" in *Derrida Today* 6, no. 1 (2013): 78–96.

40. Again, the ambivalence involved here, with the author tipping his hat to the aggressivities of Rome even as he *usually* makes a narrative distinction between "Jews" and the followers of Jesus for the purposes of explaining violence, just makes the usual operation all the more striking (e.g., Luke 2:1, 3:1; Acts 17:7). That the author can also blame pagans for causing unrest which the Romans quell on behalf of the evident nonguilt of the Christians I find not to affect the effective force of the imaginary complicity between the followers of Jesus and Roman juridical authorities (cf. Acts 16, 19).

41. While a full discussion must wait another occasion, it is easy to see here how I read Schmitt's central interlocutor, Erik Peterson. Against an effusive ecclesiastical appropriation of the work of Erik Peterson in recent decades, I see absolutely no reason to assume that there is *anything* certain about the suggestion that, with its development of a Trinitarian theology, Christianity effectively subtracted itself from all forms of political theology, as if the Trinitarian confusion of the one and the many happily withholds justificatory blessing from all efforts either to represent or directly to incarnate in worldly political forms the structures of divinity or being themselves. This kind of assertion seems to me simply the apologetic revery of a triumphalist Christianity. While I want to develop the story further on another occasion, for the moment I note simply the sheer tenacity and intensity of Peterson's efforts to read Paul *into* his triumphalist story of a post-Jewish and postpagan postpolitics, a story always premised on the assumption that something about "Christianity" breaks decisively, and as an ideal entity, from its counterparts in "Judaism" or "paganism" (e.g., in his essay, "The Church from Jews and Gentiles," in *Theological Tractates* (Stanford: Stanford University Press, 2011), pp. 40–67. In terms of a genealogical intervention, then, I claim that Schmitt was in the right against Peterson, though Schmitt could not begin to see the ways in which, as Taubes began to imagine, there was in this material forgotten indications of a sovereign partisanship emerging "from below" rather than, always and already, from the side of institutional loci of power.

42. As we will see, one of the things I find most disappointing about Derrida's encounter with Paul in *Veils* is the way he immediately equates Pauline discus-

sions of veiling and insight with a flat-footed Platonism, which in turn he imagines to constitute *the constitutive difference* between Judaism and Christianity. Ouch. More interesting, freer from the inherited tale of "Christian origins," would necessarily have been to wonder about the relationship between Paul's apocalyptic polemic of the "veiling," of his adversaries and of Moses himself in 2 Corinthians 3, with Paul's situating of his own transformative news as a variation of a theme directly borrowed from the same Moses: "Do not say in your heart, 'Who will ascend into heaven?' (that is to bring Christ down) or 'Who will descend into the abyss?' (that is, to bring Christ up from the dead). But what does it say? 'The word is near you, on your lips and in your heart' (that is the word of faith that we proclaim)" (Romans 10:5–8).

The anti-Mosaic feel of the 2 Corinthians story is therefore only a repetition of what is more obvious at Romans 10. In both cases the partisan splits the inherited text into an imagined author and a peculiar splitting off (from the same text, from the same author) of rogue forms of agency (e.g., in Romans the difference between "what Moses writes" and what "the word of faith says") which can actually turn against the imagined authorial persona itself. Derrida's misreading is understandable, as it is how the early Christian apologies wanted to read Paul, and they effectively set the interpretive rules— constructed the concrete shoes—which transformed Paul the partisan into Paul the self-grounding original whole (or Platonism for the masses). But perhaps I have said enough to indicate that we need rather to think about Paul the reader of a rogue agency which will throughout have something important to do with *clinamen* and the Lacanian *objet petit a*, the little gap in agency which can threaten to burn up the very agency itself. These links we will develop in following chapters.

43. Like the 9/11 attack, perhaps (only time will tell), the effectively political symbolic force of the violence against Galilee, Judea, and the Temple around 70 C.E. remained an obsession to Jewish and non-Jewish writers for decades (cf. Josephus, 4 Ezra).

44. Cf. Josephus's *Jewish War* 7.263–71 or *Antiquities* 4.176–95. For discussion, note Harold Attridge, *The Interpretation of the Antiqutates Judaica of Flavius Josephus* (Cambridge: Scholars, 1976), pp. 90ff. More recently, note the remarkable series of commentaries on Josephus's writings, edited by Steve Mason, notably the discussion of colonial dynamics and adaptability in the excellent introduction to John Barclay's *Flavius Josephus: Against Apion* (vol. 10 of *Flavius Josephus: Translation and Commentary*) (Leiden: Brill, 2006), pp. 1–40.

45. That I say "potentially" under the same umbrella signals of course an important break of a philosophy of difference from all forms of representationalism. In the case of the former, the strange attachments and rogue passions constituting identity themselves "stick out" obtrusively as phenomena for analysis,

and these attachments or passions always render merely representational or naturalizing tales a kind of second-order tabulation of a more originary event.

46. You can see the distinctions I am drawing between my own and Taubes's project, my admiration for Taubes notwithstanding. In this case, pressing the relevant genealogical distinctions earlier in the history of Christianity is not a magic formulae, as if the original were more authentic. Nevertheless, my procedure insinuates much more clearly than Taubes, I think, the way the relevant schisms or fault lines within the genealogical drama are internally, intimately related. My main problem with Taubes is that *even his* story of Paul naturalizes too much of a tale we have been taught—carefully, strategically taught—to reify at every opportunity, namely, the distinction between Judaism and Christianity as oppositional identities within a totalized system of distinctions.

47. Cf. references to Plato and Moses respectively throughout Runia's classic work to get a sense of the phantasmagoria which sometimes seem to dupe Philo himself. On this topic, note the excellent discussions in relevant sections of T. David Runia, *On the Creation of the Cosmos According to Moses* (Atlanta: Societyof Biblical Literature, 2005).

48. I do not know of a better discussion than the one developed by Troels Engberg-Pedersen's groundbreaking work, *Cosmology and Self in the Apostle Paul: The Material Spirit* (Oxford: Oxford University Press, 2010), pp. 8–48.

49. I have explored some of these in relation to being an academic biblical scholar in Ward Blanton, "Neither Secular Nor Religious: On Saving a Critic in Biblical Criticism," in Roland Boer, ed., *Secularism and Biblical Studies* (London: Equinox, 2010), pp. 143–164.

50. Friedrich Nietzsche, *Daybreak: Thoughts on the Prejudices of Morality*, trans. R. J. Hollingdale (Cambridge: Cambridge University Press, 1982), p. 68, section 68.

1. CONTINGENCY; OR, COVENANTAL COMEDY

With regard to the epigraphic gloss of Paul: if such a line were expressed in George Sorel, would it sound so placid as it tends to sound all locked up tight within a New Testament? Obviously, it would not, and this is a "special kind of obviousness" which should not escape our wonder. Recall Sorel to Halévy:

> The revolutionary myths which exist at the present time are almost pure; they allow us to understand the activity, the sentiments and the ideas of the masses as they prepare themselves to enter on a decisive struggle; they are not descriptions of things but expressions of a will to act. A utopia is, on the contrary, an intellectual product. . . . Whilst contemporary myths lead people to prepare themselves for a combat

which will destroy the existing state of things, the effect of utopias has always been to direct people's minds towards reforms which can be brought by patching up the system.

In this *Auseinandersetzung* of Pauline apocalypticism and modern revolutionary thought is a scene in which phenomena, will, and effect all seem remarkably, usefully skewed. Cf. Georges Sorel, *Reflections on Violence* (Cambridge: Cambridge University Press, 2002), p. 28f.

1. Cf. Jacques Lacan, *The Seminar of Jacques Lacan VII: Transference*, trans. Cormac Gallagher (New York: Karnac, 2002). While I think Foucault's reading of Lacan as a return of Cartesian thought to "the oldest tradition, the oldest questioning, the oldest disquiet of the *epimeleia heautou*, which is the most general form of spirituality." Michel Foucault, *Hermeneutics of the Subject: Lectures at the Collège de France, 1981–82* (London: Palgrave Macmillan, 2002), p. 30. Fair enough, but that disquiet—which itself drives, lures, and impels the "practice on oneself" of philosophical life—is perhaps more directly approached by Lacanian *topoi* of a madness of desire than by terms like "practice." On the other hand, assuming the two are intertwined, then what is the value of Foucault's naming Heidegger or Lacan as the either/or of contemporary theorizing? Here I depart also from the very interesting discussion of Jean Allouch, *La psychoanalyse: est-elle un exercice sprituel? Réponse à Michel Foucault* (Paris: EPEL, 2007).

2. Michel Foucault articulates a standard opinion when he writes: For our purposes, note however, that in the 1960–61 seminar on transference, Lacan articulates love as the 'being relation' operative between lover and beloved with what one does not know (and yet knows). It is that which splits the singularity of such a relation from itself, that which indicates a certain *topos* of castration, and that which points toward an excess over the self-referential or homeostatic nature of identity.

3. I say early development in the sense that he developed these in two of the first books to appear in English (*The Sublime Object of Ideology* and *For They Know Not What They Do*). The category remains essential for him, however, and here I am quoting from Slavoj Žižek, *The Parallax View* (Cambridge: MIT Press, 2006), p. 310.

4. Jacques Derrida, "My Chances/*Mes Chances*: A Rendezvous with Some Epicurean Stereophanies," in *Psyche: Inventions of the Other* (Stanford: Stanford University Press, 2007), 1:351.

5. Bruno Bosteels has an excellent discussion of the development of Althusser's questions about structure and historical change, which are taken up and developed by students, including Alain Badiou. See Bosteel's *Badiou and Politics* (Durham: Duke University Press, 2011), pp. 44–76.

6. Cf. Eric L. Santner, *On the Psychotheology of Everyday Life: Reflections on*

Freud and Rosenzweig (Chicago: University of Chicago Press, 2001), and *The Royal Remains: the People's Two Bodies and the Endgames of Sovereignty* (Chicago: University of Chicago Press, 2011). Santner's work, a rethinking of categories of the messianic in relation to a kind of surplus immanence within immanence, is very important, and I will return to it.

7. Cf. Giorgio Agamben, "The Passion of Facticity," in *Potentialities: Collected Essays in Philosophy* (Stanford: Stanford University Press, 1999), pp. 185–204.

8. Note that it is "facticity," which is the Heideggerian philosophical topos, that finds its most immediate resonance within Pauline stories of a faithful waiting on the coming *parousia* of Jesus. This particular resonance is also what drives the early Heidegger to understand a historically authentic Paul in 2 Thessalonians as intentionally setting up a contradictory apparatus for predicting the approach of the parousia as well as a peculiar doubling of Christ and the so-called anti-Christ figure in that letter. The Christic doppelganger and the refusal of pseudepigraphic writing in Paul's name are essential for Heidegger to bring out the hesitation and ambivalence constitutive of the *singularity* of facticity. See Ward Blanton, "Heidegger's Light from the Ancient Near East," chapter 3 in *Displacing Christian Origins: Philosophy, Secularity, and the New Testament* (Chicago: University of Chicago Press, 2007): I also think it is imperative that we not miss the deep links between Heideggerian thrownness into facticity and the Lacanian emphasis on split subjectivity. The historical finitude of Heidegger and the structural splitting or finitude of Lacan cohere much better than Michel Foucault recognized when he makes this split the great either/or of his time. My juxtaposition of the two here is self-conscious, drawing out the similarity—for the comparison with Paul—of different ways to imagine what Adrian Johnston, speaking about Žižek, calls "a contingent yet a priori material foundation" of phenomena. Adrian Johnston, *Žižek's Ontology: A Transcendental Materialist Theory of Subjectivity* (Evanston, IL: Northwestern University Press), p. 22. Here I just mention the issue (highlighted by the title of the book), declare my position on the matter, and point to Lacan's allusion to Heidegger.

9. As they are also haunted by, I note, the sacrifice of Abraham. My work on the politico-theological "afterlives" of Paul and Abraham will appear elsewhere, a topic I have started to teach, lecture, and write about with Yvonne Sherwood. For the moment, I simply reference the important example of another haunting by Abraham in Paul Kahn, *Political Theology: Four New Chapters on the Concept of Sovereignty* (New York: Columbia University Press, 2011).

10. Louis Althusser, *Philosophy of the Encounter: Later Writings 1978–1987* (London: Verso, 2006).

11. Remarkable references and engagements with the figure of Paul occur throughout Breton's philosophical oeuvre, though, for sustained reflection, see Stanislas Breton, *A Radical Philosophy of Saint Paul* (New York: Columbia University Press, 2011).

12. Louis Althusser, *Philosophy of the Encounter: Later Writings 1978–1987* (London: Verso, 2006) p. 183.

13. One sees how my approach to the genealogy of these categories is so profoundly different from someone like Martin Hägglund, Quentin Meillassoux, or even some of the work of Alain Badiou, all of whose wonderful pleas for a new materialism in philosophy seem deeply marred to me by their docility in the face of received category distinctions between religion and its outside. I explained why I think we should develop a cultivated *indifference* to this distinction in *Displacing Christian Origins* and have summarized in a Deleuzean vein the basic genealogical and political thrust of what for me are the important issues in Ward Blanton, "Neither Secular Nor Religious: On Saving a Critical in Biblical Scholarship," in Roland Boer, ed., *Secularism and Biblical Studies* (London: Equinox, 2010).

14. This line from one of Breton's private letters now warehoused in his archive within the Catholic Institute of Paris, in this case p. 2 of entry 786.28.1.a. Althusser-Breton (5 p., i.e., 3 f.). The letter was later published as "Jésus et Lacan" in *Psychanalystes: Revue du Collège de psychanalystes*, no. 14 (1985): 75–82.

15. Ibid., pp. 4, 2.

16. For present purposes I follow the translation in Jacques Derrida, *Psyche: Inventions of the Other*, ed. Peggy Kamuf and Elizabeth Rottenberg (Stanford: Stanford University Press, 2007).

17. Clayton Crockett, *Deleuze Beyond Badiou: Ontology, Multiplicity, and Event* (New York: Columbia University Press, 2012), p. 69.

18. To say the least, as historian of Paulinism and of his Greco-Roman philosophical contexts, such a wonder is not at all without interest for me! But it is not the issue I am pressing here. On that question of the ancient figure, one to pursue on another occasion, I will simply mention that the question of Paulinism and popularized Platonisms is far from simple, particularly in light of, precisely, the Stoic immanence evoked by the apostle at key points (e.g., 1 Corinthians 15:28; cf. Romans 11:36). As a placeholder for coming discussions, one should mention the stunning analysis, insights yet to be worked through in the guild of biblical scholarship, of the work of Troels Engberg-Pedersen, *Cosmology and Self in the Apostle Paul: The Material Spirit* (Oxford: Oxford University Press, 2010), esp. pp. 8–38. I think Engberg-Pedersen's reading of 1 Corinthians 15 as, precisely, a Stoic deconstruction of Platonic dualism, is correct.

19. My sense that Derrida here does not do enough to unseat the very terms of an imagined and inherited contest between the veils of the "Christian Paul" and synecdochic references to Judaism (via Levinas, talk of law, and the tallith) hangs on me when I read the otherwise very nice piece on *Veils* by Timothy K. Beal and Tod Linafelt, "To Love the Tallith More than God," in Yvonne

Sherwood and Kevin Hart, eds., *Derrida and Religion: Other Testaments* (New York: Routledge, 2005), pp. 175–188. I should point out, though, that Beal and Linafelt are here intentionally playing close to the text of Derrida, so one would not necessarily expect them to contravene this aspect of the piece. Also engaging the same essay of Derrida, Pyper does speak more rigorously to unsettle the terms of debate whose operationality I am arguing Derrida does too little to unseat. Hugh S. Pyper, "Other Eyes: Reading and Not Reading the Hebrew Scriptures/Old Testament with a Little Help from Derrida and Cixous," ibid., pp. 159–173. That it is precisely Paul here in Derrida who somehow escapes what might be the expected deconstruction or problematizing of the opposition between Judaism, Christianity, and Western philosophy I do not at all take to be a mere accident, a mere slip of the pen.

20. There is an excellent discussion of Serres's engagement with the Epicurean *clinamen* in Hanjo Berressem, "'Incerto Tempore Incertisque Locis': The Logic of *Clinamen* and the Birth of Physics," in Niran Abbas, ed., *Mapping Michel Serres* (Ann Arbor: University of Michigan Press, 2005), pp. 51–71.

21. Hal Taussig, *In the Beginning Was the Meal: Social Experimentation and Early Christian Identity* (Minneapolis: Fortress, 2009), p. 54. In citing this excellent book, here I drew attention to the reference to "Christian" communities only because in our case (unlike Taussig's wide-ranging study of New Testament texts) we are focused on Paul, for whom I do not like to use the term.

22. In case I need to say it out loud, one sees here, too, my interest in "undying" life not as some category of a stable or ideal eternity but rather as a matter of properly Epicurean swerve, particularly an Epicurean swerve that takes some new twists in the presence of later figures like Althusser and Derrida. Put differently, undying life will be for me a matter of the archive of an "underground current of [repressed] materialism."

23. Pliny, *Letters and Panegyrics* (Cambridge: Harvard University Press), letter 10.

24. As for a comparison of Pauline communities and other forms of Greco-Roman associations, see, in addition to Taussig, the excellent recent work of Philip A. Harland, *Associations, Synagogues, and Congregations: Claiming a Place in Ancient Mediterranean Society* (Minneapolis: Fortress, 2003), *Dynamics of Identity in the World of the Early Christians* (London: T&T Clark, 2009); and, very differently focused, William S. Campbell, *Paul and the Creation of Christian Identity* (London: T&T Clark, 2008).

25. Karl Marx, "Difficulties Concerning the Identity of the Democritean and Epicurean Philosophy of Nature," part 1, section 3, subsection C in *The Difference Between the Democritean and Epicurean Philosophy of Nature*, *Marx-Engels: Collected Works*, vol. 1 (London: Blunden, 1902 [1841]).

26. Ibid., "The Declination of the Atom from the Straight Line," part 2, ch. 1.

27. For two examples to swim up the "underground current" against the current, see Clarence E. Glad, *Paul and Philodemus: Adaptability in Epicurean and*

Early Christian Psychagogy (New York: Brill, 1995); and—focused primarily on Renaissance depictions—Jonathan Goldberg, *The Seeds of Things: Theorizing Sexuality and Materiality in Renaissance Representations* (New York: Fordham University Press, 2009).

28. I am thinking of Heidegger's fascinating reading of Pauline texts. See Martin Heidegger, *The Phenomenology of Religious Life* (Bloomington: University of Indiana Press, 2004). I discuss and criticize aspects of this work in my *Displacing Christian Origins*.

29. Michel Serres, *The Birth of Physics* (Manchester: Clinamen, 2001), p. 21.

30. This is perhaps the important point to make in relation to Schweitzer's line about Nietzsche failing to *become Saint Paul*. It is not so much that the materialist failed to become like Paul. He will have become like him, *one way or another*.

31. Derrida, *Psyche*, 1:362.

32. Serres, *The Birth of Physics*, p. 42f.

33. Ibid., p. 22.

34. Berressem, "'Incerto Tempore Incertisque Locis,'" pp. 51–71.

35. Michel Serres, *Angels: A Modern Myth* (Paris: Flammarion, 1995), p. 33.

2. ON BEING CALLED DEAD

1. Stanislas Breton, *The Word and the Cross* (New York: Fordham University Press, 2002), p. 55. As should be clear by now, I flag the word *Christianity*—understandable enough in Breton's contexts within the Institut Catholique in Paris—for serious discussions of Paul, as it was a term Paul did not use. Nor is it a term he *would have* used if it were thought to imply the invention of a new religion. For a lengthier discussion of a reading of Paul as a partisan among a multiplicity of early Jewish trajectories, see my introduction to Ward Blanton and Hent de Vries, eds., *Paul and the Philosophers* (New York: Fordham University Press, 2013).

2. Here I am thinking above all of the repeated self-definitions of Žižek and Badiou. As for secondary literature discussing the common self-designations, my favourites are Adrian Johnston, *Žižek's Ontology: A Transcendental Materialist Theory of Subjectivity* (Chicago: Northwestern University Press, 2008); and Bruno Bosteels, *Badiou and Politics* (Durham, NC: Duke University Press, 2011). Useful short interviews with Badiou and Žižek can be found in an importantly related collection of Levi Bryant, Nick Srnicek, and Graham Harman, eds., *The Speculative Turn: Continental Materialism and Realism* (New York: re.press, 2010).

3. Two very important ideology critiques of modern biblical studies should be mentioned straightaway, Dale Martin's "Paul and the Judaism/Hellenism

Divide: Toward a Social History of the Question," in Troels Engberg-Pedersen, *Paul Beyond the Judaism/Hellenism Divide* (Louisville, KY: Westminster John Knox, 2001), pp. 29–61; and Halvor Moxnes's *Jesus and the Rise of Nationalism: A New Quest for the Nineteenth-Century Historical Jesus* (London: I. B. Tauris, 2010). Susannah Heschel has done the most important archival work about the central function of anti-Semitism within modern biblical studies; see Susannah Heschel, *Abraham Geiger and the Jewish Jesus* (Chicago: University of Chicago Press, 1998), and *The Aryan Jesus: Christian Theologians and the Bible in Nazi Germany* (Princeton: Princeton University Press, 2008). See also William Arnal, *The Symbolic Jesus: Historical Scholarship, Judaism and the Construction of Contemporary Identity* (London: Equinox, 2005); James Crossley, *Jesus in an Age of Terror: Scholarly Projects for a New American Century* (London: Equinox, 2008); Shawn Kelley, *Racializing Jesus: Ideology and the Formation of Modern Biblical Scholarship* (London: Routledge, 2002). The peculiarly disciplined work of thinking through the implications of such studies in ways that articulate themselves in new historiographic models for the historical Paul are only beginning to emerge really, in part because initial efforts to bracket discrete exegetical elements (as implicit anti-Semitisms, vestiges of crass valorizations of Protestantism over Catholicism or Judaism, etc.) in our reading of Paul do not yet go far enough in articulating what a more carefully interpreted Paul *was* doing (if not, say, criticizing "Jewish legalism," exploring new and noninstrumental existential modes for religion, and so on). Several important steps in the right direction should be noted, however. See Stanley K. Stowers, *A Rereading of Romans: Justice, Jews, and Gentiles* (New Haven: Yale University Press, 1994); Neil Elliott, *The Arrogance of Nations: Reading Romans in the Shadow of Empire* (Minneapolis: Fortress, 2008); Briggitte Kahl, *Galatians Re-imagined: Reading with the Eyes of the Vanquished* (Minneapolis: Fortress, 2010); and, more popularly, Pamela Eisenbaum, *Paul Was Not a Christian: The Original Message of a Misunderstood Apostle* (San Francisco: HarperCollins, 2009).

4. See, for example, the discussion in Jean-Michel Rey's excellent little book, *Paul ou les ambiguités (penser/rêver)* (Paris: Olivier, 2008), pp. 151–165. I am indebted to Sophie Fuggle for pointing out this book to me.

5. For those who are not familiar with contemporary historical research on Paul, it may be useful to recommend three books that I find to be some of the most important touchstones for an historical understanding of the figure. For specific readings of Pauline texts, I find unsurpassed the work of Dale B. Martin, *The Corinthian Body* (New Haven: Yale University Press); and Stanley Stowers, *Rereading Romans* (New Haven: Yale University Press). For more general and introductory comments, I recommend E. P. Sanders, *Paul: A Very Short Introduction* (New York: Oxford University Press, 2001); and David Horrell, *An Introduction to the Study of Paul* (New York: Continuum, 2000).

6. The distinction between authentic and inauthentic letters of Paul has been a set piece of university discourse about this literature for more than a century in fact. For general discussion, see the introductions of Sanders or Horrell. For a more general historical framework explaining the appearance of pseudepigraphic productions in the Pauline tradition, see the reconstruction of John Dominic Crossan and Jonathan Reed, *In Search of Paul: How Jesus's Apostle Opposed Rome's Empire with God's Kingdom* (San Francisco: HarperSanFrancisco, 2004).

7. Stanislas Breton, *A Radical Philosophy of Saint Paul* (New York: Columbia University Press, 2011), p. 58.

8. Ibid.

9. While the inflection in this quotation is Deleuzean, it is important here that Žižek compares the operation of the quasi-cause to that of the *objet petit a* in the work of Lacan. I will return to some of these intertwined themes as a kind of pressure on the "return" of Paul in the discussion of Pasolini. Slavoj Žižek, *Less Than Nothing: Hegel and the Shadow of Dialectical Materialism* (New York: Verso, 2012), p. 855.

10. Ibid., p. 857.

11. Breton, *A Radical Philosophy of Saint Paul*, p. 60.

12. See the interview "Philosophy and Marxism," in Louis Althusser, *Philosophy of the Encounter: Later Writings, 1978–87* (New York: Verso, 2006), p. 281.

13. Paul Ricouer, *Lectures on Ideology and Utopia* (New York: Columbia University Press, 1986).

14. Ibid., p. 115.

15. Louis Althusser, "Ideology and the State," in *On Ideology* (London: Verso, 2008), p. 46.

16. Étienne Balibar, "The Non-Contemporaneity of Althusser," in E. Ann Kaplan and Michael Sprinkler, eds., *The Althusserian Legacy* (New York: Verso, 1993), pp. 1–16 (cited p. 14).

17. Genealogically speaking I feel a great deal of affinity here with Montag's very interesting recent discussions (to my knowledge unpublished except in Spanish) of Spinozistic immanence as a repetition of an Epicurean materialism in "Lucretius Hebraizant: Spinoza's Reading of Ecclesiastes"; cf. "Lucretius Hebraizant: La lectura de Spinoza del Eclesiastés," in Montserrat Galcerán Huguet and Mario Espinoza Pino, eds., *Spinoza contemporaneo* (Madrid: Tierradenadie, 2009). See also Warren Montag, "Spinoza and Althusser Against Hermeneutics: Interpretation or Intervention?" in E. Ann Kaplan and Michael Sprinkler, eds., *The Althusserian Legacy* (New York: Verso, 1993), pp. 51–58.

18. Warren Montag, "Lucretius Hebraizant: Spinoza's Reading of Ecclesiastes," *European Journal of Philosophy* 20, no. 1, (March 2012): 109–129.

19. Louis Althusser, *Philosophy of the Encounter: Later Writings, 1978–87* (New

York: Verso, 2006), p. 174. I have developed some of the links between secular immanence and the "return" of religion as an analytic form and critical archive in Ward Blanton, "'Reappearance of Paul, "Sick"': Foucault's Biopolitics and the Political Significance of Pasolini's Apostle," *Journal for Cultural and Religious Theory*, 10, no. 2 (2010): 52–77.

20. Althusser, "Ideology and the State," p. 45f.

21. Gianni Vattimo and Santiago Zabala, *Hermeneutic Communism from Heidegger to Marx* (New York: Columbia University Press, 2011), p. 20. I do not mean to minimize here the importantly divergent negotiations of the question of an inaugural "event" of disclosure in Heidegger, Althusser, Vattimo/Zabala, or a reader of Althusser like Alain Badiou, though a full discussion of the event (perhaps paired with Bultmann) will wait for another time. I do want to note only that what several years ago seemed certain, a distinction between Badiou, Žižek, and the more Heideggerian version of "weak thought," seems less so today.

22. Giorgio Agamben, *The Kingdom and the Glory: For a Theological Genealogy of Economy and Government* (Stanford: Stanford University Press, 2011), p. 1.

23. Eric Santner, *The Royal Remains: The People's Two Bodies and the Endgames of Sovereignty* (Chicago: University of Chicago Press, 2011), p. 39.

24. Ibid., p. 27.

25. Above all, I would, in this context, like to refer to the relationship between older discussions of a factical horizon and the steering of this phenomenological tradition toward a focus on specific techniques and technologies of self-making, the specificity of which I find to be a good way of interacting with the focus of Santner. Cf. Giorgio Agamben, *What Is an Apparatus?* (Stanford: Stanford University Press, 2009). Incidentally, I find that, from start to finish, the question of this specificity of technique is a much better way to engage the peculiar aura that attached to the Pauline movement than more wholistic modes of thinking about a new covenant, new religion, new organizational mode. The surplus of immanence within immanence emerges from quirks in our practices of the everyday, the body's (un)rootedness in the symbolic identities on offer, and it will ultimately be important to engage this issue with more patient readings of the believing body in Pauline texts than have emerged to this point. Santner's statement is no less true for the ancient contexts than the medieval and modern ones: "what is missed in . . . all efforts to deflate the force of political metaphors by 'deconstructing' their metaphoricity, their status as fictions or rhetorical figures, is the difference between symbolic fiction and fantasy. What is missed is precisely the fact that such fictions get a grip on the imagination of individuals and collectives because they are ultimately sustained by the 'real stuff' of fantasy, by the dimension I have been calling the flesh" (Santner, *The Royal Remains*, p. 42f.). Put differently for the sake of the Pauline conversations, this implies that all readings

of the ancient collective imaginaries which are premissed entirely on epochal, economic, or forensic distinctions between a "Jewish" and "Christian" mode of thinking about law, patrimony, etc., necessarily obscure important aspects of the mechanics of finding oneself, in the Pauline language, in Christ, crucified as Christ, etc.

26. There is a great deal to say about the excellent work of Fenves, and I hope to have time and space to do so more seriously in relation to the Paulinisms of the early Heidegger in the next volume. See Peter Fenves, *The Messianic Reduction: Walter Benjamin and the Shape of Time* (Stanford: Stanford University Press, 2011).

27. Apologies to Rosemary Radford Ruether for playing on the title of her classic, *Sexism and God-Talk.*

28. Stanislas Breton, *La Pensée du Rien* (Kampen: Kok Pharos, 1992), p. 113.

29. Stanislas Breton, *Théorie des Idéologies* (Paris: Desclée, 1976), p. 34.

30. Ibid. p. 44.

31. The neuter (see below) is a common motif within Breton's ontological writings throughout his career, indicating (among other things) his interest in neo-Platonism, set theory, and univocal ontologies like that of Duns Scotus. While it is not the time to explore the striking theologico-political genealogy signaled by this interest, it is worth pointing out that Breton's work in this respect stands in stark contrast to recent anxieties about univocity and its ambiguity of the neutral space of being (or even disavowals of it, theological circumscriptions of the neutral as a taboo association) in the political theologies of the Radical Orthodoxy movement and others. For this anxiety, see, among other places, Conor Cunningham, *Genealogy of Nihilism* (London: Routledge, 2002); John Milbank, "The Thomistic Telescope: Truth and Identity," in Conor Cunningham and Peter Chandler Jr., *Transcendence and Phenomenology* (London: SCM, 2008); cf. the discussion in Nicholas Wolterstorff, *Justice: Rights and Wrongs* (Princeton: Princeton University Press, 2008), pp. 24ff., especially the chapter about conflicting genealogies of rights.

32. See the transcript of the "Alterities" conference in 1986 during which Breton tried to articulate his own more and less metaphysical modes of thinking difference and alterity alongside those of Pierre-Jean Labarrière and Jacques Derrida et al., "Difference, Relation, Alterity," trans. Pierre Colin, *Parallax* 10, no. 4 (2004): 42–60, p. 43.

33. Breton, *Théorie des Idéologies*, p. 35f.

34. Ibid.

35. Ibid., p. 35.

36. Ibid., p. 118; cf. Breton, *Théorie des Idéologies*, p. 35.

37. Much more could be said about these issues in relation to Breton's work, though such discussions would exceed the scope and interests of an introduction. But the rejection of the nothing as a substratum or outside of ideology are crucial

and affect rather intimately the occasional critique of Breton as a Hegelian or neo-Platonic philosopher of identity. We should also not miss the way recent critiques of Gilles Deleuze, as neo-Platonic or Scotist thinker of the indifferent One, are answered in the same way: with a rejection of the substantiality or role as substratum of the void. See the excellent reflections on Deleuze and the future of emancipatory philosophy in Kenneth Surin, *Freedom Not Yet: Liberation and the Next World Order* (Durham: Duke University Press, 2009), p. 238f. We should not miss that a similar concern not to reify the void as the substratum of the One is a driving concern behind Alain Badiou's critique of Gilles Deleuze, which plays itself out also as the particular sort of Paulinism Badiou finds in the ancient apostle. Cf. Alain Badiou, *Deleuze: The Clamor of Being* (Minneapolis: University of Minnesota Press, 2000), and Badiou's (Paulinist) rejection of a "fourth" discourse of mysticism about the unspeakable One: "For Paul, the fourth discourse will remain a mute supplement, enclosing the Other's share in the subject. He refuses to let addressed discourse, which is that of the declaration of faith, justify itself through an unaddressed discourse, whose substance consists in unutterable utterances. . . . I believe this to be an important indication, one that concerns every militant of a truth. . . . I shall call 'obscurantist' every discourse that presumes to legitimate itself on the basis of an unaddressed discourse." Alain Badiou, *Saint Paul: The Foundation of Universalism* (Stanford: Stanford University Press, 2003), p. 52.

38. In this sense, Breton's discussions of the inconsistent and ontologically ephemeral (yet structurally profound) nature of the "empty part" or "zero" level of ideology are comparable to the later Lacanian discussions of the Real. Cf. Žižek's discussion of the two roles of the "real" in Lacan's early and later work, Slavoj Žižek, *The Sublime Object of Ideology* (New York: Verso, 1989), pp. 161ff. Žižek's own work, it may be added, has moved toward a more structurally/internally generated model of the real over time. See, e.g., Slavoj Žižek, *The Parallax View* (Boston: MIT Press, 2006), pp. 25f.

39. Compare the majority of Agamben's book on the remainder/remnant (which orients itself not so much on Romans as on 1 Corinthians 7 where the messianic pressuring of temporality forces an activity "as if" one were "not" what one is) to Rudolf Bultmann's earlier (Heideggerian) fascination with the Pauline category, neither boredom nor anxiety exactly but functioning similarly at a quasi-ontological level. Giorgio Agamben, *The Time That Remains: A Commentary on the Letter to the Romans* (Stanford: Stanford University Press, 2005); Compare the crescendo of Bultmann's famous exposition of Paulinism in Rudolf Bultmann, *Theology of the New Testament* (New York: Scribner's, 1951), 1:351f. As we seek to establish (generally missed) encounters between disciplines, interests, and temporalities, one should note also the emancipatory exploration of these categories in the work of Vincent Wimbush, *Paul the Worldly Ascetic* (New York: Mercer University Press, 1987).

40. Breton, *Théorie des Idéologies*, p. 47.

41. Ibid. While it would carry us too far afield to explore the link between the "materialism" of Althusser's "aleatory encounter" and Breton's "meontology," suffice it to say that the crucial link is with the thought of contingency (the swerve or *clinamen* of "aleatory encounter") and Breton's thought of the "crucified" or brutally suppressed messianic function. Both alike provide a ground that disturbs the harmonious (but atomistic) fall of atoms in the void (for Althusser's materialism) or the enjoyment of atomized worldhood and its "special kind of obviousness" in Breton.

42. Ibid. cf. 48f.

43. Note the way that Althusser is at pains to include Heidegger in his repressed history of materialism, primarily because Althusser sees in Heidegger's *es gibt* or *il y a* of the facticity of everyday life a profound statement about the originary contingency from which emerges this everyday. "A philosophy of the *es gibt*, of the "this is what is given," makes short shrift of all the classic questions about the Origin, and so on. And it 'opens up' a prospect that restores a kind of transcendental contingency of the world, which in turn points to the opening up of Being, the original urge of Being, its 'destining,' beyond which there is nothing to seek or think. Thus the world is a 'gift' that we have been given, the 'fact of the fact [*fait de fait*]' that we have not chosen, and it 'opens up' before us in the facticity of its contingency, and even beyond this facticity, in what is not merely an observation, but a 'being-in-the-world' that commands all possible meaning." Louis Althusser, *Philosophy of the Encounter: Later Writings, 1978–87* (New York: Verso, 2006), p. 170, cf. 190.

44. I am also echoing this particular language of Paul as an evocation of the language of the "neutral" in Roland Barthes, which also has strong echoes with Breton's lifelong reflections on weakness and void as a paradoxical (and, as both would point out, scandalous) form of power. While the comparisons and the ongoing vivacity of their formulations are a topic for a different context, note the immanent antagonism implied in Barthes's linguistic focus: "let's recall that the subject of our course, the Neutral, is what baffles the paradigm: the paradigm is the law against which the Neutral rebels." Roland Barthes, *The Neutral: Lecture Course at the College de France (1977–1978)* (New York: Columbia University Press, 2005), p. 42. In this respect, Breton shows us what Barthes never says clearly, that Paulinism constitutes a significant part of the archive of the rebellious neutral.

45. Stanislas Breton, *The Word and the Cross*, trans. Jacquelyn Porter (New York: Fordham University Press, 2002), p. 54.

46. For the Spinozist-Althusserian critique of notions of individual freedom, see further on in this chapter. For the notion of Christianity as the spawn of, or tarrying with, a nightmare, see, among other places, Breton, *The Word and the Cross*, p. 71. Perhaps it is worth highlighting, in that respect, a fascinating—if

often understated and underdeveloped—discourse of the "nocturnal" one finds in Breton's writings, a discourse which insinuates itself into the present volume at multiple levels. While this is not the place to develop the ideas at any length, my suggestion is to consider Breton's interest in neo-Platonic and Scotist univocity, on the one hand, and a Schellingian indeterminacy between God and Satan, on the other. Underneath and in excess of Apollonian representations and functional categories, there is a kind of "white noise" of univocity whose appearance sometimes threatens to undo all such roles.

47. See Stanislas Breton, *Philosopher par passion et par raison* (Grenoble: Jérome Million et les Auteurs, 1990), p. 8f.

While Sloterdijk does not generally remark on the profound links between Paulinism and precisely the break with religion imagined to mark the work of the young Heidegger, it is nevertheless the case that his own reflections on Heidegger in the aptly named *Nicht Gerretet* (Unsaved) constitute an important point of comparison for Breton's reading of Paul. See Peter Sloterdijk, *Nicht Gerretet: Versuche nach Heidegger* (Frankfurt: Suhrkamp, 2001). My own analysis of the intimate union of, precisely, Heidegger's effort to step outside of theology or religion and his own early turn toward Paulinism appears in a chapter entitled, "Paul's Secretary: Heidegger's Apostolic Light from the East" in Ward Blanton *Displacing Christian Origins: Philosophy, Secularity, and the New Testament* (Chicago: University of Chicago Press, 2007).

48. Breton, *Théorie des Idéologies*, p. 93.

49. Ibid., p. 94.

50. The play was the subject of a recent conference at the University of Glasgow, "Paul, Political Fidelity and the Philosophy of Alain Badiou: A Discussion of *Incident at Antioch*," February 13–14, 2009. See Alain Badiou, *The Incident at Antioch* (New York: Columbia University Press, 2013).

51. For an extended exploration of the motif, see Jacques Derrida, *The Gift of Death* trans. David Wills (Chicago: University of Chicago Press, 1995), esp. pp. 12ff.

52. Breton, *Philosopher par passion et par raison*, p. 9. This is the kind of phrase which summarizes very nicely the ambiguously (post)metaphysical nature of Breton's work. The movement of being is autotelic, returning to itself, but only inasmuch as it is producing a form of alterity and negation of identity. Breton was criticized by Derrida and others for phrasings that sound all too Hegelian, as perhaps does this one. Nevertheless, in keeping with what Derrida would himself say of Hegel (namely, that we would never be done reading and rereading him), Breton said fairly often that the best way to think the limits of metaphysics was by eschewing the illusion that one had stepped outside of them!

53. Ibid., p. 8.

54. The association between appearance and messianic temporality in Benjamin is a common exploration. Note the Bergsonian link between ephemeral

"image" and opening to radical revaluation in his famous "Concept of History" essay. Walter Benjamin, *Selected Writings, 1938–1940* (Cambridge: Belknap, 2003), 4:390, 397.

55. Moreover, it is common within Breton's writings to criticize the history of Christian theology which keeps Paulinist kenoticism or the Gothic inflation of the crucified safely distanced at the level of myth. Breton argues frequently that the subversive force of Paulinist cross-talk must be allowed to do its destructive and deflating labor within the ontological structures of Christian theology. Cf. Breton, *The Word and the Cross*, 95.

56. Jacob Taubes, *From Cult to Culture: Fragments Toward a Critique of Historical Reason* (Stanford: Stanford University Press, 2010), pp. 5–6.

57. Breton, *Théorie des Idéologies*, p. 116.

58. Stanislas Breton, *Philosophie Buissonniere* (Grenoble: Jérôme Millon, 1989), pp. 65–74.

59. Ibid., p. 74.

60. Ibid.

61. Ibid., pp. 71, 74.

62. Cf. Breton, *Philosopher par passion et par raison*, p. 8.

63. One does not need to go far to discover a panoply of edifices, foundations, and richness of origin in relation to the Pauline legacy within the literature. For the moment I am sampling from some of the old standards: C. H. Dodd, Arthur Darby Nock, and Johannes Munck.

3. INSURRECTIONIST RISK

1. Boris Groys, *The Communist Postscript*, trans. Thomas H. Ford (New York: Verso, 2009), pp. 9ff.

2. Indeed, Groys's criticisms of Foucault are oriented primarily around a desire to *extend* the folding, splitting, inverting paradoxes of the Foucauldian spiritual exercises, namely, by trying to formalize them in reason as such (which he does not think Foucault does); cf. p. 19f. In other words, despite their differences, under the banner of the spiritual exercise of "stuckness," it seems appropriate to allow Groys and Foucault to stand side by side.

3. See Didier Franck, *Nietzsche and the Shadow of God*, trans. Bettina Bergo (Bloomington: Indiana University Press, 2012). I am very grateful to Bettina Bergo both for pointing me toward Franck's work several years ago and also for showing me in advance pieces of her excellent English translation of this book.

4. Gilles Deleuze, *Nietzsche and Philosophy* (London: Continuum, 2006), p. 36.

5. Franco "Bifo" Berardi, *The Soul at Work: From Alienation to Autonomy* (Los Angeles: Semiotext(e), 2009), p. 21.

6. Luther Martin, Huck Gutman, and Patrick Hutton, eds., *Technologies of the Self: A Seminar with Michel Foucault* (Amherst: University of Massachusetts, 1988), p. 25.

7. If the story begins for me with this project to suggest constellations for a rethinking of Paul which is simultaneously a rethinking of both "religion" and "philosophy," then my next book about biopolitics, singularity, and Mediterranean life in the Roman Empire will tackle the topic from the ancient side of the comparative equation.

8. Halvor Moxnes makes the same point by declaring that Foucault "compares the moral philosophers of the early Roman empire of the first two centuries with Christian writers from the fourth and fifth centuries, not with their contemporaries in earliest Christianity." Halvor Moxnes, "Asceticism and Christian Identity in Antiquity: A Dialogue with Foucault and Paul," *Journal for the Study of the New Testament* 26, no. 1 (2003): 3–29 (8).

9. As Hans Ruin glosses: "Christianity, in Nietzsche's account, is simply the destruction of Rome and Athens by Jerusalem, contrived by Paul, as the foremost representative of priestly slave morality." Hans Ruin, "Faith, Grace, and the Destruction of Tradition," *Journal of Cultural and Religious Theory* 11, no. 1 (2010): 25. Ruin goes on to suggest some of the ways Foucault's interest in *askesis* could be read as a transformative challenge to this Nietzschean narrative. My own interests tend to revolve around two related stories: Christianity as a perpetuation of the docility, control, and hierarchy already endemic to Western metaphysics (i.e., Christianity as a "Platonism for the masses"); and Paulinism as *another* instance with which Foucault *could have* altered the received story.

10. I am thinking of Jonathan Crary, *Suspensions of Perception: Attention, Spectacle, and Modern Culture* (Cambridge: MIT Press, 1999); and Peter Sloterdijk, *Du Musst dein Leben ändern: Über Anthropotechnik* (Berlin: Suhrkamp, 2011).

11. Michel Foucault, *The History of Sexuality*, vol. 2: *The Use of Pleasure* (New York: Vintage, 1988), p. 4.

12. Ibid., p. 11.

13. Gilles Deleuze, *A Thousand Plateaus* (Minneapolis: University of Minnesota Press, 1987). p. 399.

14. Gilles Deleuze, *Difference and Repetition* (London: Continuum, 1997), p. 198.

15. Foucault, *The History of Sexuality*, 2:12.

16. Note the discussion of Schweitzer's Jesus as a figure of the end of a "modern" and "liberal" epoch of metaphysical reflection, in chapter 4 of Ward Blanton. *Displacing Christian Origins: Philosophy, Secularity, and the New Testaement* (Chicago: University of Chicago Press, 2007).

17. For some discussion, see Ward Blanton, "Biblical Scholarship in the Age of Biopower: Albert Schweitzer and the Degenerate Physiology of the Historical

Jesus," *Bible and Critical Theory* (February 2006): 1–25. I plan to develop a reading of Masoch and the emergence of the category of "messianism" with Yvonne Sherwood in coming months.

18. Foucault, *The History of Sexuality*, 2:5.

19. Numerous references could be mentioned. For now, see the interesting summary of this project in Michel Foucault, "Technologies of the Self," in Martin, Gutman, and Hutton, *Technologies of the Self*, pp. 16–49.

20. The language of call and response is of course important here inasmuch as Foucault always seemed particularly interested in the relationship between sexual activity and the vicissitudes of *speaking* about sexual activity.

21. Foucault, *The History of Sexuality*, 2:23ff.

22. Put differently, here we flag the relationship between sexuality, truth, and spiritual direction/exercise which always, in the late Foucault, feed into one another. See, e.g., "Pastoral Power and Political Reason," in Jeremy Carrette, ed., *Religion and Culture: Michel Foucault* (New York: Routledge, 1999), pp. 135–152; see also the fascinating discussions in Michel Foucault, *Security, Territory, Population* (New York: Picador, 2009), pp. 135–191, where he faces most directly the Heideggerian question of "man" as the "shepherd of being," a discussion that is now impossible to hear apart from the more recent appropriations of Foucault on these points by Sloterdijk. In addition to his unfairly condemned "Human Zoo" speech, see Peter Sloterdijk, *You Must Change Your Life* (London: Polity, 2012).

23. Michel Foucault, *The History of Sexuality*, vol. 3: *The Care of the Self*, trans. Robert Hurley (New York: Random House, 1990), p. 45.

24. While they disagree profoundly about the way Paul interacts with Hellenistic philosophical traditions, several crucial touchstones must be mentioned here: Stanley Stowers, *A Rereading of Romans: Justice, Jews, and Gentiles* (New Haven: Yale University Press, 1997); Dale B. Martin, *The Corinthian Body* (New Haven: Yale University Press, 1999); Troels Engberg-Pedersen, *Paul and the Stoics* (London: T&T Clark, 2000) and *Cosmology and Self in the Apostle Paul* (Oxford: Oxford University Press, 2010); Emma Wasserman, *The Death of the Soul in Romans 7: Sin, Death, and the Law in Light of Hellenistic Moral Psychology* (Tübingen: Mohr Siebeck, 2008); George Van Kooten, *Paul's Anthropology in Context* (Tübingen: Mohr Siebeck, 2008); Niko Huttunen, *Paul and Epictetus on Law: A Comparison* (London: T&T Clark, 2009); Runar Thorsteinsson, *Roman Christianity and Roman Stoicism: A Comparative Study of Ancient Morality* (London: Oxford University Press, 2010). I discuss this issue in more detail in my afterword to Pier Paolo Pasolini, *Saint Paul* (London: Verso, 2013).

25. Cf. Michel Foucault, *The Government of Self and Others: Lectures at the Collège de France (1982–1983)* (New York: Palgrave Macmillan, 2008), p. 43.

26. Gilles Deleuze, *Negotiations: 1972–1990* (New York: Columbia University Press, 1997), p. 105.
27. Mika Ojakangas, "On the Pauline Roots of Biopolitics: Apostle Paul in Company with Foucault and Agamben," *Journal of Cultural and Religious Theory* 11, no. 1 (2010):92–94. Ojakangas's engagement with Foucault and Paulinism should be bundled together into a single volume, as he makes important contributions to a developing conversation. See also his "Impossible Dialgue on Biopower: Agamben and Foucult," *Foucault Studies*, no. 2 (May 2005): 5–28, and "Michel Foucault and the Enigmatic Origins of Bio-politics and Governmentality," *History of the Human Sciences* 25, no. 1 (2012): 1–14.
28. Foucault, *The History of Sexuality*, 3:236.
29. Ibid., 3:239.
30. Ibid.
31. Precisely because of some of the lacunae and traditional stereotyping of distinctions, the work of Foucault on the history of religion needs very much, as a kind of compelling afterword, the understated but powerful study of Dale B. Martin, *Inventing Superstition: From the Hippocratics to the Christians* (Cambridge: Harvard University Press, 2004). Martin's study maps shifts in ancient medical disourses, varying modes of attention to the body, onto shifts in discourses about religion.
32. Foucault, *The History of Sexuality*, 3:239.
33. Ibid.
34. This is a typical refrain in the later Foucault, particularly. Note, for example, Foucault's answer to the question of Hasumi in "Sexuality and Power" in Carrette, *Religion and Culture*, p. 127f.
35. Foucault, *The History of Sexuality*, 3:239.
36. Ibid.
37. See Jonathan Z. Smith, *Drudgery Divine: On the Comparison of Early Christianities and the Religions of Late Antiquity* (Chicago: University of Chicago Press, 1990), especially p. 115, but also pp. 36ff. The periodization and comparative discreteness of identities in these narrations of "Western culture" or the history of religion constitutes their political stakes, which is why calling them into question, rethinking them, tends to subvert the contemporary identities to which these stories provide their orientation. This is no doubt why a reworking of "Paul and the philosophers" sometimes elicits fierce antagonism, though such refigurations may obviously be worked without reference to Paul, as (for example) in the critical works of Ruprecht, who challenges recent influential Christian readings of culture by way of a genealogical subversion of their implicit periodization of the West, e.g., Louis A. Ruprecht Jr., *Afterwords: Hellenism, Modernism, and the Myth of Decadence* (New York: SUNY Press, 1996).

38. Foucault, *The History of Sexuality*, 3:238.

39. For a very similar type of discussion, see the way Senecan ethical discourse is played off against fourth-century Christian ascetics in Michel Foucault, *Du Gouvernement des Vivants: Cours au Collège de France, 1979–1980* (Paris: Gallimard/Seuil, 2012), pp. 219–281.

40. Cf. Michel Foucault, *Psychiatric Power: Lectures at the Collège de France, 1973–1974* (London: Palgrave Macmillan, 2006), pp. 165ff.

41. Moxnes, "Asceticism and Christian Identity in Antiquity," p. 8.

42. Foucault, *Du Gouvernement des Vivants*, p. 247.

43. Ibid., cf. pp. 240–241, 246.

44. Theodor Zahn, *The Apostle's Creed: A Sketch of Its History and an Examination of Its Contents*, trans. C. S. and A. E. Burn (London: Hodder and Stoughton, 1899), p. vii. Incidentally, the question of masculinity and the history of biblical scholarship is woefully underdeveloped, though see the work of Halvor Moxnes which breaks new ground, *Jesus and the Rise of Nationalism: A New Quest for the Nineteenth-Century Historical Jesus* (London: I.B. Tauris, 2011).

45. J. B. Lightfoot, *Saint Paul's Epistle to the Philippians* (London: MacMillan, 1903), p. 308.

46. Ibid.

47. Theodor Zahn, *Introduction to the New Testament* (Edinburgh: T&T Clark, 1909), 1:121.

48. Ibid., 1:114 (my emphasis).

49. I say "extraordinary" in the sense that we really begin to understand Zahn when we realize that, in moments like this, he is more conservative about such matters than Eusebius of Caesarea, that great author of an ecclesiastical history who hoped he could string together historical testimonies in such a way to give Constantine, essentially, an unbroken link—a telegraphic line of signal fires, as he describes it—back to the "origin" of Christianity. On James's authorship, cf. 2.23–25.

50. Zahn, *Introduction to the New Testament*, 1:114.

51. Theodor Zahn, *Der Stoiker Epiktet und sein Verhältnis zum Christentum* (Erlangen: Universitäts-Buchdruckerei von E. Th. Jacob, 1894), p. 3.

52. See especially Zahn's remarks, ibid., pp. 12, 18, 20.

53. Foucault, *The History of Sexuality*, 3:236.

54. Cf. Jacques Derrida, "Faith and Knowledge: The Two Sources of 'Religion' at the Limits of Reason Alone," in Jacques Derrida and Gianni Vattimo, eds., *Religion* (Stanford: Stanford University Press, 1996), pp. 2, 12, 21.

55. I have explored at length the role of this "little machine" and the starkly destabilizing effect it has on distinctions between religion and secular critique in Ward Blanton, *Displacing Christian Origins: Philosophy, Secularity, and the New Testament* (Chicago: University of Chicago Press, 2007).

56. Gershom Scholem would have missed the similarity perhaps (being gener-

ally keen to maintain clear lines of distinction between the "Jewish" and the "Christian," but here it is worth pointing out that there is perhaps a Scholemesque "messianism" operating at the heart of Derrida's diagnosis of the "little machine" of European self-subversion. The key comparison concerning immanent inversion, undoing from within, and the gesture is the same in both thinkers.

57. Cf. Foucault's interview, "Iran: the Spirit of a World Without Spirit" reprinted in Michel Foucault, *Politics, Philosophy, Culture: Interviews and Other Writings, 1977–1984* (New York: Routledge, 1988), pp. 211–224.

58. Janet Afary and Kevin Anderson, *Foucault and the Iranian Revolution* (Chicago: University of Chicago Press, 2005), pp. 38ff.

59. Inasmuch as *parrhēsia* represents, among other things, a "zero degree of those rhetorical figures which intensify the emotions of the audience," and this by way of pressing a risky demand for decision, the rhetorical form invites comparison with some characterizations of messianic "shortening" of time (as in Agamben) or Badiou's (related) "forcing" of an event. Michel Foucault, *Fearless Speech* (New York: Semiotext(e), 2001), p. 22.

60. Ibid., p. 13.

61. Without repeating comparisons that may be found elsewhere (e.g., in the work of Hubert Dreyfus), the way in which bodies, motions, and energies in Heidegger are made available to broader collective agencies and economies fits very well with the way, in Foucault, that docile bodies are precisely those bodies that, as it were, respond or allow themselves to be measured by the feedback mechanisms of economies and broad structures like collective "life." In both cases the drama of the interpretation emerges from attention to the same basic "dialectical" movement, between generalizing tactics of measuring/framing and specific sites in which those measuring/framing devices find a purchase. The Foucauldian mechanisms productive of docile bodies, mentioned earlier, for example, may be usefully compared to the discussions of "standing reserve" and "enframing" in Martin Heidegger, "The Question Concerning Technology," in *The Question Concerning Technology, and Other Essays* (San Francisco: Harper, 1977), pp. 3–35.

62. Crockett's reflections on entropy are essential today more than ever, constituting a kind of quasi-Deleuzean mode of thinking about (in earlier dialectical language) immanent contradiction. See, e.g., his sections on void and entropy in Clayton Crockett, *Deleuze Beyond Badiou: Ontology, Multiplicity, and Event* (New York: Columbia University Press, 2013); and sections on entropy with Jeffrey Robbins in *Religion, Politics, and the Earth: The New Materialism* (London: Palgrave Macmillan, 2012).

63. This is, of course, Foucault's own language, which also constituted his rationale for thinking that discursive and nondiscursive environments of material practices, levied one another, not to mention why he continued to write gene-

alogies of ancient people and distant places. Still very useful is Pamela Major-Poetzl's study, *Michel Foucault's Archaology of Western Culture: Toward a New Science of History* (Chapel Hill: University of North Carolina Press, 1983), particularly chapter 1.

64. Michel Foucault, *The History of Sexuality*, vol. 1: *An Introduction*, trans. Robert Hurley (New York: Random House, 1978), p. 21.

65. Ibid., p. 5.

4. SINGULARITY; OR, SPIRITUAL EXERCISE

1. Gilles Deleuze, *Negotiations, 1972–1990*, trans. Martin Joughin (New York: Columbia University Press, 1990), pp. 108–111.

2. Michel Foucault, *Discipline and Punish: The Birth of the Prison*, trans. Alan Sheridan (New York: Penguin, 1977), p. 208.

3. Ibid.

4. Ibid., p. 209.

5. Michel Foucault, *The Order of Things: Archaeology of the Human Sciences* (London: Routledge, 2001), p. 357.

6. Ibid.

7. While there is *more* than an interest in the displacement of model-and-repetition constitutive of representational thought here in Foucault, we should not miss the way it is nevertheless a crucial topic for him. Foucault will refuse some of the obvious similarities at work in the classical episteme and the modern one by pointing to their different mode of relation to the question of representation:

> But this play of correspondences must not be allowed to delude us. We must not imagine that the Classical analysis of discourse has continued without modification through the ages merely by applying itself to a new object; that the force of some historical weight has maintained it in its identity, despite so many adjacent mutations. In fact, the four theoretical segments that outlined the space of general grammar have not been preserved: but they were dissociated, they changed both their function and their level, they modified the entire domain of their validity when, at the end of the eighteenth century, the theory of representation was eclipsed. . . . In contrast [to the classical age], the analysis of man's mode of being as it has developed since the nineteenth century does not reside within a theory of representation.

> Ibid., p. 367.

8. Ibid., p. 358.

9. Ibid., p. 364f. Cf. Foucault's comments about two ways of thinking the ethical, one by the law of the model, the other by modern singularities.

10. Cf. the association of Plato, Aristotle, and Kant under the rubric of "traditional" ontologies as a process of deduction from the general appears, for example, in Martin Heidegger, *An Introduction to Metaphysics* (New Haven: Yale University Press, 1987), p. 41; cf. similar discussions in *Being and Time* (Albany: SUNY Press, 2010), pp. 12–15 (section: int. I, 4); or *Kant and the Problem of Metaphysics* (Bloomington: Indiana University Press, 1997), pp. 3–8 (sections 1, 2).

11. Cf. Slavoj Žižek, *Bodies Without Organs: On Deleuze and Consequences* (New York: Routledge, 2004), p. 183–187, *The Parallax View* (Cambridge: MIT Press, 2006), pp. 261–269. I should note that Žižek's writings contain essential indications also about how to rework precisely these criticisms.

12. Here she is echoing Todd May. See Valérie Nicolet Anderson, "Becoming a Subject: The Case of Michel Foucault and Paul," *Journal of Cultural and Religious Theory* 11, no. 1 (2010):140.

13. Her very interesting book on Foucault and Paul came too late to my attention to do it justice here, though I hope to engage some of its arguments in future writing. I suspect we value "narrative" and "self-fashioning" in fruitfully distinct modes. For now, see an agenda-setting book of Valérie Nicolet Anderson, *Constructing the Self: Thinking with Paul and Michel Foucault* (Tübingen: Mohr Siebeck, 2012).

14. I should add that I think even fairly recent controversies between latterday Lacanians, Badioueans, and Deleuzeans are moving onto new terrain. Consider, for example, the differently nuanced inflection of Deleuze's "quasicause"—a topos related to the ambiguous force of *pistis*—in Žižek's *Less Than Nothing*. Slavoj Žižek, *Less Than Nothing: Hegel and the Shadow of Dialectical Materialism* (London: Verso, 2012), pp. 853–858, compared to his earlier discussion of the same in *Organs Without Bodies* (New York: Routledge, 2003), pp. 26–32. Exemplary in emerging discussions is the perceptive defense of Deleuze in Clayton Crockett, *Deleuze Beyond Badiou: Ontology, Multiplicity, and Event* (New York: Columbia University Press, 2013).

15. I am thinking not only of the way he "Paulinizes" phenomenology in his early lectures on the phenomenology of religious life, effectively procuring "authentic" Paulinism in the same gesture as he lays bear authentic phenomenology (see my discussion of this matter in *Displacing Christian Origins*), but also—related—of the way he then "atheizes" both Paulinism and phenomenology in *Being and Time*, a move already there implicitly in his own—and Bultmann's—reading of Paul. Ward Blanton, *Displacing Christian Origins: Philosophy, Secularity, and the New Testament* (Chicago: University of Chicago Press, 2007), pp. 105–128.

16. Foucault, *The Order of Things*, p. 370.
17. Ibid.
18. Ibid.
19. Ibid.
20. Here the crucial issue is to face directly the contested philosophical modes of understanding excess, *clinamen*, and *objet petit a*, as Slavoj Žižek has been doing brilliantly in an engagement with Deleuze and Lacan which seems to me to cut against some of the Deleuze bashing often associated with the work of Hardt and Negri. Cf. Žižek, *Less Than Nothing*, pp. 852–858.
21. Foucault, *The Order of Things*, p. 370f.
22. Ibid., p. 371.
23. Foucault, *Discipline and Punish*, p. 298.
24. Ibid.
25. Foucault, *Discipline and Punish*, p. 301.
26. Jeffrey T. Nealon, *Foucault After Foucault: Power and Its Intensifications Since 1984* (Stanford: Stanford University Press, 2008), p. 52.
27. Foucault, *Discipline and Punish*, pp. 206–7.
28. Ibid, p. 207.
29. See
30. Foucault, *Discipline and Punish*, p. 27.
31. With the caveat that my (phenomenologically inflected) repetition of Althusser's interpellation scenario focuses more on the way the *effects* of the call retroactively constitute the initial "invitation" to be interpellated. Structure and function follow the interpellating performative rather than precede it.
32. Foucault, *Discipline and Punish*, p. 23.
33. Ibid., p. 194.
34. Here I find crucial the remarkably illuminating work of Michael Dillon, who explicates Heidegger and more recent thinkers of the "event" in relation to the fact that "evental" thought is rapidly proliferating across cultural and economic spheres, from managerial training sessions to military tactics and national preparedness strategies. Relationality, openness, and contingency are increasingly the practices of our emerging social ontologies. See, for example, the excellent piece by Michael Dillon, "Specters of Biopolitics: Finitude, Eschaton, and Katechon," *South Atlantic Quarterly* 110, no. 3 (2011): 780–792, or "Accident, Eschaton, Katechon: Toward a Genealogy of the Event" in his forthcoming book on biopolitics and political theology.
35. See Gilles Deleuze, *Foucault*, trans. Sean Hand (Minneapolis: University of Minnesota Press, 1988), pp. 108–123. More recent engagements with the relationship between these thinkers may be found in Timothy Rayner, *Foucault's Heidegger: Philosophy and Transformative Experience* (London: Continuum,

2007); and Alan Milchman and Alan Rosenburg, eds., *Foucault and Heidegger: Critical Encounters* (Minneapolis: University of Minnesota Press, 2003).

36. Jacques Lacan, *The Seminar of Jacques Lacan: The Other Side of Psychoanalysis* (book 17), trans. by Russel Grigg (New York: Norton, 2007), p. 119f.

37. G. W. F. Hegel, *The Phenomenology of Spirit*, trans. by A. V. Miller (Oxford: Oxford University Press, 1979), p. 47.

38. Michael Hardt and Antonio Negri, *Commonwealth* (Cambridge: Belknap, 2009). For the genealogical story, see chapter 1, "Productive Bodies", especially pp. 30ff. Their genealogy is provocative and invites much-needed further reflection about the relation between capitalism and the turn to the phenomena of everyday life within *fin-de-siecle* continental philosophy (cf. within phenomenology, hermeneutics, linguistic philosophy of Wittgenstein). At that later point, the same move was occurring in other fields as well and has a bearing on the way in which biblical studies moved, in a sweeping shift in paradigms, to "apocalypticism" as an essential name under which to understand early Christian religion. In a word, this was the emergence of those central touchstone within New Testament interpretation, from the Pauline "event" to Jesus's "apocalyptic" relation to the world at hand. I explore some of the important issues in the chapters about Heidegger and Schweitzer, respectively, in *Displacing Christian Origins*.

39. Hardt and Negri, *Commonwealth*, p. 31.

40. Ibid., p. 38.

41. Roberto Esposito, *Bios: Biopolitics and Philosophy*, trans. Timothy Campbell (Minneapolis: University of Minnesota Press, 2008), p. 39.

42. Ibid.

43. Ibid.

44. Roberto Esposito, *Immunitas: The Protection and Negation of Life*, trans. Zakiya Hanafi (Cambridge: Polity, 2011), p. 65.

45. See the preface of Antonio Negri's *Labor of Job*, trans. Matteo Mandarini (Durham: Duke University Press, 2009).

46. My colleague Yvonne Sherwood, who is worlds more a sophisticated interpreter of Job than I ever will be, points out that this may be a flat-footed reading inasmuch as the (ambiguously) narrative/divine voice at the end of the biblical book does *not* uniformly or without qualification dismiss the counselors. She will forgive me if, for the present, I let the reading slide. One should nevertheless note the important work on such topics in Abigail Pelham, *Contested Creations in the Book of Job: The-World-As-It-Ought-and-Ought-Not-to-Be* (Berlin: Brill, 2012).

47. Negri, *Labor of Job*, p. xix.

48. Ibid., p. xxiii.

49. Important to note here is the groundbreaking genealogy constituted by the

work of Roland Boer. See the books in the Historical Materialism series of Haymarket Books: *Criticism of Heaven; Criticism of Theology; Criticism of Religion; Criticism of Earth*; and also his *Political Myth: On the Use and Abuse of Biblical Themes* (Durham: Duke University Press, 2009). I imagine that Boer would resist my "excessive reduction" (so to speak) of ontology to structures of quasi-cause, retroactive positing of causality, *objet a*, or swerved *pistis*, Boer preferring a more elaborately Marxist theory of structured social production. No doubt his remarks on this topic would be, as ever, provocatively illuminating.

50. For the general dynamics—and an effort to situate them in historical and cultural context—see chs. 1 and 2 of my *Displacing Christian Origins*.

51. Jean Baudrillard, *Forget Foucault* (Cambridge: MIT Press, 2007), p. 34.

52. Ibid., p. 35.

53. Ibid., p. 37. Needless to say, I do not agree that Baudrillard is here different from Foucault and Deleuze, neither of whom seems to me to be at all interested in a fetishization of a panlogicism of transparency!

54. Ibid., p. 60.

55. The language of exorcism is common enough in Baudrillard's interventions, not only here, but see, e.g., Jean Baudrillard, *Impossible Exchange* (London: Verso, 2001), p. 142f.

56. Baudrillard, *Forget Foucault*, 63.

57. In this respect we could chalk Deleuze up to yet another amazing thinker who misses his own affinities with Paulinism. Consider Deleuze's essay "Nietzsche and Saint Paul, Lawrence and John of Patmos," in Ward Blanton and Hent de Vries, eds., *Paul and the Philosophers* (New York: Fordham University Press, 2013). Note also Clayton Crockett's excellent Paulinist exposition of a Deleuzean philosophy of immanence and difference in the same volume, "Radical Theology and the Event: Saint Paul with Deleuze."

58. Gilles Deleuze and Leopold von Sacher-Masoch, *Masochism: Coldness and Cruelty and Venus in Furs* (New York: Zone, 1991), p. 89.

59. I have noted before Troels Engberg-Pedersen's compelling arguments that Paul is in 1 Corinthians 15 opposing a Stoic immanence of the "spiritual body" to the more Philonic dualisms evident among the Corinthian believers. Engberg-Pedersen's work is a breakthrough, not just in the way it provides a viable ancient philosophical context for Pauline drama but also for the way it encourages us to reflect on how it is specifically a *modern immanence* which is so actively conjuring a "return" of Paulinist tropes within cultural reflection. See Troels Engberg-Pedersen, *Cosmology and Self in the Apostle Paul: The Material Spirit* (Oxford: Oxford University Press, 2010).

60. Deleuze and Sacher-Masoch, *Masochism*, p. 89.

61. Cf. Gilles Deleuze, *What Is Philosophy?* (London: Verso, 1994), p. 55.

62. Deleuze and Sacher-Masoch, *Masochism*, p. 88.

63. Ibid., p. 88.

64. Ibid., p. 88.

65. Ibid., p. 86.

66. Edward W. Said, *The World, the Text, and the Critic* (Cambridge: Harvard University Press, 1983), pp. 245–246.

67. Indeed, "So that Paul teaches exactly the same as ourselves." See Benedict de Spinoza, *A Theologico-Political Treatise* (New York: Dover, 1951), p. 53.

68. Cf. Crockett's "Radical Theology and the Event."

69. Baudrillard, *Forget Foucault*, p. 65.

70. Michel Foucault. *Maurice Blanchot: The Thought from Outside* (New York: Zone, 1990), p. 22.

71. See Slavoj Žižek, "The Necessity of a Dead Bird: Paul's Communism," in Blanton and de Vries, *Paul and the Philosophers*.

72. See, respectively, Stanislas Breton, *Théorie des Idéologies* (Paris: Desclée, 1976), pp. 31–34, 47–49, 92–98, and "Portrait du Rien," in *Philosophie Buissonnière* (Grenoble: Jérôme Millon, 1989), pp. 65–74. Elsewhere he makes clear his thinking of ontology in relation to Paul's logos of a cross by comparing it to the theme of ontological exodus in the writing of Meister Eckhart. See Stanislaw Breton, *Philosophie et mystique: Existence et surexistence* (Paris: Jérôme Millon, 1996), 89–110.

As for the ambiguously (post)metaphysic nature of his work, Breton said fairly often that the best way to think the limits of metaphysics was by eschewing the illusion that one had stepped outside of it!

73. See Negri, *The Labor of Job*, p. 13f.

74. I should add that Negri's statements on the matter are clear. See, for example, Michael Negri, *Diary of an Escape* (London: Polity, 2010).

75. I borrow the language from Lawrence Welborn's excellent book, *Paul, a Fool of Christ: A Study of 1 Corinthians 1–4 in the Comic-Philosophic Tradition* (London: T&T Clark, 2005).

76. See Michael Taussig, *Defacement: Public Secrecy and the Labor of the Negative* (Stanford: Stanford University Press, 1999), p. 4. This is not the time to explore the full significance of Taussig's work for a reading of the historical Paul's effort to engage the "magic of the [Roman] state." For an excellent engagement with Taussig, see Kenneth Surin, "The Sovereign Individual and Mchael Taussig's Politics of Defacement," in *Nepantla: Views from South* 2, no. 1(2001), pp. 205–220.

77. I say so-called Christians, of course, to remind us that the word itself is not actually Pauline and would have been rejected by him were it to have any connotations of not being Jewish.

78. The weakness and, properly speaking, stupidity of the gesture itself deserves more attention here, as what is at stake is not a romanticizing of powerlessness but a paradoxical reworking of notions of power and agency. In this

respect, I do not know of better interlocutors for these suggestions of Paul than Taussig, Stanislas Breton, or (to mention but one more) the striking effort to rethink nonbeing, possibility, and necessity in Edith Wyschogrod, *Saints and Postmodernism: Revisioning Moral Philosophy* (Chicago: University of Chicago Press, 1990, though she does not engage directly with Paul. Her own work on these categories comes to the same peculiar conclusion, however, and it may be a good indication of why Paulinist weakness and stupidity—and this in the act of community formation—have returned with such a forcefulness in these diverse fields: "The saint's life is not simply one of action but one of authorized action. The authorization of moral action in a postmodern context in which the general presuppositions for authoritative discourse fall under criticism requires renouncing power" (ibid., 60). Viewed also in relationship to the question of revolutionary violence, such is ultimately the question posed by Badiou's *Incident at Antioch*. See Alain Badiou, *The Incident at Antioch* (New York: Columbia University Press, 2013). The farthest thing from that closure, leveraging, and sacrifice constituting an act under a metaphysical warranty, there is what Julia Reinhard Lupton might call a "Paul-effect" that rather concerns a moment of the crisis of legitimation.

79. 1 Corinthians 1:23f.

80. Judith Butler, *The Psychic Life of Power: Theories in Subjection* (Stanford: Stanford University Press, 20), p. 91.

81. Ibid., p. 87.

82. Ibid., p. 89.

83. Cf. ibid., pp. 93, 97.

84. Simon Critchley, *Infinitely Demanding: Ethics of Commitment, Politics of Resistance* (London: Verso, 2008), p. 1.

85. Butler, *The Psychic Life of Power*, p. 88. See Stanislas Breton, *Saint Paul*, trans. Joseph Ballan (New York: Columbia University Press, 2010). For Breton's references to Paulinist meontology more generally, see *Théorie des Idéologies*, p. 47. Breton discerned Paulinist meontology above all in 1 Corinthians 1 and the hymn of Christ's kenotic self-emptying in Philippians 2. See also Stanislas Breton, *The Word and the Cross*, trans. Jacquelyn Porter (New York: Fordham University Press, 2002).

86. Butler, *The Psychic Life of Power*, p. 100.

87. To my knowledge, the lecture to which I refer by Timothy Mitchell, "The Virtues of Recalcitrance: Democracy from Foucault to Latour" (addressed to a conference at UCLA entitled Foucault and Middle East Studies, April 28, 2009), is not yet in print, though currently accessible in downloadable audio form at http://www.international.ucla.edu/cnes/podcasts/.

88. Jean-Luc Marion, *God Without Being: Hors-Texte* (Chicago: University of Chicago Press, 1995), p. 87.

89. Ibid.

90. An excellent engagement with Marion and Derrida on just this point may be found in Thomas A. Carlson, *Indiscretion: Finitude and the Naming of God* (Chicago: University of Chicago Press, 1999), pp. 190–237.

91. Jon Sobrino, *No Salvation Outside the Poor: Prophetic-Utopian Essays* (Maryknoll, NY: Orbis, 2008), pp. 4, 35, 12. Thanks to Neil Elliott for the suggestion to see what Sobrino does with *ta mē onta*.

92. Baudrillard, *Forget Foucault*, p. 63.

93. I echo the title of a wonderful book in fond memory of the recently departed Friedrich Kittler.

94. John Riches, *Galatians Through the Centuries* (Oxford: Blackwell, 2008), pp. 141f. See also Ueda Shizuteru, "Jesus in Contemporary Japanese Zen: With Special Regard to Keiji Nishitani," in Perry Schmidt-Leukel and G. Köberlin, eds., *Buddhist Perceptions of Jesus: Papers of the Third Conference of the European Network of Buddhist-Christian Studies* (St. Ottillien: EOS, 1999). I am grateful to two excellent colleagues, Gereon Kopf at Luther College and Perry Schmidt-Leukel at the University of Glasgow, for their intriguing suggestions about some of these things, which I hope to speak about at more length elsewhere.

95. Ibid., citing Ueda Shizuteru.

96. See his articulation of the "undead" in Eric Santner, *On the Psychotheology of Everyday Life: Reflections on Freud and Rosenzweig* (Chicago: University of Chicago Press, 2001), but also his readings of Paul in this light within *On Creaturely Life: Benjamin, Sebald* (Chicago: University of Chicago Press, 2006).

5. SEIZURES OF CHANCE

Now that the Verso publication of Pasolini's notes will soon be available, I will not repeat my earlier plot summaries of Pasolini's screenplay; see Ward Blanton, "'Reapperance of Paul, Sick,'" *Journal of Cultural and Religious Theory* 11, no. 1 (Winter 2010): 52–77. Plus, the translator's introduction of Elizabeth Castelli is extraordinary to the point that I want to be sure only to point readers in that direction rather than tread similar territory less effectively here. Instead I will focus here on comparative theoretical issues surrounding Pasolini's creative intervention.

1. It has become an unfortunate stereotype among critical theorists reading nineteenth-century biblical scholarship that there is something politically debilitating about the proliferating modes of concreteness in expression

among "apocalyptic" texts as opposed to, say, "messianic" or "prophetic" literature. It is a topic for another time, but this seems to me really unhelpful for thinking about images and openness, but also for thinking about the ancient "politics" of these movements.

2. Pier Paolo Pasolini, *Petrolio*, trans. Ann Goldstein (London: Secker and Warburg, 1997), p. 74. Pasolini's note about the handling of *Petrolio* (1973) suggests it was underway while he was also working on the screenplay about Paul (1968–72).

3. Franco "Bifo" Berardi, *The Soul at Work: From Alienation to Autonomy*. trans. Francesca Cadel and Giuseppina Mecchia (Los Angeles: Semiotext(e), 2007), p. 59. As part of the analogical/apocalyptic play of figures and frameworks, it is worth pointing out that Berardi's articulation of this emergence of a new economy of desiring production in the late 1960s and '70s was itself marked by a return of Italian theorists at during this period to the Marx of the *Grundrisse*. It is worth wondering whether there is a developing *intensification* of a Marxian problematic that governs the way critical theory has been, as it were, *increasingly* haunted by the spectral return of Paulinism, from the dialectically understood Paul of the Tübingen school during the writing of Marx's *Grundrisse* to Pasolini's Paul at a moment of "return" to the *Grundrisse*, to an explosion of competing theoretical Paulinisms (e.g., Jacob Taubes, Alain Badiou, Giorgio Agamben, Slavoj Žižek) at a moment when the dialectical poles become more decidedly indistinguishable or "negative." While a great deal needs to be done, Boer has more than anyone else diagnosed the mutually implicated trajectories of Marxist and biblical scholarship. See, e.g., his twin books, Roland Boer, *Criticism of Heaven* (London: Haymarket, 2009) and *Criticism of Religion* (London: Haymarket, 2011), as well as *Political Myth* (Durham: Duke University Press, 2009). More focused on contemporary ideology criticism, see also James Crossley, *Jesus in an Age of Neoliberalism: Quests, Scholarship, and Ideology* (London: Equinox, 2012); or the philosophically focused story of nineteenth- and early twentieth-century biblical scholarship in Ward Blanton, *Displacing Christian Origins: Philosophy, Secularity, and the New Testament* (Chicago: University of Chicago Press, 2007).

4. Berardi's own work, of course, emerges from within a vibrant and developing tradition of Italian critical theory for whom the diagnosis of these decades and their ongoing political significance is both essential and contested. A fuller contextualization of these texts, Pasolini's and Berardi's, within a specifically Italian critical theory (or, by the same token, a specifically Italian film history) is not my aim at the present, in part because my work is focused on the first-century *Greek* pole of my analogical Greek-Italian-English story of the screenplay, a comparative pole which is still underdeveloped even amidst the high profile "return" of Paulinism as a comparative touchstone for philoso-

phy and critical theory. Nevertheless, without suggesting "to cover" this side of the comparative story, for those interested one should mention (in addition to studies I discuss further on) at least two efforts to situate and present the larger theoretical debates, Michael Hardt and Paolo Virno, eds., *Radical Political Thought in Italy: A Potential Politics* (Minneapolis: University of Minnesota Press, 2006); and Lorenzo Chiesa and Alberto Toscano, eds., *The Italian Difference: Between Nihilism and Politics* (Melbourne: re.press, 2009).

5. Rather than to expand the list of Italianists obsessed with questions of biopolitics, I will simply mention here the attempt at a synthesis of Andrea Righi, *Biopolitics and Social Change in Italy: From Gramsci to Pasolini to Negri* (New York: Palgrave Macmillan, 2011).

6. As we will see, I read Pasolini's moves against the backdrop of rich comparative discussions of "Oedipus" in Paris. For an important evaluation of this period, see Miriam Leonard, *Athens in Paris: Ancient Greece and the Political in Postwar French Thought* (Oxford: Oxford University Press, 2005).

7. Pier Paolo Pasolini, "Tetis," in Patrick Rumble and Bart Testa, eds., *Pier Paolo Pasolini: Contemporary Perspectives* (Toronto: University of Toronto Press, 1994), p. 248.

8. Righi, *Biopolitics and Social Change in Italy*, p. 89.

We should note also the research of Naomi Greene, whose work articulates *Salò* against the backdrop of consumerist "neocapitalism," even as it also describes the way many of Pasolini's contemporaries resisted this reading, interestingly, preferring to find instead a confessional Pasolini making clear that he hated his own sexuality the way many of his critics did as well. She writes:

> In *Salò*, sexual acts are totally brutal and without preamble; its victims do not undress but appear nude, lined up as if awaiting the gas chambers. In this sexual lager, no real *jouissance* is possible. Its tortured victims bear no resemblance to the heroines of a certain pornographic tradition who achieve pleasure through pain. And even their executioners, that is, the libertines, do not attain the pleasure they so endlessly seek. Meticulous bureaucrats, banal torturers, Pasolini's libertines are driven not by the energy or the pulsing of desire but by impotence and frustration.

Naomi Greene, "*Salò*: The Refusal to Consume," in Rumble and Testa, *Pier Paolo Pasolini*, p. 234f.

9. Jacques Lacan, *The Other Side of Psychoanalysis (The Seminar of Jacques Lacan, Book XVII)*, trans. Russell Grigg (New York: Norton, 2007), p. 19f.

10. Gilles Deleuze and Félix Guattari, *Anti-Oedipus: Capitalism and Schizophrenia* (London: Continuum, 2004); Jean-Francois Lyotard, *Libidinal Economy*

(London: Continuum, 2004); Jacques Derrida, *Dissemination* (London: Continuum, 2004); and Jean Baudrillard, *The Consumer Society* (London: Sage, 1998).

11. While they disagree profoundly about the way Paul interacts with Hellenistic philosophical traditions, several crucial touchstones must be mentioned here: Stanley Stowers, *A Rereading of Romans: Justice, Jews, and Gentiles* (New Haven: Yale University Press, 1997); Dale B. Martin, *The Corinthian Body* (New Haven: Yale University Press, 1999); Troels Engberg-Pedersen, *Paul and the Stoics* (London: T&T Clark, 2000) and *Cosmology and Self in the Apostle Paul* (Oxford: Oxford University Press, 2010); Emma Wasserman, *The Death of the Soul in Romans 7: Sin, Death, and the Law in Light of Hellenistic Moral Psychology* (Tübingen: Mohr Siebeck, 2008); George Van Kooten, *Paul's Anthropology in Context* (Tübingen: Mohr Siebeck, 2008); Niko Huttunen, *Paul and Epictetus on Law: A Comparison* (London: T&T Clark, 2009); and Runar Thorsteinsson, *Roman Christianity and Roman Stoicism: A Comparative Study of Ancient Morality* (London: Oxford University Press, 2010).

12. For further discussion, see my introduction, "Back to the New Archive," to Ward Blanton and Hent de Vries, eds., *Paul and the Philosophers* (New York: Fordham University Press, 2012).

13. We should note immediately that discourses about *nomos* in ancient Mediterranean contexts afforded a panoply of modes by which to double, and effectively to circumvent, sublimate, or negate the value of a particular instance of *nomos*. Philosophers, of course, regularly switched codes from ethnic to natural law, often precisely in order to allow the doubling and displacement of *nomos* as a mode of escaping the effective operation of the local or the allegedly general. Jewish traditions from Josephus to Philo to the texts of the Dead Sea Scrolls perform similar operations, sometimes adding additional tricks about the (oral or written) media of nomological discourse. In a word, in moments like these Paul inhabits, rather than subtracts himself from, Jewish and philosophical traditions alike. Two very important efforts to locate Pauline discussions of *nomos* within their general Greco-Roman environments are Brigitte Kahl, *Galatians Re-imagined: Reading with the Eyes of the Vanquished* (Minneapolis: Fortress, 2010); and Davina Lopez, *Apostle to the Conquered: Re-imagining Paul's Mission* (Minneapolis: Fortress, 2010).

14. Josephus. *Antiquities* 2.239.1.

15. See, e.g., the "discussion on sin" in Georges Bataille, *The Unfinished System of Nonknowledge* (Minneapolis: University of Minnesota Press, 2004); and the reference to hyperbolic sin in the lecture "On the Moral Law" in Jacques Lacan, *The Seminar of Jacques Lacan: Book VII, The Ethics of Psychoanalysis* (1959–60), trans. Dennis Porter (London, 1992), p. 84.

16. For an excellent discussion of Schmittian exceptionalism, with an accom-

panying genealogy of Schmitt's precursors, see Marc de Wilde's excellent essay, "Politics Between Times. Theologico-Political Interpretations of the Restraining Force (*katechon*) in Paul's Second Letter to the Thessalonians" in Blanton and de Vries, *Paul and the Philosophers*.

17. Ancient discussions assumed that the fund of *aphormē* could be borrowed, saved, and the origination of new enterprises (cf. Xenophon, *Memorabilia* 2.7.12; 3.12.4), or even the distributed fund of the state itself (cf. Aristotle, *Politics* 6.1320a39).

18. See Gil Anidjar, "Freud's Jesus (Paul's War)," in Blanton and de Vries, *Paul and the Philosophers*. Several other comparative encounters with Pauline and Schmittian topics of the *katechon* or restrainer of political catastrophe may be found in the excellent work of Michael Dillon, "Spectres of Biopolitcs: Eschatology, Katechon and Resistance," in *South Atlantic Quarterly* 110 (Summer 2011): 3; Sergei Prozorov, "From *Katechon* to Intrigant: The Breakdown of the Post-Soviet *Nomos*," in Alexander Astrov, ed., *The Great Power (mis)Management: The Russian-Georgian War and Its Implications for the Global Order* (Surrey: Ashgate, 2011), pp. 25–42; and (implicitly, through his longer history of scholarship on Schmitt) Mika Ojakangas, "Michel Foucault and the Enigmatic Origins of Bio-politics and Governmentality," in *History of the Human Sciences* 25, no. 1 (2012): 1–14; and Michael Hoelzl, "Before the Anti-Christ is Revealed: On the Katechontic Structure of Messianic Time," in Arthur Bradley and Paul Fletcher, eds., *The Politics to Come: Power, Modernity and the Messianic* (London: Continuum, 2010), pp. 98–110.

19. It is not merely incidental that the seizure of chance which Philo opposes here concerns the construction of forms of causality, the intimate issue of chance's "seizure."

20. It is the careful sequestering of its own limited ownerships of power by contemporary piety which fails to see the cheeky Pauline inversion of Moses's veiled glory as as a glory *katargoumenēn* in 2 Corinthians 3.

21. For an excellent discussion of the role of Joyce as exemplar of a quasi-emancipatory fidelity to one's (singular) symptom, see Lorenzo Chiesa, *Subjectivity and Otherness: A Philosophical Reading of Lacan* (Cambridge: MIT Press, 2007), pp. 188ff.

22. Lacan, *The Ethics of Psychoanalysis (1959–60)*, p. 177.

23. Lacan. *The Other Side of Psychoanalysis*, p. 19f.

24. A. Kiarina Kordela, $surplus: Spinoza, Lacan (Albany: SUNY Press, 2007), p. 38.

25. Lacan, *The Other Side of Psychoanalysis*, pp. 119f. "By the end of her article Marie-Clare Boons would even give us to understand that many things flow from this death of the father and notably a certain something that would make it the case that in some way psychoanalysis frees us from the law. . . . Fat chance" (119).

CONCLUSION: NEW BEGINNINGS

1. Cf. Friedrich Nietzsche, *Human All Too Human* (New York: Penguin, 1984), section 20, in this translation p. 28.

2. As should be clear from the discussions in the various chapters here, this is of course just to name two forensic, technical shifts which make possible the recovery of Paul in concrete shoes, the relationalities constituting the shifting object of our discussions being more diffuse and expansive. As if to recall the path of the "material" swerve of difference, we note:

   > It should above all remind us that the said archival technology no longer determines, will never have determined, merely the moment of the conservational recording, but rather the very institution of the archivable event. It conditions not only the form or the structure that prints, but the printed content of the printing: the *pressure* of the *printing*, the *impression*, before the division between the printed and the printer. This archival technique has commanded that which in the past even instituted and constituted whatever there was as anticipation of the future.

   Jacques Derrida, *Archive Fever: A Freudian Impression* (Chicago: University of Chicago Press, 1996), p. 18.

3. Alberto Toscano, *Fanaticism: On the Uses of the Idea* (London: Verso, 2010), p. 228.

4. Ibid.

5. The axiom, in fact, seems to me the productively paradoxical core of all of Crockett's work. See, for example, *Radical Political Theology: Religion and Politics After Liberalism* (New York: Columbia University Press, 2011), p. 128, *Deleuze Beyond Badiou: Ontology, Multiplicity, and Event* (New York: Columbia University Press, 2013), p. 128.

INDEX